TIMPSON'S
ENGLISH VILLAGES

JOHN TIMPSON

Photographs by
MICHAEL J.
STEAD

HEADLINE

AUTHOR
John Timpson, OBE

DESIGNER
Geoff Staff

EDITOR
Paula Granados

RESEARCHER
Bridget Barne

PHOTOGRAPHER
Michael J. Stead
*(except photographs on pages 24, 49, 80, 81 and
as detailed on dust-jacket).*

Title page picture:
Great Massingham, Norfolk

TIMPSON'S ENGLISH VILLAGES
Designed and produced by Parke Sutton Publishing Limited, Norwich
for Headline Book Publishing PLC, London.

First published, 1992

British Library Cataloguing in Publication Data

Timpson, John
Timpson's English Villages
I. Title
914. 204589

ISBN 0-7472-0586-8

Typesetting by P.S. Typesetting, Norwich
Colour origination by Blackfriars Colour Repro, Norwich
Printed and bound in Great Britain by Butler & Tanner, Frome

HEADLINE BOOK PUBLISHING PLC,
Headline House,
79 Great Titchfield Street,
London WIP 7FN

CONTENTS

FOREWORD

This is not just another collection of picturesque villages. Each one has something more to it than a cluster of quaint old cottages or a photogenic village pond, though there are plenty of those to be found here as well. I have selected them, not just because they might look good on a chocolate box, but because they all have some unusual feature which is part of the English heritage, illustrations of the odd ways in which they have developed, the quirkier aspects of English social history, the traditions that have developed over the centuries.

That doesn't mean a surfeit of maypoles and morris dancers, though they have to come into it too, I have looked for the less familiar activities of English rural life. There are the customs which have died out, like the maiden's garlands which were carried at the funerals of unmarried girls in some Shropshire villages and elsewhere; and some which have been revived, like the well-dressing in Derbyshire which now extends to public taps and village pumps as well. Some have been preserved for centuries, like the medieval system of strips of land being shared out among farmers by the Court of the Manor; Laxton in Nottinghamshire is the only place it still happens. And at Castle Rising in Norfolk the elderly ladies from the Jacobean 'Hospital' still walk to church wearing full-length scarlet capes emblazoned with the crest of the Hospital founder, and the kind of tall black hat you would normally associate with a broomstick . . .

Sometimes it is the place itself which is remarkable, like Blanchland in Northumberland,

BLANCHLAND, AN EIGHTEENTH-CENTURY VILLAGE ON THE SITE OF A MEDIEVAL MONASTERY.

built 250 years ago on the site of a medieval monastery, following the same layout and incorporating some of the old buildings; or Heronsgate in Hertfordshire, the dreamchild of a Victorian land

A SCENE, BELOVED OF THE TOURIST, AT
ICKWELL GREEN.

reformer who brought industrial workers down from the north to support their families on smallholdings which turned out to be much *too* small. It may be a reminder of an event in the history books which a village preserves, like the ruins of the great tithe barn at Acton Burnell in Shropshire where Edward I held the first truly representative

ACTON BURNELL – EDWARD I KNEW IT WELL.

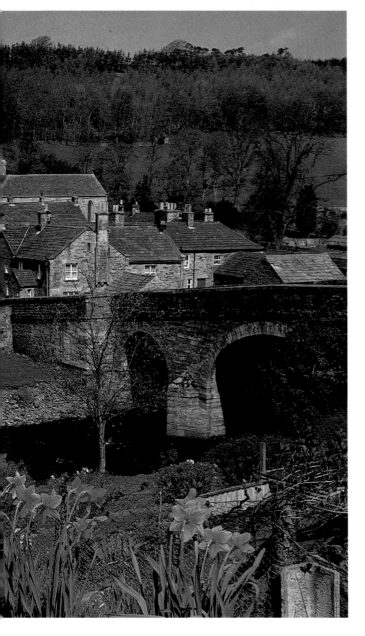

Parliament, or the Eleanor Cross at Geddington in Northamptonshire, one of the twelve he erected along his wife's funeral route. In some cases the incident dates back so far that no actual evidence

remains, just a plaque perhaps, like the one on the little bridge at Hoxne in Suffolk where King Edmund was killed by the Danes and became St Edmund, patron saint of East Anglia.

A village's special significance could lie in its unique ancient buildings, like the almshouses and grammar school at Ewelme in Oxfordshire, built by Geoffrey Chaucer's grand-daughter and still being used for their original purposes; or the Octagon at Heptonstall in West Yorkshire, with a foundation stone laid by John Wesley and a roof brought by pack-horse over the hillsides, the oldest Methodist chapel in the world in continuous use. And it could be just an ordinary feature of the village with an out-of-the-ordinary tale attached, like the pond at Bishops Cannings in Wiltshire where smugglers hid their contraband, and when the Excise men found them about to fish it out, they said they were raking the water to catch the moon's reflection – Wiltshire men have been known as the Moonrakers ever since; or the rough track at Gidleigh in Devon which was part of the Mariners' Way, the route across the county taken by sailors who had missed their ship at Dartmouth and hoped to catch up with it at Bideford before it set off across the Atlantic.

More often than not, there is something special to be found in the village church, which has always been the centre of village life throughout the centuries, and gives an earlier and more comprehensive picture of what went on there than any other building. The memorials alone give little cameos of local history, ranging from the near life-size marble sculpture at Gaddesby in Leicestershire of the local squire astride one of the four horses that were shot under him at Waterloo, to the much smaller than life-size figure of Thomas Cockayne at Youlgreave in Derbyshire, who was not a midget as one gazetteer suggests, but he died before his father and it was the custom to make the effigy smaller in such cases, even though he was full-grown.

I enjoy the quirkier features of some churches too, like the clock-face at Old Brampton in Derbyshire, which was given sixty-three minutes by a craftsman who had taken too much refreshment at the local inn; although it is probably unique in English villages, the church guidebook discreetly omits any mention of it, which I find fascinating in itself. Then there are the remarkable decorations on the church at Barfrestone in Kent and its unorthodox belfry, which prompted my irreverent heading: 'Three fancy doors, two butting rams and a church bell in a yew tree . . .'

Needless to say, I could not have accumulated all this information without the efforts of an unsung army of village historians and church

BARFRESTONE'S UNUSUAL BELFRY.

guidebook authors, who have written about their village, quite literally, just for the love of it. Their work ranges from the erudite history of Appledore in Kent by a local resident who just happened to have been director-general of the National Trust, to any number of simple duplicated leaflets by unnamed villagers which often contained more entertaining snippets than the weightier publications. It has been impossible to acknowledge them all by name, but I am deeply grateful to every one of them, and to the village parsons and parish clerks and oldest inhabitants who have given such valuable and willing assistance.

Inevitably stories may be embellished over the years, memories can blur, different sources can provide different versions. In addition, road-builders and developers can transform a landscape so fast that my knowledge of a village may already be out of date, though every effort has been made to get things right. I can only quote one of those devoted local historians, Edmund Fortescue Gange. Anyone with such a splendidly English name deserves a place in this book anyway, but the sentiment he expresses in his own foreword is admirably suited to mine. 'If I have in any way infringed any rights or privileges of any person, I beg them to accept my sincere apologies and pardon me, as an old man anxious only to leave behind records and

RUSHTON'S UNIQUE TRIANGULAR LODGE.

references for posterity of a village and church he has loved so long and so well'. Just substitute 'English Villages' for 'a village and a church', and perhaps insert 'fairly' in front of 'old' . . .

I hope I have done these villages justice; and if I have expressed any criticism – because this is, after all, a personal impression, not a tourist gazetteer which turns a blind eye to the heavily congested main road which passes through a village, or a hideous new building which can overshadow all those around it – then I hope they will be generous enough to forgive me. If blemishes exist, then I have said so.

Indeed some of these villages have lost their battle with the developers, and only a few original corners are left, but I have included them because they still possess some special aspect of English village life. On the other hand I have omitted some villages on the well-known tourist trails because their only merit is being photogenic; their beauty, as it were, is only timber-and-whitewash deep – and even that is generally obscured by the coachloads of trippers. The accent of this book, as

you may have now gathered or indeed as you might have expected, is on the less fashionable, more unlikely villages which have made their own unsung contribution to the English rural way of life. Often it is unexpected, sometimes it is slightly bizarre; I was never quite sure what I was going to find.

As a result *Timpson's English Villages* has been great fun to research and to write, and I hope it will be fun to read, as well as offering you something extra to look out for when you are exploring the English countryside. And if it preserves, in a slightly unorthodox way, some of those aspects of rural England which more serious chroniclers may consider too trivial or too quirky to record, then so much the better.

John Timpson

EAST GARSTON WAS ORIGINALLY ASGAR'S TUN NAMED AFTER EDWARD THE CONFESSOR'S STABLE BOSS.

THE PILCHARDS HAVE LEFT THE SERPENTINE BUT THERE MAY BE MULLET IN THE SEINE

CADGWITH
CORNWALL
11 miles south-east of Helston

I always think of Cadgwith as the village in chains, but that doesn't mean it is a Cornish version of Devil's Island. The chains are actually on the thatched roofs, and to the casual eye they look like cables that ought to lead to television aerials, but they were put there, very wisely, to hold the thatch down when the gales howl in from the Atlantic. It might have been safer, I suppose, to have used slates instead, and indeed some of these stone cottages do have them, but the thatch looks prettier and anyway I gather that Cadgwith hasn't lost a roof in years.

What it has lost, though, are the pilchards which used to be the mainstay of the village economy. In the nineteenth century two steam-driven pilchard boats were kept standing by during the pilchard season awaiting the call of the huer, the village look-out man who kept watch from a hut on top of the cliffs – it is difficult to spot pilchards from sea level. When he saw a shoal heading down the coast he raised the alarm – a huer cry, presumably – and the boats set off with their seine nets.

The catches were quite astonishing. Some of them are still recorded on the beams of the one remaining seine loft at the harbour. It sometimes took three days to empty the nets. The largest number of fish caught in a single day was one million three hundred thousand, enough to fill an awful lot of those lethal tins we grapple with these days. At a price of nearly a pound per hundred that was enough to keep the village's finances looking rosy until the next shoal came along – but it also had to last through the forty-six weeks of the year after the pilchard season had finished. As a bonus, the natural oil that came out of the fish as they were packed into barrels was drained into tanks and used to fuel the oil-lamps.

Cadgwith's pilchard fishing succumbed to the big flotillas from the larger ports, using massive drift nets, and the last catches were made in 1910. However, the seine nets are still preserved for the fairly rare occasions when a shoal of red or grey mullet happens to pass by. There is no full-time huer these days, though the hut still stands on the cliffs, but the retired fishermen will take turns to walk along the cliffs during the mullet season and keep watch in much the same way. Needless to say, the catches have never reached the million mark – if they did, the entire village could retire in luxury – but a mullet fetches a great deal more than a pilchard, and it can be a nice little earner. In fact there was an occasion about five years ago when the catch was so large that everyone in Cadgwith lent a hand to pack it, just like the old days.

The main catch these days, though, is crab and lobster, and Cadgwith also goes in for gig-racing, which I have seen on the Isles of Scilly but never on the mainland. These gigs are not the horse-drawn variety, they are long rowing-boats manned by six rowers and a cox, the West Country's

THE WINCH-HOUSE WHICH ECHOED TO THE BULLER AND HARTLEY DUETS.

answer to the Boat Race. They provide an alternative outlet for the fishermen's energy, and a new use for the old lifeboat house, which is now the headquarters for the gig-racing club.

The only other local industry, stone-cutting, has long since died, but most of the cottages are built in the hard local stone called serpentine. It comes in various colours, but the patterns on it are all in the same form, snake-like markings which give it its name. Landewednack Church, a couple of miles from Cadgwith, not only has a tower made of serpentine and granite but a red serpentine pulpit; it is said that the last sermon in Cornish was preached from it in 1678. The only evidence of where the stone used to be cut is a water-wheel at Carleon Cove, a mile along the coast from Cadgwith. It powered the stone-cutting machinery, and the ruins of the factory are nearby.

The village may have lost its principal industries, but in some ways that is all to the good. It has managed to remain a tiny unspoilt village of perhaps a hundred people and although, inevitably, the tourists pour in during the summer, there is still a great community spirit. Not surprisingly it centres on the seventeenth-century pub, the Cadgwith Cove Inn. Sometimes the community spirit has overflowed onto the beach, and there is an unlikely memorial that proves it. At the winch-house on the beach is a plaque which reads: 'Buller and Hartley and their many friends loved to sing here on summer evenings'.

Buller was a fisherman and Hartley a postman. They were great friends and good singers, and every Friday night they led a sing-song in the pub, a practice which still continues. At closing times, still in good voice, the singers would head down to the beach and continue their concert there. I am told that on one of these occasions an Italian lady opera singer, who was staying in the area, joined Messrs Buller and Hartley in leading the singing, and was highly complimentary about the quality of their performance!

It must have been a rare combination, the fisherman, the postman and the Italian diva, singing away together in this tiny Cornish cove; almost enough, I would have hoped, to tempt back the pilchards . . .

THE FISHING FLEET IN HARBOUR. TODAY, THE CATCH IS MAINLY CRAB AND LOBSTER.

A Strange Saint, A Rascally Major, and A Mixed-up Mason

EGLOSKERRY
CORNWALL
5 miles west of Launceston

Somebody once described Cornwall as 'only a boring picture in a beautiful golden frame'. He was being ungenerous, but I know what he meant. There is nothing to beat the Cornish coast for grandeur and spectacle, but inland the scenery can be none too exciting, and what there is you often can't see because of the hedges. I admit I am prejudiced, because I can recall a series of family holidays when it rained almost continuously, and the only way to occupy the children was to take them for interminable rides through the sodden Cornish countryside. However, there are some attractive little villages tucked away in the hinterland – even though I might only recognise them again through the blades of a windscreen-wiper. One such is Egloskerry, on what used to be the main road from Launceston to Camelford. It is just a lane now, and the old stone cottages are only slightly marred by the scattering of modern bungalows.

The name has a certain Irish ring about it, but 'eglos' is Cornish for church, and Egloskerry is named after a visiting Welsh saint, St Keri, who is supposed to have built a chapel nearby. Welsh saints seemed to take a great fancy to Cornwall in the sixth century – maybe it didn't rain so much then – and their names crop up all over the county. The most illustrious was St Non, mother of St David of Wales, whose holy well at Altarnun, on the edge of Bodmin Moor, was supposed to cure madness, but my favourite is St Endelion, daughter of a Welsh king, who lived like a hermit near Port Isaac, subsisting mostly on the milk from her cow, until a local landowner got annoyed because the cow strayed on to his land, and killed her – Endelion, alas, not the cow.

Keri was not into wells or cows, but has a more unusual distinction for collectors of Welsh saints. Nobody is sure if the name is male or female. Keri was one of twenty children born to a Welsh chieftain called Brychan, and presumably with that number in the family, Brychan never noticed whether Keri preferred dolls or football. But he, or she, obviously made an impact in that part of Cornwall, and would be gratified to know that, although the sex is unknown, the name has lived on for fourteen hundred years.

In more recent times, during the seventeenth and eighteenth centuries, the name associated with the village was Speccott. The estate was bought by John Speccott, Sheriff of Cornwall, in 1622, and his family held it for a number of generations until a situation arose which sounds almost like romantic fiction. When the last male heir died childless, the estate was split between his three sisters. One died unmarried, another married a local MP who survived her and got a third of the estate, and the other one also married but her husband died soon afterwards. An old history of Cornwall then records: 'In her old age the widow was induced to marry John Bidlake Herring, a major in the army, who resorted to all possible methods of extorting money from the old lady – one that will scarcely be credited, by terrifying her with supposed apparitions'.

Major Herring was obviously a most frightful bounder, and Barbara Cartland would have made sure he came to a bad end, but it was the old lady

THE HELMET AND GAUNTLETS OF SIR GUY DE BLANCHMINSTER

who died first, perhaps due to his ministrations, and he duly inherited her share of the estate. He changed his name and, no doubt, had a high old time until he died himself in 1806. After that the estate was split in various directions, and the name of Speccott has disappeared, except for the monuments in Egloskerry Church.

The same old history book has a list of the inscriptions on these monuments, and records without comment the rather unusual one for Grace Speccott, who died in 1636:

Go peaceful sainte, Go accept Rest;
Retyred betime Heaven calls the best.
Away to Make its Harmony
Compleate. What angry Deitye
Ere we could patterne take of thee
Snatch from us both the branche and Tree . . .

Not all that unusual, you may think, but look at the initial letters on each line. They spell Grace's name, and the rest of the verse which has worn away no doubt completed the Speccott; quite an ingenious piece of seventeenth-century word-juggling. Incidentally, the Speccott crest seemed to me to feature three modern clothes pegs, which would have been even more ingenious, but I am told they are actually mill-rinds, the pieces of metal put on mill-wheels.

Such a case of mistaken identity can easily occur, to judge by the stonemason who repaired the oldest monument in the church, the fourteenth-century ala-baster effigy of Sir Guy de Blanchminster. After bits had been broken off it the mason did his best to sort them out and put them back. He found the nose all right, though he could have done a better job of re-attaching it, but he was obviously baffled by two spare pieces of decoration, and hopefully stuck them on Sir Guy's chest. This in turn baffled later experts, until somebody realised they must be the pom-poms from Sir Guy's fancy shoes.

I understand that among certain types of lady dancer, the idea has since caught on . . .

WRECKERS AND SMUGGLERS – AND MUCH, MUCH LATER, AN OLD BROWN TRUNK

CRACKINGTON HAVEN
CORNWALL
8 miles south-west of Bude

I have always had a soft spot for Crackington Haven. It was my favourite holiday venue in the days long ago, when my mother filled up the old brown trunk with bathing costumes and wraps and towels, and my father tied it up with yards of thick rope, and about a week ahead of the holiday it was sent off to Cornwall by Carter Patterson. We travelled down by train, an all-day journey, wondering all the way if the trunk had got there safely. The taxi would drive the last three miles down the long steep lane from the main coast road – the one they call these days the Atlantic Highway

– and there was the sea and the breakers ahead of us in the gap between the two great promontories on either side of the Haven, and the stretch of sand with those broad flat rocks so ideal for sunbathing. Then we'd arrive at the hotel, and I can still feel the enormous relief as we saw the familiar brown trunk waiting for us inside. The rush to undo all those knots; out would come the towels and the costumes and the vast tent-like wraps with the hole in the middle for our heads, so we could change with proper decorum, and then down to the beach and into the sea, and the holiday had begun . . .

I learned to surf at Crackington Haven. Not the fancy hey-everyone-look-at-me-standing-up-on-my-Malibu type surfing, but the humbler, lie-on-your-tummy-and-hope-you-don't-scrape-your-knees-too-much surfing, which was just as exciting for a small boy. I also nearly got drowned at Crackington Haven; I ventured too far out with my surf-board, got caught in the undertow by the rocks, and had to be hauled out by my elder sister. But I bore no grudge against the Haven, and when I had a family myself we still went back there, until the Cornish weather finally beat us and we succumbed to the package tour. Our surfing days are long since over now, but we still return occasionally, and although there seems a lot less sand on the beach and a lot more cars in the field that passes for a car park, it still holds a curious magic.

During all those holidays I never knew anything of the history of the Haven. I knew it was an exhausting climb to the top of the cliffs, but I never knew they were the highest cliffs in Cornwall – and as one Cornishman told me, if Cornwall were in England they'd be the highest in England too. I knew there were two hotels, one rather upmarket, the other where we actually stayed, but I never knew that the Combe Barton was originally the home of the manager of the local slate quarry, or that the manor was once a 'kiddleywink', that marvellous Cornish word for an alehouse, which lives on in nearby Boscastle and in the Lamorna Wink, near Mousehole.

I never knew that small coastal vessels used to come into the Haven on the tide, bringing limestone and fuel for the lime-kiln, and taking away the slate from the quarry; both kiln and quarry have long since gone. I certainly never knew that Crackington Haven nearly became Port Victoria, with a rail link to Launceston. In 1836 a consortium, which included the explorer Captain James Clark Ross, obtained an Act of Parliament which authorised them to develop the Haven into a 'Port of Refuge' and expand the village into a town. 'Port Victoria will be one of the most magnificent harbours in the world,' said Captain Ross. Then he went off to see a bit more of it, and changed his mind. Mercifully for my summer holidays the Haven stayed exactly as it was.

Well, not quite. Over the years the locals took away so much sand and seaweed to use on their farms, and so much stone to use for their houses and walls, that the Haven was almost stripped bare. Fortunately it recovered, but time and tides seem to be repeating the process.

I also never realised that Crackington was not just the little cluster of buildings by the beach. The main village lies well inland, mostly modern development and nothing much to shout about. It is all part of the parish of St Gennys, a much larger area that takes in about five miles of coastline and extends back to the Atlantic Highway. There is no church in the Haven itself, and I suppose it doesn't really qualify as a village at all – let alone, as my Cornish friend would point out, an English village. But this little corner of Cornwall has so many features that I look for and enjoy, and I associate them with Crackington Haven rather than Crackington or St Gennys, so forgive me for giving the Haven all the credit, and consigning the others to the index.

TRULY A HAVEN FOR JUNIOR SAILORS . . .

So what else does it have besides sea and surf? First, there is its fascinating history, going back to the days of wrecking and smuggling, when two members of the principal local family, William and Robert Gennys, were outlawed for their exploits, though later pardoned.

There is local legend – and I always enjoy a good legend – that if all the wood taken from wrecked ships was removed, every house in the parish would fall down.

But its history goes back further than that. On a ridge beyond Penkenna Point is an Iron Age fort, reckoned to be two thousand years old, and at Dizzard Point there is a rather weird primeval oak wood, on a cliff so full of holes and crevices under the brambles that visitors are warned to keep clear.

It has a beach which sounds as sinister as the oak wood looks, called Strangles Beach, but the name is just a corruption of Strange Hill, and not even that meant there was anything odd about it –

there was merely a local family in the fourteenth century called Strange.

More recently a literary connection was acquired. Thomas Hardy met his wife Emma in this area, while he was the architect restoring the church in the next parish, St Juliot, and they did some of their courting on Strangles Beach. Hardy never mentioned any precise locations, but lines like: 'She opened the door of the West to me, With its loud sea-lashings, And cliff-side clashings, Of waters rife with revelry', must surely apply to the coast around Crackington Haven.

Finally, it has a marvellous situation, surrounded by spectacular coastal scenery, remote from the nearest main road, and compared with the rest of the Cornish coast, unpublicised – all qualities I treasure. Most of all, for me, it has the memory of those far-off family holidays, of that first glimpse of the sea as we drove down the valley, and waiting for us at the hotel, the reassuring sight of that old brown trunk . . .

THE MARINERS PROBABLY WENT THEIR WAY – BUT WHAT OF THE MURDEROUS MONK?

GIDLEIGH
DEVON
8 miles south-east of Okehampton

If you were looking for somewhere off the beaten track you might well go for Gidleigh. You can only reach it by narrow winding lanes, and when you get there you can go no further. It is right on the edge of Dartmoor, where the roads run out and the open moor begins. The village is just a church, a few cottages, the remnants of a Norman keep, and these days a youth hostel; the nearest main road is miles away and there's no sign of a railway, even a derelict one. So you could well think that 'off the beaten track' was the perfect description – and you'd be quite wrong. Gidleigh, in fact, lies on one of the oldest, the longest, and at one time the most controversial beaten tracks in Devon.

The Mariners' Way was reputed to run for seventy-two miles coast-to-coast, from Dartmouth to Bideford. Some say the mariners who used it had missed their ship at Dartmouth and were cutting across country to catch up with it at Bideford, before it set off across the Atlantic. Others say they had been paid off in one port and went to look for a fresh ship in the other. But in 1958 there was a great debate over a much more basic issue – whether the Mariners' Way ever actually existed. It culminated in a public enquiry, at which the principal witness for the defence of the way was the then Rector of Gidleigh, the Revd John Scott.

He was in a good position to argue because he was a mariner himself, a retired naval captain in holy orders. He had already put his case in the correspondence columns of the *Western Morning News*, in response to a blast from another retired sailor, Rear-Admiral Lawder of Okehampton. The rear-admiral wrote that 'anyone in his senses' would not have followed the meandering cross-country route of the Mariners' Way but taken the road instead, especially when carrying heavy kit. Rest-houses were supposed to have existed every eight or ten miles, wrote the rear-admiral, but there couldn't have been enough itinerant sailors to make them pay.

The rector counter-attacked. In the eighteenth century, he wrote, many of the roads might not have existed, and those that did were rough and stony. Men going barefoot or in unaccustomed boots would prefer soft footpaths 'as indeed do most sensible people today'. As for the rest-houses not paying, 'two hundred years ago there was a very real sense of charity . . . and many parishes had arrangements for caring for such wayfarers'. In Gidleigh itself, he pointed out, there had been a building called Church House which was used precisely for that purpose. As further evidence he quoted from the Gidleigh churchwarden's accounts for 1740: 'Gave eleven sailors that had a pass, two shillings'.

Alas, he had made a false move. Back came the answer that in 1740 there were any number of hard-up sailors wandering the country, and similar entries could be found in parish accounts far removed from any Mariners' Way.

The rear-admiral followed up with another broadside. Even the term 'Mariners' was inaccurate, he wrote. According to a naval historian, Captain Roskill, sailors were called sailors, and the mariners were those who did the fighting. But the rector had another shot in his locker. 'With all due respect to Captain Roskill, an old friend and shipmate of mine' – so there! – 'an even greater authority, Sir Francis Drake, once gave the directive: "I will have the gentlemen to haul and draw with the mariners, and the mariners with the gentlemen".'

He repeated much of this at the enquiry, which was held because a local landowner argued that the Mariners' Way, even if it ever existed, was no longer a right of way. However, most of it is still a popular route for walkers, and at least one of them, a Miss Varwell of neighbouring Thurleigh, was in no doubt about its authenticity. She wrote lyrically:

ELABORATELY CARVED AND GILDED ROOD-SCREEN IN GIDLEIGH CHURCH.

'It would not surprise me if a running figure passed me in the dusk, and I got a whiff of the salt sea and of baccy as he hurried by. I seem to hear the flip-flop of the feet and to catch a glimpse of a tarry pigtail and a bundle in a red handkerchief.' Maybe it was the Revd John Scott, Capt RN (Retd), trying to prove his point . . .

Gidleigh church has one or two unusual features. One rarely finds a stream running through the middle of a churchyard, for instance, and three of the five bells in the tower are fifteenth century and among the oldest in England. They have lasted rather better than the bell frame, which is so shaky now that they can't be rung full circle.

The church's history has been fairly uneventful; for high drama one must turn to the ruined chapel just outside the village. Wandering monks used it for prayer and meditation, but in 1328 a Clerk in Orders called Robert de Middelcote apparently used it for quite a different purpose. He was charged with 'maltreating Agnes, the daughter of Roger the miller of Gidleigh Mill, and murdering the child she was carrying'.

Nobody knows what actually happened in the chapel, but the local guidebook has a few suggestions. 'Was the femininity of a woman attending a lonely Mass at this isolated chapel too great a strain on the avowed celibacy of the young priest?' it speculates delicately. 'Was there a clandestine love affair? Was the unborn child his? Was there a quarrel and violence resulting in a still-born birth?' I almost expected the follow-up 'Don't miss next week's thrilling instalment', but that part of the story ended there. The chapel was closed, and many years later was used as a cattle byre. In the last century acorns were planted inside it, and there are now five oak trees growing out of the ruined walls.

But what about the monk? Did he get convicted, or did he get off? Did he escape before coming to trial? Did he commit suicide? Yes, I am quoting the guidebook again. But I have my own theory. I reckon he got away, disguised as a sailor, and that's who Miss Varwell saw, running off down the Mariners' Way . . .

THE GUBBINSES – AND OTHER ASSORTED GUBBINS

LYDFORD
DEVON
7 miles north of Tavistock

If you have heard of Lydford it is probably because of its famous gorge, a deep ravine over a mile long where the River Lyd swirls into a massive pot-hole called the Devil's Cauldron, and later plunges ninety feet down the White Lady waterfall. It is one of the most spectacular walks in Devon, and the National Trust are making sure it stays that way. But Lydford itself, decried by one gazetteer as 'a town that became redundant, now a small grey village', has so many curious facets that personally I find it more fascinating than the renowned gorge itself.

However, the beauty spot does have one sinister tale to tell, of the family that settled in it, the Gubbinses. It's a faintly comical name, but there was nothing comical about the family; they were the terror of the neighbourhood. Charles Kingsley gives a romanticised version of them in *Westward Ho!*, but a seventeenth-century writer provides us with a more down-to-earth picture: 'They lived in cots, rather holes than houses, like swine having all in common, multiplying without marriage into many hundreds. Their wealth consisted of other men's goods – they lived by stealing sheep on the Moor.'

It was for the likes of the Gubbinses that Lydford Castle was designed, though they seemed to keep clear of it themselves. The castle was in fact a prison, described in 1512 as 'one of the most heinous, contagious and detestable

THE WHITE LADY WATERFALL, DROPPING NINETY FEET DOWN LYDFORD GORGE.

places in the realm'. At that time it was already three centuries old, and it stands there still, as grim as ever, a monument to the savage Stannary Laws which provided a good many of its inmates.

The Stannary or Tin Laws protected the tin mine owners and imposed death or imprisonment on those who offended them. Even a Devon MP, Richard Strode, spent three weeks in Lydford Castle in 1508 for complaining that the mining industry was polluting the rivers. The owners were not at all bothered about the rivers, but they did object to anyone adulterating their tin, and under the Stannary Laws the penalty for doing so was three spoonfuls of the molten metal poured down the throat. The hanging penalty for even minor thefts was probably preferable.

Lydford had its own mint, and some Lydford Pennies are on show at the Castle Inn, but the best collection is many hundreds of miles away in the Royal Stockholm Museum. This was the Danegeld paid to the Vikings to bribe them not to raid the village. Alas, the Vikings took the money and raided it just the same. A thousand years later, in 1990, a plaque was erected opposite the church gate, portraying a Danish axe on a Saxon shield, to mark the Viking raid and also – on a less violent note – the seventieth anniversary of Lydford Women's Institute.

This is one of many monuments and markers in and around Lydford. You can hardly miss the huge granite cross which was erected on top of Bratt Tor to mark Queen Victoria's golden jubilee, but it is not so easy to spot the Lydford boundary stone on the Coryton road with the initials L. B., or the one on the boundary with Bridestowe which says, less cryptically, 'End of Okehampton Trust' – a forerunner of all those signs saying 'Dartmoor National Park'. My favourite is the stone near Beardon Farm with the baffling inscription: 'Take Off'. Take off what, one wonders, or where to, and why?

I doubt you would guess the answer. The stone stood on an ancient route from Tavistock to Okehampton which was subject to tolls, but on one

LYDFORD CASTLE, NOW A TOURIST ATTRACTION BUT ONCE A PRISON, 'ONE OF THE MOST HEINOUS, CONTAGIOUS AND DETESTABLE PLACES IN THE REALM'.

section in Lydford parish it was permitted to use an extra horse to pull a very heavy load without paying an additional toll. At the end of that section the extra horse had to be left behind – taken off, in fact, and tethered to the 'Take Off' stone. Did you get it . . . ?

Another route at Lydford was called the Lych Way, where the loads were mostly coffins. The original parish covered an amazing area, more than seventy-eight square miles. Most of it was moorland, but people lived on the far side, and when they died they were carried along the Lych Way to be buried at St Petroc's Church in Lydford. If the weather was too bad to cross the moor the bodies were stored in salt as a temporary measure.

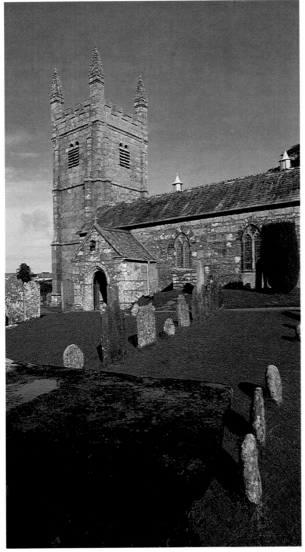

ST PETROC'S CHURCH; THE FAMOUS WATCHMAKER EPITAPH IS ON A STONE NEAR THE PORCH.

It is said that a traveller staying the night at the Warren Inn, on the far side of the moor, discovered that the chest in his bedroom contained the salted remains of the landlord's father, awaiting shipment along the Lych Way . . .

There was a more orthodox burial at Lydford for a watchmaker who became famous, not for his watches but for his epitaph, which is quoted in every self-respecting anthology of tombstone titbits; I have even quoted it myself. It's the one that starts: 'Here lies in horizontal position the outside case of George Routleigh, Watchmaker. Integrity was the mainspring and prudence the regulator all the actions of his life.' And it ends: 'Wound up in hopes of being taken in hand by his Maker and of being thoroughly cleaned, repaired, and set agoing in the world to come.' Yes, you've heard it – but did you know it came from Lydford?

Lydford's bleak spell came with the decline of the tin mining industry, reducing it to the 'small grey village' of the gazetteer. In 1660 it was 'a mean, miserable village', and in 1840 it was called 'the former noted township, but now ruined village – its bleak and exposed situation would give us leave to imagine few people could have made it their choice as a residence.' Edward Lear, who visited it a little later, was just as scathing about the climate: 'There is only one fine day in fifteen, and all the rest are beyond expression, demoralising and filthy'.

Then came the railways in 1865 and nobody seemed to care about the weather any more, judging by the visitors who poured in. These days the railways have disappeared, but the visitors still come. Most will head straight for the gorge, but if they do pause in Lydford there is one more snippet I can offer. The reredos in St Petroc's Church is in memory of a lady called Sarah Lansdowne, who died in 1923. I don't know her marital status, but I can guess, because she left a bequest 'to maidens in the parish who, having been married, have not given birth to a child before the proper time has elapsed'.

The rector, Canon Martyn Bateman, recording this in the excellent booklet which I have relied on greatly, adds three exclamation marks after the story, but to me Lydford has many others to tell which are just as delightful. So the gorge can wait; give me the 'small grey village' every time.

SO OARE HAD CARVER DOONE, BUT HOW ABOUT THE AXE-MURDERER PRIEST OF CULBONE?

OARE AND CULBONE
SOMERSET
6 miles east of Lynton

If it hadn't been for the rector's grandson writing a novel about some legendary local outlaws, I doubt that many folk outside West Somerset would ever have heard of Oare. It is a tiny village in a remote valley between Exmoor and the coast, and with its two even tinier neighbours it inspired a local versifier to write, very fairly, though with rather dodgy scanning:

Culbone, Oare and Stoke Pero,
Are three such places as you seldom hear o'.

Certainly the map-makers seem in two minds whether they exist at all. I have three quite good road atlases: one shows Oare but not Culbone or Stoke Pero, another shows Culbone but not the other two, and the third shows none of them at all. If I may re-scan that couplet:

Such well-hidden places you never saw
As Culbone, Stoke Pero and Oare . . .

Yet Oare gets hundreds of visitors a year, thanks to Richard Doddridge Blackmore, and Culbone actually features in the *Guinness Book of Records*. Only Stoke Pero seems to have remained in total obscurity. I found just one mention of it in a gazetteer, merely saying it was five miles south-east of Oare, but on the maps there is not even a road in that direction. I eventually discovered that

THIS PEACEFUL STREAM FLOWS THROUGH CARVER DOONE COUNTRY.

it became part of the parish of Luccombe in 1933.

So back to Oare, and R.D. Blackmore, and of course *Lorna Doone*. Blackmore buffs will not need reminding that Oare Church was where Carver Doone shot the lovely Lorna at her wedding to dashing Jan Ridd. They will be disappointed, though, if they expect to find the setting unchanged. In Lorna's time the church ended where the screen now stands, the pulpit and reading desk are post-Lorna, and instead of the present box pews there would have been simple benches. But at least there is still a single-light window which could be the one Carver fired through, and it's nice to know that a John Ridd was churchwarden as recently as 1925. Even with-out the Doone connection, though, Oare is an attractive little village in a lovely setting, and well worth the effort of finding it.

While Doone devotees may pour into Oare, my preference is for Culbone, not just because of its place in the record books, but its setting is even more delightful, and it has real-life stories which are just as dramatic and moving as *Lorna Doone*. But let's get the *Guinness* entry out the way first: 'The smallest completed medieval English church in regular use is that at Culbone, Somerset, which measures 35 v 12 ft'. The church leaflet adds the further statistic that its seating capacity is about thirty-three, in great dis-comfort'.

OARE CHURCH, AS FEATURED IN *LORNA DOONE*

This tiny old church lies down a track through a steep wooded combe, half a mile from the nearest road, and no effort has been made to ease the way. A visiting guidebook writer recalls: 'The trips to Culbone in the ecclesiastical Land Rover were exciting experiences, particularly through Culbone Combe, where the narrow boulder-strewn track left no room even for a bicycle to pass. It was impossible to avoid one boulder as big as a football, and having surmounted that, there was a turn of about 130 degrees where the track descended steeply to Culbone.'

I approached it from below, along the coastal path from Porlock Weir, not such a hazardous route but quite a stiff climb – the church is four hundred feet above the sea. I shared his feelings when I got there: 'In Culbone it is hard to be a disbeliever. The scenery is delightful and nothing seems to disturb the quiet, but the little stream that gurgles over the rocks on the way down to the shore.' And the sound of me, panting . . .

There used to be cottages around the church, but they have long since gone. Culbone's thirty-odd inhabitants, when they are not seated in great discomfort in the church, are scattered around the Culbone Stables Inn on the main road. But there have been times over the past seven hundred years when those wooded slopes were alive with people – and some very strange people at that. It is difficult to picture this lovely, peaceful place as a prison colony or a leper settlement, but it has been both in its time, thanks to its isolated situation. The prisoners have ranged from medieval criminals to eighteenth-century prisoners-of-war; the latter were dumped there to make a living as best they could by burning charcoal and stripping bark for fuel in the tanneries.

The lepers were abandoned there in 1544, forty-five men, women and children.They were not allowed to mix with the locals, and in the church there is still the leper squint, the tiny window in the north wall where they could watch the services from outside. They lived in the woods for the whole of their lives; when the last one died he had been there for seventy-eight years.

So Culbone, in spite of its idyllic appearance, has had its grim periods, and on one occasion it even had a murder. It must have caused just as great a stir as Carver Doone's fictitious crime, because in Culbone's case it was a priest who did the killing. The Assize Rolls of 1280 record that the chaplain of Culbone, one Thomas, 'struck Albert of Ash on the head with a hatchet, and so killed him'. We are not told what Albert had done to annoy him, but we do know that Thomas was not executed, but outlawed; maybe he was a distant ancestor of the Doones.

The church may be tiny but it has its fair share of ancient relics. One of its bells is early fourteenth century, the oldest in West Somerset; the red sandstone font is probably eight hundred years old, and a two-light window, cut from a single piece of stone, is two hundred years older than that. But the mere fact that it was built there at all, with the stones being hauled down that steep track and the trees being hauled across the hillside for timber, is remarkable in itself.

I am told, however, that one part of the church caused no transport problems at all. The tiny deal and slate spire – the leaflet calls it a 'spirelet', if there is such a thing – was deposited on the roof by St Michael, after he had knocked it off the spire at Porlock with a bolt of lightning as a punishment for the wicked Porlockians.

Unlikely? Well, it's a local legend, just like the Doones. And why should Richard Doddridge Blackmore have all the fun.

CULBONE CHURCH, THE SMALLEST MEDIEVAL CHURCH STILL IN USE IN ENGLAND, WITH ITS TINY SPIRE 'BROUGHT FROM PORLOCK CHURCH BY ST MICHAEL'.

THE OLD MAN'S LATE HOME?
PASS THE PUNKIE . . .

HINTON ST GEORGE
SOMERSET
2 miles north-west of Crewkerne

Which should I give precedence to in Hinton St George: the Pouletts or the Punkies? I am sure the Pouletts themselves would have been in no doubt. They were Lords of the Manor up at Hinton House from the fifteenth century until the eighth and last Earl Poulett died in 1973, when the title became extinct. Their name crops up all round the village, from the Poulett Arms in the High Street to the Poulett family pew and vault in St George's Church.

The Punkies, on the other hand, are only noticeable once a year, on the last Thursday in October, but they too have been connected with the village for centuries and, unlike the Pouletts, they live on. However, a family of distinguished knights and landowners should take precedence of a hollowed-out mangold with a candle stuck in it, so I'll take the Pouletts first.

The entire village, built in the picturesque golden stone quarried from nearby Ham Hill, came into their possession, not by force of arms or gift of the sovereign, but much more conveniently by marriage. It was originally in the Denebaud family – that may be Sir John Denebaud lying in his armour on the tomb chest beneath the Poulett pew. His daughter Elizabeth married Sir William Paulet, there were no more male Denebauds to inherit, and the Paulets or Pouletts have been at Hinton ever since.

The earlier ones seem to have led more spectacular lives than the later ones. In Tudor times the first Sir Amyas Poulett once had the distinction of putting young Thomas Wolsey in the stocks, though I'm not quite sure why. Inevitably the Cardinal had the last laugh; many years later he arrested Sir Amyas in London. The second Sir Amyas was the guardian of Mary Queen of Scots during her imprisonment at Fotheringhay Castle. When he died in 1588 he was buried at St Martin-

in-the-Fields, but later was brought back to Hinton – that's his tomb on the west wall of the family chapel.

Sir Anthony Paulet – the spelling seems to vary from generation to generation, and from book to book – was Military Governor of Jersey before he died in 1600. His canopied tomb is in the chancel, with his wife beside him and their ten children kneeling around them. And so the memorials continue through the centuries, until the death of

NO, NOTHING TO DO WITH HALLOWE'EN; IT'S A PUNKIE.

the last earl's second wife Olga was marked by a modern stained-glass window depicting St Francis of Assisi. He is surrounded, not only by the traditional birds and animals, but also those which frequented Hinton Park – a pheasant, a barn owl, a heron and so on. In addition there are the countess' personal pets, an Alsatian, two dachsunds, a cat and a budgerigar. The only notable absentee, surprisingly perhaps in a memorial to a Poulett, is a chicken.

Of all the deceased Pouletts I rather fancy the seventh earl, whose tomb is in the chapel. The story goes that he disliked his relatives so much that he refused to be buried with them, down in the vault.

THERE'S GNOME PLACE LIKE HINTON ST GEORGE.

Amidst all this Poulettry in the church one might marvel that there is room for anyone else, but the odd outsider has managed to slip in. On the wall beside St Francis and his variegated flock is a rather nice little brass to the Martin family, mother and father, five daughters and six sons; and high up in the roof is a boss depicting, unexpectedly, the face of Field Marshal Lord Kitchener. So far as I know he had no direct connection with Hinton St George; he was not even distantly related to the Pouletts. It just happened that while the church roof was being repaired in 1916 he was drowned on board *HMS Hampshire*, and the builders thought they would pay their little tribute.

So much for the Pouletts and their neighbours in the church; I can postpone the Punkies no longer. It is possible that you have noted my reference to candles inside mangolds and the date in late October, and written off the Punkies as just another frolic connected with Hallowe'en. But not so. Their history is quite different, and unique to Hinton St George.

Many years ago, on the night of the Chisel-borough Fair, the menfolk of the village failed to return from the revelries at the expected hour. That is not exactly unique, but their wives' response was. They decided to go in search of them, but as they were too poor to have lanterns they dug up mangolds from the fields, hollowed them out to hold candles, and went off to meet them, carrying their 'Punkies'.

The reaction of their menfolk, reeling home happily from the fair, when these ladies bore down upon them brandishing their illuminated vegetables is not recorded; it probably frightened the wits out of them. But the event is commemorated each year when the children first collect money by selling five-penny tickets in the village, then whoever sells the most becomes the Punkie Royal Family for the year, King and Queen, Prince and Princess. On Punkie Night they ride through the village on a decorated float, escorted by the other children carrying their candle-lit Punkies and chanting the Punkie song:

It's Punkie Night tonight, it's Punkie Night tonight,
Gie us a candle, gies us a light,
It's Punkie Night tonight.

They collect more coins as they go, and then there is a Punkie-judging ceremony at a party in the village hall. The money they collect is used for other activities during the year – a sports day, a coach outing, a Christmas party. It is all so much more civilised than the quite appalling 'Trick or Treat' custom that has been imported from the States in recent years, when masked children go round the houses virtually demanding money with menaces; they are liable to empty the dustbin over your front garden if you refuse.

So I'm all for Hinton St George's Punkie Night, properly organised by a Punkie Night committee, and with a useful financial outcome as well as an evening's entertainment. Punkies rather than punks any time . . .

THE ENTIRE VILLAGE IS BUILT IN THIS WARM GOLDEN STONE.

SEEN THE SERIES? READ THE BOOK? – NEVER MIND, THERE'S STILL SOMETHING LEFT

LUCCOMBE
SOMERSET
17 miles west of Watchet

You may have seen the television series, either on HTV or Channel 4, and you may have read the book, in which case you will have your own vision of what Luccombe is like, and I'll bet it's nothing like the one the villagers have themselves. When an organisation called Mass-Observation – such an unendearing name – carried out a survey of Luccombe towards the end of the second World War, and published their findings in 1947 under the title *Exmoor Village*, the reception it was given in Luccombe was not exactly ecstatic. Eric Rowlands, who has just written a slimmer but more acceptable volume about the village, says guardedly that they were 'less than complimentary about it', though it eventually became accepted as an interesting period piece.

Then, when a television crew turned up some forty years later and made a series, under the same title and based on the book, complete with a hunt meet, a panto performance, a farm party and the like, actors giving readings and Dan Farson giving the commentary, the village was again not impressed. As Mr Rowlands puts it, discreet as ever, 'the reaction of most of the village on viewing these programmes was probably very similar to that of the residents of forty years ago on first reading the book'.

So what chance do I have after that? It would probably be safer to stop now, and just suggest you go and see Luccombe for yourself. But perhaps they won't mind if I mention what gives it, for me, a particular attraction. Never mind Mass-Observation's enquiries into people's pets, and health, and the gossip over the garden wall, or HTV's re-creation of wartime street scenes. I am much more taken with the story of the Revd Dr Henry Byam, the rector who joined the Royalist forces during the Civil War and became Prince Charles' chaplain in exile. Henry Byam would surely be just as exciting a hero as R. D. Blackmore's Jan Ridd in *Lorna Doone*, set only a few miles away across the moors.

THE CHURCH HAS A HANDSOME DOMED CEILING.

Then there is the mysterious ruined chapel on the edge of the village, its history quite unknown, but said to be haunted by a vindictive spectre which takes the form of a deer, or a boar, or a ram, and chases unwary travellers. There was supposed to be buried treasure there too, but it's not been found yet. And what about those old iron workings on the hill above the village, where in 1830 'some mining adventurers from Wales' were allowed to dig for iron ore, and were doing so quite successfully until, 'disagreeing among themselves, they ceased working'? There must be a tale to be told there. Then how about the handsome brass in the church in memory of William Harrison, Gent,

who lived at the manor house called Wychanger and died in 1615, but no one seems to know more than that. Luccombe at that time belonged to the Arundell family of Cornwall, before it came down to the Aclands and ultimately to the National Trust; so who was this dashing character in the Jacobean gown and ruff, what was he doing at Wychanger, and why did he rate such a prominent memorial?

I'll leave some latter-day Blackmore to immortalise William Harrison, Gent, and the old iron workings, and the haunted chapel ruins, but Henry Byam's story has been well chronicled already, so I should be on safe ground with the villagers there. His father was rector before him, and he was born in the old rectory in 1580. At Oxford he built up a considerable reputation as an orator and scholar, succeeded his father in 1612, and in 1636 was made Prebendary of Exeter. He seemed destined to complete a distinguished, but uneventful, career in the church, until he publicly backed the King against the Parliamentarians. When the Civil War broke out he was arrested at Luccombe by General Robert Blake, commander of the Parliamentary forces in the West of England. Somehow he managed to escape, and with his five sons he joined the King's army at Oxford.

His immediate, if short-lived, reward was to be made a Doctor of Divinity by the King, but that was little consolation when he learned that his wife and daughter had drowned while trying to escape across the Bristol Channel to Wales. Then the King was defeated and Byam went into exile with the young Prince Charles, first to the Isles of Scilly until Cromwell's men turned up, then in Jersey until that was captured too. There is a blank in his story during the years of exile that followed, while his old enemy General Blake was making a name for himself as Cromwell's 'General at Sea'.

The term would be derogatory today, but it just meant that he led the naval forces, and defeated the Dutch fleet three times.

It was Henry Byam, however, who had the last laugh. Blake died in 1657, and three years later came the Restoration. Henry returned to Luccombe, and a grateful Prince Charles, now Charles II, doubtless had a hand in his appointments as Canon of Exeter and Prebendary of Wells Cathedral. He died at Luccombe in 1669, a much venerated old gentleman of nearly ninety, and there is a fine memorial to him in the church.

Luccombe has been through some changes since then. Many of the cottages Henry Byam knew have disappeared as the village shrank at the end of the last century. Of those that remain, a lot have had the thatch replaced by Bridgwater tiles, though there is still some thatch about, notably on the Post Office, with its elaborate signboard for its former residents, the Ketnors. But of course new houses have appeared too. The latest, put up by a housing association and the National Trust, blend well enough – 'unlike the two houses just above them,' says Eric Rowlands, quite acidly for him, and referring to two cottages built in 1988 which a kinder critic describes as 'sympathetic but functional'.

I will keep out of that one, but if the villagers will forgive me, I must warn you that if you fancy a beer you'll be out of luck in Luccombe. Strangely, and not even Mr Rowlands explains why, there are no pubs in the village. That might have made me think twice about including it, if it hadn't been for Henry Byam, and the old iron mine, and the mysterious Mr Harrison, and the haunted chapel ruins up the road . . .

A VIEW OF THE POST OFFICE THROUGH THE LYCH-GATE – BUT THE KETNORS DON'T LIVE THERE ANY MORE.

SAINT BLANCHE, GWEN OR CANDIDA? NONE WAS WHITER THAN WITE

WHITCHURCH CANONICORUM
DORSET
4 miles north-east of Lyme Regis

If there is a competition for the English village with the most mellifluous name, this one must surely be in the running. Whitchurch by itself sounds pretty average, and there are plenty of them about. The one in Buckinghamshire could well be the prettiest – Rex Whistler must have thought so because he made his home there. Charles I preferred the Whitchurch in Hampshire; it was a handier place to stay the night before the second Battle of Newbury. And the one in Shropshire was the choice of a Mr and Mrs German, who produced a son there called Edward.

But my favourite Whitchurch has to be this one in Dorset, tucked away in the Marshwood Vale a few miles from the sea, out of sight and sound of the main coast road between Bridport and Lyme Regis. It was getting on for Christmas time when I first came across it, and the name seemed to have a seasonal lilt to it. I read it out loud, and found that instead of just saying it, I was singing it:

We Whitchurch Canoni-corum,
We Whitchurch Canoni-corum,
We Whitchurch Canoni-corum,
And a Happy New Year...

With a name like that, I thought, it must be quite a special village – and so it turned out to be. In fact, not just special, but unique. Many other villages can claim to have as long a history, as attractive an appearance and as peaceful a setting, but Whitchurch Canonicorum is not just a pretty name for a pretty place; it has the only parish church in England which contains relics of its patron saint. And to add a little extra spice to its history, nobody knows for certain who the patron saint was.

The saint's name is confusing in itself. Originally it was St Wite, but at some time during the Middle Ages they started using the Latinised version, Candida. The church guidebook plays it both ways and refers to 'The Church of St Candida

(St Wite) ...' Canon Syer, who wrote it, admits that 'it is unfortunately not possible definitely to identify St Wite', but goes on to have a jolly good try.

For many hundreds of years the popular local theory was that, in the ninth century, St Wite was a Saxon Christian lady who fell victim to Danish invaders on one of their rape-and-pillage excursions. A great many other Saxon Christian ladies must have suffered a similar fate, but Wite was more Christian than most. An eighteenth-century writer says she lived in prayer and contemplation beside a well on a hillside near the village, and when the Danes made 'cruel ravage and slaughter' in the area she became a Virgin Martyr. Certainly there is still a well on Chardown Hill known as St Wite's Well, though it is choked up and overgrown, but that is hardly conclusive, and in the past hundred years there have been other, more spectacular theories put forward about the saint's identity.

Canon Syer reviews them briefly. One suggests she was the daughter of a Prince of Brittany, and her name was Gwen, or Blanche, or some other version of Wite or White. She built up a saintly reputation over there, and it is said that when she was captured by pirates and taken to England, she escaped and walked on water back to Brittany. She was eventually buried there, but many years later there was an influx of Breton refugees into the west of England, and they brought her relics with them.

Then there's the theory that Wite was actually a chap, a Wessex monk called Witta who went as a missionary to Germany, was martyred and brought back to England for burial. When it was pointed out that the relics were those of a woman, the theory was adjusted to make the monk a woman missionary instead. Canon Syer has little time for any of this conjecture, and comes down firmly in favour of the Danish rape-and-pillage story. As he

THE TOMB OF ST WITE, WITH THE THREE APERTURES INTO WHICH PILGRIMS INSERTED THEIR DISEASED LIMBS.

says rather icily: 'It seems more likely that a tradition which was strong in the parish for over nine hundred years should be correct, rather than any of these theories of later years'.

The whole debate was re-opened in a booklet by Christine Waters called simply, *Who Was St Wite?* The front cover features an early painting of a young woman at prayer. Under it are the words: 'The Saint of Whitchurch Canonicorum', and for a moment I thought Ms Waters must have cracked it, but the painting turns out to be 'Female hermit in a landscape, Flemish School', and it transpires that, after consulting more than a score of antiquarian authorities, she can only come to the same 'probable' conclusion as the canon.

Happily, there is no dispute about the relics themselves. The church was founded by King Alfred in honour of St Wite and to preserve her remains, and since the thirteenth century they have been kept in their present shrine. In 1900 the tomb had to be opened because of structural repairs to the shrine, and inside the stone coffin

was a leaden box inscribed in Latin: 'Here rest the remains of St Wite'. It contained the bones of a women aged about forty, and experts agreed they were genuine. The shrine was repaired, and they rest there still.

For centuries it was a place of pilgrimage for the ill and disabled, who believed it had miraculous healing powers. There are three large holes under the tomb, and the idea was to place the diseased limbs inside the holes, to be close to the relics. If it worked, it was the custom to measure the pilgrim, not for the coffin he might otherwise have needed, but for a candle, which was made the same length as the cured limb. Sometimes the whole body was involved, which could have resulted in a rather cumbersome candle, but fortunately it was only the wick which had to be the right length, so they coiled it up to shorten it and made the candle more manageable.

Today the candle trade has fallen off, but petitions and offerings are still placed in the holes beneath the tomb. St Wite's origins may be obscured by what one antiquary calls 'a curious haze', but in Whitchurch Canonicorum her memory remains very clear.

I wanted one more question to be answered. Why Canonicorum – 'of the canons'? Appropriately it was Canon Syer who gave me the reason. In 1240 the Bishops of Sarum and Wells found they were short of cash and ordered that the tithes from the parish should be split between their two cathedrals, instead of remaining in the benefice. The canons, in fact, took over the purse-strings.

It's a very mundane explanation, I'm afraid, for such a delightful name. I rather wish I hadn't bothered ...

THE LOCAL TEA-ROOM WILL WELCOME YOU WITH OPEN ARMS.

YOU WON'T FIND GABBIGAMMIES IN THE FILLY-LOO

ASHMORE
DORSET
5 miles south-east of Shaftesbury

It was the Filly-Loo that finally convinced me, but I would probably have included Ashmore anyway. It is perched on a lofty vantage point on Cranborne Chase, the highest village in Dorset; they say on a clear day you can see the Isle of Wight, forty miles away. Even on a clear day it is not the easiest place to reach, seven hundred feet up on its hilltop, but in the winter it is sometimes almost impossible. Supplies have had to come in through the snowdrifts by tractor, or even by air. But many of the cottages still rely on thatch for protection, and they make a pleasant backdrop to the big village pond.

It has its squirearchy, the Howards, great benefactors to the village and the church, which they helped to rebuild. There are some curious village superstitions involving the strange cries of the Gabbigammies in Washer's Pit; and there is an excellent cricket ground where they have fielded one of the strongest village teams in England. So there are plenty of reasons to justify Ashmore's inclusion; but it was the Filly-Loo that finally did it.

I ought to explain first, though, about the Gabbigammies, the local name for ghosts. There was also talk of another odd manifestation at the Pit; nobody could think of a name for it, having

used up their inventive powers, perhaps, on the Gabbigammies, so it was just known as 'It'. 'It' was something like a bale of wool, which lolloped along behind anyone who walked past the Pit at night. Then a skeleton was found buried by the roadside, and when it was given a Christian burial the Gabbigammies stopped gibbering and 'It' stopped lolloping. The sceptics say the noise was just badgers, and I suppose 'It' might have been just a short-legged sheep, but let's not spoil the story.

There is slightly more authentication for another tale connected with Washer's Pit. An eighteenth-century squire at the manor house dreamed three times that there was trouble of some sort at the Pit. His cook, a lady called Mullens, volunteered to investigate, and the squire, with some relief perhaps, lent her his horse. She rode to the Pit and found a lady in white, hanging by her hair from a tree. As she cut her down she was set upon by men who had been hiding in the woods, but she managed to ride off with the lady in white (now with shorter hair) sitting in front of her. They even jumped a five-barred gate on the way home, perhaps to celebrate.

The squire, much impressed with her courage (and perhaps feeling a little guilty himself), presented her with a cottage in the village. Nobody records who the lady in white was, nor why she was dangling from a tree, but there is no gainsaying that there is still a cottage in Ashmore called Mullens . . .

So Walker's Pit and its associated weirdies make quite an impression in their own right. But I have come across spooky ponds before; how about the Filly-Loo? With a name like that, I thought, it must have an even more fascinating history. It takes place on the Friday nearest to Midsummer's Eve, with morris dancers and the local folk dance club making merry around the pond. As a midsummer revel it is not unique to Ashmore, but why Filly-Loo?

It seemed an easy exercise to find out. Ashmore has been blessed with a number of

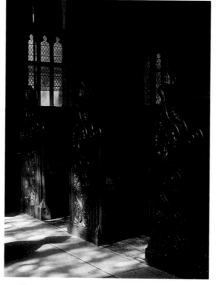

CARVED PEW ENDS IN ASHMORE CHURCH.

historically-minded residents who have written about the village. An early rector wrote the first history in 1890. The Howard family has kept an 'Ashmore Diary' since 1869, and in 1925 Eliot Howard wrote *A Dorset Village Seventy Years Ago*, drawing on his family's knowledge and records. A local student wrote a shortened history for an examination thesis and, in more recent years, another rector not only wrote a book about Ashmore but set it in type and printed it himself.

I failed to find the thesis, but I have been through all the rest. The Gabbigammies and the lady in white feature in each one, and there are many other titbits. Eliot Howard tells how the villagers objected to a new well because it was three hundred feet deep, quite a long haul to get a bucket of water, so they threw the maypole down it and went back to their rainwater cisterns. He also noted that 'the old Ashmore families are a fine, intelligent race, perhaps partly owing to the absence of any public house, my father having successfully resisted all attempts to establish one'. The old Ashmore families were intelligent enough, presumably, not to argue with the squire . . .

The rector with the printing set records how Eliot himself had an eye shot out in 1869 during a shooting party, and put a lead plaque on the tree where it happened, which was later surrounded by a daffodil garden and became a place of pilgrimage for the family. Eliot also marked the event by presenting a stained-glass window to the church, depicting Christ feeding His sheep on one side, and appropriately restoring sight to the blind on the other. All nice stories – but no mention of the Filly-Loo.

It was Mr George Taylor, a current Ashmore resident, who solved the mystery for me. Small wonder the Filly-Loo isn't mentioned in these earlier histories, because it is not an ancient village tradition at all. It was only invented, in fact, in 1956! The name was dreamed up by the then oldest inhabitant, Mr Louis Rideout, who said it meant 'having a good time', and related to the celebrations at the end of the nutting season. True, all the books mention the hazelnut crop which used to provide a major income for the village. They even give a useful tip for nut-gatherers: the best ones are found in the mouseholes under trees, because mice never collect unsound nuts. But not a mention of a Filly-Loo.

The Festival was actually the idea of a folk-dance enthusiast called Peter Swan, who had moved into Dorset and decided Ashmore made the ideal setting for it. The 'traditional' horn dance was devised by the chairman of the Ashmore Folk Dance Club, and another dance created by the men in the club was given the 'traditional' name, The Cranborne Chase. Hence my confusion.

The Filly-Loo has continued ever since, but as ancient customs go, it was a bit of a let down. Maybe I should have stuck with Washer's Pit and the Gabbigammies, not forgetting their weird woolly friend. In fact, I ought to have remembered, 'If you've got "It" – flaunt it!'

FAR FROM THE SUPERMARKET MADDING CROWDS – ASHMORE'S GENERAL STORE STILL SERVES THE VILLAGE.

NO DRUIDS, JUST A GIANT
AND THE FIENDISH FIDDLER

STANTON DREW
AVON
7 miles south of Bristol

The Drew family have a lot to answer for. Many centuries ago they made a bee-line for any village which was near some prehistoric site, and attached their name to it. Littleton Drew in Wiltshire was one, with its chambered long barrow. Drewsteignton in Devon was another, with its 'Spinster's Rock' burial chamber. And here is Stanton Drew, another of the family's acquisitions, with its circles of standing stones.

In all these villages, perhaps understandably, when the Drews had long since left but the village name remained, it became confused with the Druids, and so Stanton Drew has its Druid Farm, its Druid's Garth and Druid Lea, and inevitably the Druid's Arms.

These days archaeologists get very irritated by all this, and write scathingly about their earlier counterparts who fell for this false link. In the case of Stanton Drew they are also very rude about the inn sign at the Druid's Arms. 'Its periodical renewals every five years or so,' wrote one of them, 'provide a pictorial illustration of the fact that every age gets the Druids it deserves.' He goes on to establish that the stones actually go back to

between 2670 and 1975 BC, known as the Late Neolithic to Early Bronze Age – and not a Druid in sight. But the myth lives on, and so do the stories about the stones, helped no doubt by the villagers and particularly the landlord of the Druid's Arms.

If it weren't for the stones few people would probably have discovered the village at all. 'Where in the world is Stanton Drew?' asks an old Somerset rhyme, then adds helpfully, 'A mile from Pensford, another from Chew.' It is referring to Chew Magna, the much noisier village on the main road, not the River Chew, which is close by. In fact you cross it to enter Stanton Drew, on a bridge built by a fifteenth-century Bishop of Bath. It is guarded by the Round House, originally a look-out post for nearby Stanton Court, then used as a toll-house when the road became a turnpike in 1790. The box for the toll money is still inside the door, but the only toll taken at the bridge these days is on the paintwork of those who don't negotiate it with care.

Stanton Court was the home of the Stantons in the *Domesday Book*, then in the thirteenth century came the Drews, the cause of so much confusion later.

THE ROUND HOUSE, ORIGINALLY A LOOK-OUT POST, LATER A TOLL-HOUSE.

Opposite is Rectory Farm, which was built by the Bishop at the same time as the bridge, so his archdeacons could stay there as they toured the diocese. I doubt he would have had much time for the stories attached to the stones not far away, but there is no escaping them if you are writing about Stanton Drew, so here we go.

One of them was recorded by an architect called John Wood who visited the village in 1749. 'No one, say the country people about Stanton-drue, was ever able to reckon the number of these metamorphosed stones, or to take a draught of them, though several have attempted to do both, and proceeded until they were either struck dead upon the spot, or with such an illness as soon carried them off.' Mr Wood fared rather better; all that happened when he tried to count them was a violent thunderstorm, which the villagers naturally blamed on him. But the tradition continues that even if you do manage to count them, you will never arrive at the same total twice.

Anther tale relates to a single massive boulder known as Hautville's Quoit, some way from the stone circles, near the road to Chew Magna. A lot of it was chipped away in the last century to use for mending the road, but it is still quite a sizeable chunk. It was named after Sir John Hautville, known as the Giant Knight of Chew, who followed King Richard to the Crusades, then returned to perform all manner of amazing feats around Stanton Drew. For instance, he once caught three sheep stealers and carried them to the top of Norton church tower, one under each arm and the third in his teeth. He didn't need to throw them over – after that experience they never stole a sheep again.

His exploit with the Quoit was even more dramatic. He competed with the Devil in throwing it from the top of an earthwork known as Maes Knoll – which incidentally he had created himself 'with one spadeful of earth'. His throw was three furlongs longer than the Devil's, who then made an excuse and left. There is an effigy in Chew Magna church which purports to be Sir John, but experts say his name was added comparatively recently, and it's about as believable as that story about the Quoit.

Finally, the most popular tale of Stanton Drew's stones, the Petrified Wedding. 'Once, long ago, before cider was invented,' as one version endearingly begins, a newly married couple – some say a Miss Stanton and a Mr Drew, but you

THE DRUID'S ARMS, WITH ITS CURRENT SIGN – BUT NEVER A REAL DRUID IN SIGHT.

can push this sort of thing a bit too far – held their wedding party on a Saturday evening in a field just outside the village. They and their guests danced to the music of three fiddlers until midnight, when the fiddlers, being pious men, refused to continue playing on the Sabbath. The bride said she'd find another fiddler even if she had to go to hell for him – whereupon Guess-Who appeared from the Underworld, armed with his fiddle, and said he would play them a jig which they would never forget. They danced in a large circle around him, faster and faster, until they dropped with exhaustion and were turned into stone. 'I leave you,' said the fiendish fiddler, 'as a monument to my power and your wickedness, to the end of time.'

The story has been told and re-enacted countless times since, and perhaps the best way to round it off is to quote the final lines of the nineteenth-century poem:

There are some who may this tale esteem
As some crazed poet's idle dream.
Yet 'tis not so, I only tell
What once, tradition says, befell
In ages past. But, false or true,
The stones remain in Stanton Drew.

And perhaps I can add:

The locals don't let these old stones
daunt 'em.
They take the view: 'If you've got 'em,
flaunt 'em . . .'

A MUSICAL VICAR, A MUSIC-LESS CARREL – AND RAKING FOR THE MOON

BISHOPS CANNINGS
WILTSHIRE
3 miles north-east of Devizes

It's the Moonraker story which has earned Bishops Cannings a place in the reference books, but the village has more to it than just a charming legend. It is attractive enough in itself: thatched and half-timbered cottages with a church like a miniature Salisbury Cathedral, set in the traditional farming countryside of the Vale of Pewsey between the open uplands of the

BISHOPS CANNINGS CHURCH, A MINIATURE SALISBURY CATHEDRAL IN THE VALE OF PEWSEY.

Marlborough Downs and Salisbury Plain, far enough away from the main road not to be disturbed by the traffic between Swindon and Devizes, and handily placed for boat trips on the newly-opened Kennet and Avon Canal – you could hardly ask for more.

But more there is. The church has a rare carrel, not for singing but for study, the original version of the tiny study rooms now being re-introduced in some colleges and schools. There are its two early benefactors, one talented, the other tenacious. And if the Moonraker legend is not enough for you, have you heard the one about the villagers telling strangers that the church tower grew so high because they spread manure around it?

The tower is in fact very high, and the spire above it rises to 135 feet, which for a village church is very high indeed. The resemblance to Salisbury Cathedral is not a coincidence; the village used to belong to the Bishops of Salisbury, hence the name. They no doubt had a hand in building the church, and a very impressive job they made of it – but over the centuries it had two other people to thank for adding important extra touches.

One was the Revd George Ferebe, the vicar at the start of the seventeenth century. He was a musician of note, indeed of several, and was prepared to put his money where his notes were. He provided the church with a complete peal of eight bells, said to be the first new peal recorded in England after the Reformation. He also provided an organ, which remained in use for more than two hundred years, and trained a first-class choir. As a result Bishops Cannings 'could challenge all England for musique, football and bell-ringing' – he may have been a soccer coach as well.

The other benefactor was William Bayly, a local man who sailed the world with Captain Cook as his assistant astronomer. After retiring back in England in 1807 he offered to build a new school in his home village, but the churchwardens, somewhat short-sightedly, declined the offer. At that point most of us would have told them what they could do with their village, but Mr Bayly was not to be put off. All right, he said, if you don't want a new school, how about a new organ? This time they admitted he had a point; Mr Ferebe's instrument was beginning to flag after a couple of centuries – indeed it was officially reported to be 'in a bad state'. So they graciously accepted, and Mr Bayly not only paid for the organ, but agreed to provide for its upkeep. Alas, he never saw or heard it. The organ took two years to build, and by the time it was completed and installed he had died. But the organ itself, with some modifications, is still in use.

The most unusual furnishing in the church is the carrel, a single-seater box pew with a sloping desk facing the seat and a hinged door on the front. The back panel has a painting of an enormous hand, with Latin religious tags written on the palm and fingers, and two cockerels beneath it, symbols of watchfulness. It is the type which monks used for solitary study and meditation, but nobody knows who used this one

or how it got to Bishops Cannings.

And so to the Moonraker story, part of a sequence of events around the seventeenth and eighteenth centuries which gave Wiltshiremen their nickname, and the rest of us two new words and a new saying. It was the time when Flemish weavers were coming over to England to teach us their craft, and a lot of them finished up in Wiltshire, where vast flocks of sheep grazed on Salisbury Plain. Wool weaving was considered too hard for the womenfolk, so the men worked the looms while their wives coped with the family. Only the unmarried women did the spinning, and became known as 'spinsters'.

The boats which took the finished broadcloth to Holland often came back with Dutch cheese, quite different from the home product made on the chalklands of Wiltshire – 'as different,' in fact, 'as chalk and cheese'. The boats also brought the Dutchmen's favourite tipple, schnapps, which soon caught on among the locals – so much so that a very high duty was imposed on it to protect the traditional English ales. Where there is import duty, inevitably there are smugglers, and a flourishing trade built up in bootlegged schnapps. The barrels were transported around the county by night on donkeys, and if they were still on the road at dawn the barrels were hidden in ponds until it was dark again. One such pond was at Bishops Cannings.

If you don't know the rest of the story, you must have guessed it. One night as the moon was coming up, two men were raking the pond to get the barrels out for the next stage of the journey when a patrol of Excisemen appeared and asked, not surprisingly, what they were up to. Without hesitation one of the men pointed at the reflection of the moon in the water, beamed happily at the Excisemen and explained in all wide-eyed inno-cence: ''Tis the gert cheese in the water we be trying to get un'.

The Excisemen were apparently quite satisfied by this; I expect it merely confirmed their low opinion of Wiltshire folks' intelligence. Tapping their heads sadly, no doubt, they left them to it, and went off to tell their colleagues about the two village idiots they had found raking for the moon in Bishops Cannings pond.

And another legend was born . . .

SO WHOSE ROOTS GO BACK TO THE JUTES?

EAST MEON
HAMPSHIRE
8 miles north-east of Bishop's Waltham

East Meon is an absolute gift to the gazetteers. The river Meon flows picturesquely through the heart of the village with the High Street on each side. There's a medieval Court Hall, a Norman church, Tudor and Georgian houses, and not far away Roman villas, an Iron Age fort, an assortment of Bronze Age burial grounds and a modern stately home, all set in a delightful Hampshire valley. It is so obviously attractive that it almost seemed superfluous to add anything else – until I read F.G. Standfield's *A History of East Meon*, and discovered just how much there is about this village that a casual visitor could not hope to find out.

Mr Standfield came to live in East Meon about thirty years ago, a solicitor who became a parish councillor, president of the cricket club, trustee of the almshouses and chairman of the village hall committee . . . But the greatest service he has rendered to the community has been the four years' hard work that went into his book.

It's not just an historical survey, though all the history is there. He deals, for instance, with the wary relationship with West Meon, some four miles downstream, which has been going on for quite a few centuries. The popular belief is that it dates back to the days when the raiding Jutes only sailed up the river as far as West Meon, which acquired a Jutish culture while East Meon remained Celtish; the two have never really got on since. It's a lovely story, but Mr Standfield is not entirely convinced. He quotes evidence suggesting the Jutes got rather further than that, and he also points out that a couple of centuries earlier there were German mercenaries roaming Hampshire after deserting from the Roman army, and they could have colonised the whole valley.

He does agree, however, that there has always been this coolness between East and West. It is not quite a 'never the twain' situation, but as he says, 'social intercourse is very limited, and the rivalry of inter-cricket and football matches is spiced with a little extra "edge".' As president of the cricket club, he should know.

It is this human aspect of East Meon which Mr Standfield brings out, and he has unearthed some entertaining village characters. There was Thomas Habin, an eighteenth-century parish clerk and sexton, who could not resist filling up a few blank pages in the church register with cheerful comments like: 'Thomas Habin is my name and England is my nation, Eastmean is my dwelling place and Christ is my Salvation'. One of his successors, Robert Smith, who held the post for sixty-three years, left a more wistful note for posterity: 'When I depart this life I would like to have a hymn sung at my funeral, as I have sung so

THE TWELFTH-CENTURY FONT IN ALL SAINTS' CHURCH IS SCULPTED FROM ONE BLOCK OF MARBLE; IT DEPICTS THE CREATION AND THE FALL OF MAN.

many years'. I hope he got a couple.

In more recent times there was Percy Richard Morley Horder, a distinguished architect who came to the village in 1926, at a time when the fourteenth-century Court House and Hall had been crudely converted into farm-workers' accommodation. It had deteriorated, says Mr Standfield, into 'a shabby farmhouse sited among equally shabby (and smelly) surroundings'. Morley Horder restored the ancient building, converted the derelict farm-yard into a terraced garden, and lived there until his death in 1944. During that time he bought a number of thatched cottages in the village which had been badly neglected, and instead of pulling them down, as most landlords would have done, he repaired and restored them 'with characteristic thoroughness and good taste'. East Meon began to look its old self again, and visitors who enjoy its well-preserved period flavour today can largely thank Morley Horder for setting the pattern.

But the one person who has made the biggest impact on East Meon in this century must surely be Eleanor Countess Peel, the eccentric lady with almost unlimited means who, with her husband, built 'Leydene', the magnificent mansion on Hyden Hill, just outside the village. Mr Standfield was obviously much taken with her, and so am I; she was one of those larger-than-life characters who used to crop up quite frequently in the English squirearchy in past centuries, but now are increasingly rare – perhaps because they no longer have the money to indulge their whims and fancies.

Lady Peel had no such problem. Her father was a Lancashire lino manufacturer, which may sound unromantic but was highly profitable. He gave her a dowry of £800,000 and when he died he left two million. Eleanor married William Peel, grandson of the great Sir Robert, who was pretty well heeled himself, and in 1913 they decided to build a country home in the Meon Valley. That was not the best time to start a building project, and it wasn't finished until 1925, but once installed Lady Peel began buying up the surrounding farms until she had over ten thousand acres, while her husband spent much of his time shooting in Scotland. She became the biggest landowner, and probably the biggest employer, in the district – there were fourteen gardeners and three chauffeurs at Leydene alone, and goodness knows how many footmen and maids. But Lady Peel was more sociable with her pigs than her staff. If a sow was being taken to be mated she would ride on the lorry with it to keep it company, whereas one of her kitchen maids said that in the four years she worked at Leydene her mistress had never spoken to her.

Lady Peel wore shabby old clothes and was very careful with money in spite of her wealth. In 1928 she sued Petersfield R.D.C. for £7 17s 7d, 'the estimated cost of keeping six visitors for four days

in excess of their invitations' because the council hadn't cleared the snowbound roads. But the nicest story of life at Leydene concerns not so much Lady Peel as her butler. Mr Standfield does not record his name, but he deserves a special niche in East Meon's Hall of Fame. In 1941 a high-powered deputation from the Admiralty came to the house to assess its suitability as a naval establishment – which indeed it now is. They were very senior naval officers, awash with gold braid, and the future of Leydene lay in their hands. The butler ushered them to the huge drawing-room where Lady Peel awaited them, flung open the double doors, and announced: 'My Lady, the sailors have arrived'.

I shall cherish the memory of that butler, as I shall cherish Lady Peel who must have schooled him so ably, and indeed Frederick Standfield, who has recorded it all for us. East Meon, I am sure, cherishes them too.

EAST MEON, SET IN A DELIGHTFUL HAMPSHIRE VALLEY.

EAST IS FAIRLY SOUTH, AND THERE ISN'T ANY WEST

EAST GARSTON
BERKSHIRE
5 miles north of Hungerford

Let's face it, the Lambourn Valley has seen quieter days. They were much quieter, I imagine, before the M4 cut across it above Boxford, not only because of its effect on the landscape, but also because its junction near Great Shefford means that it is only an hour or so from London these days, with all that that implies. It may well have been quieter before the Lambourne Valley Railway was built, linking Newbury with Lambourn and so encouraging local commuting through the valley; by the time the railway was abandoned the motor car enabled that commuting to continue. And in much earlier days than that, it was probably a lot more peaceful before the Romans turned up and built a road alongside it, close to where the M4 is now.

With the motorway came, inevitably, the developers, and it could be argued that they have made the worst impact of all. In a reference to Boxford, for instance, one gazetteer which normally turns a blind eye to such things comments scathingly: 'Rusting farm machinery and vehicles, buildings displaying their guts (or at least their girders), and grey rectangles of building blocks qualify at least one straggle for nomination as Berkshire's worst-kept village'.

But to be fair the writer does urge his readers to persevere, and I can confirm that it is worth it. Keep heading upstream and you come to Great Shefford, which has the disadvantage of being on the main road from Hungerford to Wantage, and only a mile or so from the M4 junction, but it still retains some quiet corners, notably around the Church of St Mary's, the only one in Berkshire

HIDDEN AWAY, A TYPICAL EAST GARSTON HALF-TIMBERED COTTAGE.

with a Norman round tower. Keep going for a mile beyond Great Shefford and your perseverance will really be rewarded, because the next village is East Garston, with its delightful timber-framed cottages, some of them thatched, some with moss-covered tiles, the walls often sloping at alarming angles, as they have done for centuries. East Garston was in a prosperous cloth-producing area based on Newbury, and the Tudor and Jacobean yeomen who lived in these cottages obviously did very nicely for themselves.

The odd thing about East Garston is that there isn't a West Garston. The 'East' in this case has nothing to do with the compass. Before the Norman conquest it belonged to a man called Asgar or Esgar, and the village's name means 'Asgar's tun'. Until quite recently the name was still pronounced as 'Argasson' by the locals.

Asgar was King Edward the Confessor's staller, or stable boss, and the Lambourn Valley is still associated with horses. Strings of them are liable to appear around the next corner at any time, and as they are racehorses and very valuable, it is advisable to treat them with respect. Most are based around Lambourn itself, further up the valley, which features as 'Maryland' in Thomas Hardy's *Jude the Obscure*. East Garston can't claim a literary connection, even an obscure one, but older inhabitants do recall how some of the scenes for the film of *Quiet Wedding* were filmed in the village, around the end of the second World War, and they talk about it still.

Rather further back, in the sixteenth century, a

chronicler referred to 'a propper river running through . . . verie commodyous to the habitants'. It doesn't run quite so 'properly' these days in East Garston; traditionally it flows between Candlemas in February to Michaelmas in October, but in 1991 it dried up in August and didn't start running again until May. Great Shefford, a mile downstream, does slightly better.

East Garston Church is a little way out of the village, and to reach it you pass some of the most attractive of the old cottages, each with a thatched porch and its own little bridge across the river (superfluous, alas, for much of the year). All Saints' Church is renowned for what the church leaflet calls its 'eminently curious' east window. Unfortunately it goes on to describe it in terms quite baffling to the average visitor: 'three steeply stepped lights and huge over-cusped pointed trefoils above the lower ones' – but don't be put off, it's worth seeing anyway.

Much more curious, in my view, is the tale of

the over-pernicketty parson who was Vicar of East Garston in 1912. That year was marked by the death at the age of 104 of the village's oldest inhabitant, Isaac Early, a much venerated local preacher at the Primitive Methodist Chapel for eighty-two years. He helped to build the chapel in 1880, collecting stones for the foundations in a wheelbarrow, which he then allowed his wife to pull on a rope to the building site; an early example of non-discrimination.

When he died, the vicar checked the baptismal records and found that Isaac had been christened just before his second birthday. This apparently caused him great disquiet, since he felt unable to decide whether Isaac was 104 or 105 – and in view of this he refused to allow an inscribed tombstone to be erected on the old chap's grave. I don't suppose Isaac was too bothered, and his wheelbarrow-pulling wife had probably predeceased him, but it doesn't seem very friendly to me . . .

THE RIVER AT EAST GARSTON HIDDEN IN DEEP BANKS, HAS SHRUNK SINCE ITS HEYDAY IN THE SIXTEENTH CENTURY.

FIRST VIKINGS, THEN FRENCHMEN, NOW TOURISTS
– BUT THEY'VE ALL LEFT STONE UNTURNED

APPLEDORE AND STONE-IN-OXNEY
KENT
5 miles south-east of Tenterden

I felt I was in one of those classic scenes in the old westerns: a lonely rider heading across a vast empty plain, then the range of hills on the horizon and signs of human habitation. He rides off the plain and up the dusty main street of the little township perched on the hillside, and heads for the saloon . . .

I had only driven from the environs of the Romney, Hythe & Dymchurch Railway, but the vast empty spaces of Romney Marsh were getting almost as boring as that vast empty plain, when the landscape changed. After miles of flat nothingness the road crossed a disused canal and climbed out of the marsh, into the centre of what seemed to me, by contrast, one of the most attractive villages in England. I didn't even look for the saloon . . .

Even without the contrast of the Marsh, Appledore can hold its own in the premier league of scenic villages. The B-road that passes through it may attract too much traffic in summer, but the old cottages on either side are set back far enough to be enjoyed in comfort. This was, after all, the medieval market place when Appledore was a town, and there is still room for stalls to be set out alongside the road. It was licensed by Edward III in 1359, and although it has long since disappeared, the annual fair that he granted with it went on until the end of the last century.

The approach to Appledore looked very different in Edward III's day. It started off as a port with direct access to the sea, which turned out to be rather a disadvantage when the Vikings sailed up with five thousand men, and made it their headquarters for the usual rape and pillage. It took King Alfred five years to dislodge them. In 1380, the French did much the same thing; they burned down the church and most of what was then a sizeable town. So one might have thought that it was something of a relief when the channel silted up, the sea retreated, and Appledore found itself seven miles inland.

It actually made matters worse. Appledore lost its sea trade and gained instead an expanse of marsh on its doorstep which made it one of the unhealthiest places in England. As one historian wrote in 1798: 'The large quantity of stagnating water . . . engenders such noxious and pestilential vapours as spread sickness and frequent death on the inhabitants'.

Ironically, it took a war to solve Appledore's health problem. With Napoleon threatening invasion, it was decided to dig a twenty-mile canal around the inland boundary of the Marsh, virtually turning it into an island. The Martello towers along the coast were the first line of defence, the canal – with a protective wall along its landward side and gun emplacements at regular intervals – would be

the second. If necessary to repel invaders, the Marsh could be flooded as well.

By the time the Royal Military Canal was completed in 1807 the threat had passed, but it proved very useful nonetheless. It provided effective drainage for the Marsh, so Appledore no longer suffered the 'noxious and pestilential vapours'. As a bonus, barges were able to use it between Rye and Hythe, so Appledore was back on the water-borne trade route again, and there was also the road which the Army built alongside the canal. When the canal traffic eventually ceased and the road became overgrown, Appledore was sufficiently well established to continue as a thriving village, if no longer a prosperous town.

One of its residents these days is Sir John Winnifrith, who was the first director-general of the National Trust and later chairman of Kent County Council's local history committee. Small wonder that Sir John's history of Appledore is a most detailed and knowledgeable study, and every detail of the village's changing fortunes is in it. But for a crash course in local history you can't beat the quite remarkable tapestry in the parish church, Appledore's answer to Bayeux, designed and made by local ladies to mark the eight-hundredth anniversary of its first recorded rector in 1188. There are the Vikings coming ashore, Edward III's market, the French burning down the church, the digging of the canal, and much more besides.

Inevitably, with its dramatic history and being on a main road, Appledore gets its full quota of tourists, as the 'Fish and Chips' signs outside the pubs testify, but only two miles away, also on the edge of the Marsh, is a village which few tourists discover. You can see it from Mill Mound, just outside Appledore. In the foreground is the Ferry Inn, still with its board of tolls from the days when you actually needed a ferry to cross the modest stream beside it. Beyond

LIST OF TOLLS		
	s	d
EVERY CARRIAGE, WAGGON or MACHINE WITH 4 WHEELS	1	0
" " " " WITH 2 WHEELS		6
EVERY HORSE, MULE or ASS		1
CATTLE Each		1
SHEEP or LAMBS Per Score		3
PIGS Each		1
FOOT PASSENGER		½
ENGINE	1	6
TRUCK, WAGGON, MACHINE or PLOUGH Drawn by same	1	0
LORRY - STEAM or MOTOR	1	6
TRACTOR	1	0
MOTOR COACH or CHAR-A-BANC	1	6
MOTOR CAR	1	0
MOTOR CYCLE		2
TRAILER or SIDECAR		1
HAND TRUCK		1
BATH CHAIR		1
TRICYCLE or BICYCLE Each Way		1

THE BOARD OF TOLLS AT THE FERRY INN, BETWEEN APPLEDORE AND STONE.

it rises the great whale-back shape of the Isle of Oxney, jutting into the Marsh, and on the tip of it is Stone-in-Oxney.

The tourists may have missed it, but Kent County Council hasn't. It was selected as one of twenty villages deserving special care and attention. The Weald of Kent Preservation Society then produced an exhaustive study in 1970 describing every building in the village, and what needed doing to it. It's a very frank survey: one cottage, for instance, was described as 'too high and too narrow, somewhat grim . . . an ugly duckling which would look out of place in any village'. And under the heading 'Suggested Treatment', is the one word, 'Difficult'; I think they really meant 'Demolition'.

They were also very rude about the illuminated sign on the garage, and they didn't like some dilapidated outbuildings near the Baptist Chapel or the breeze-block garages by the council houses, but it seems to me they were nit-picking a bit.

They sum up: 'Stone is not a "show village" with a high standard to live up to, but neither has it any atrocities'. I would rate it rather higher than that. It is nicely compact and self-contained around a handsome fifteenth-century church, it has fine views from its hilltop overlooking the Marsh, and there is no main road through it, so you can wander about in comparative peace.

Thus Appledore and Stone-in-Oxney have contrasting appeals for me. Appledore is more of a 'show village', as the Preservation Society might say, and it has a more dramatic and eventful history, but the tourists come pouring in on that busy main road. Stone has been a backwater throughout the centuries and remains happily so today.

But although Stone-in-Oxney is very much a junior partner, it can out-do Appledore in one respect at least. The Preservation Society, meticulous as ever, noted that under the church tower, next to a Roman altar which used to serve as a horse-block, are the fossilised remains of parts of an iguanodon unearthed in Stone Quarry in 1935. With a rare touch of whimsy the survey comments: 'Living here some 130 million years ago, it can unquestionably claim to be Stone's oldest inhabitant'. So, Appledore, beat that!

THE HANDSOME MEMORIAL HALL IN STONE.

... THREE FANCY DOORS, TWO BUTTING RAMS, AND A CHURCH BELL IN A YEW TREE

BARFRESTONE
KENT
8 miles south-west of Sandwich

'Whosoever takes any interest in ecclesiastical architecture has heard of, if not seen, Barfrestone church,' wrote an early chronicler in a volume entitled, with simple charm, *A Saunter Through Kent.* Certainly the reason this little village has crept into the reference books is its richly embellished and decorated church – 'this little gem of the mason's craft,' as our saunterer puts it, adding with grammatical abandon, 'and quite unique'.

Another enthusiast has written an entire book-let on what he calls, unequivocally, Barfreystone

church's 'world-famous' carvings, and if you are writing about the village there is really no getting away from them. Even so, there are other features which are less obvious, but to a non-expert may be rather more intriguing – not least, as you may already have spotted, the spelling of its name.

One authority calls it Barfrestone, the other has inserted a 'y'. Signposts and maps seem to favour the former, and it does seem closer to the original Norman spelling of Barfreston. But all three versions are designed to confuse the stranger, because throughout the centuries the locals have pronounced it simply 'Barson', and for a time the Victorians had the good sense to spell it that way too.

The name meant 'cold bleak town', but in spite of that, or perhaps because of it, Barfrestone is supposed to rival its neighbouring village Coldred (which sounds pretty chilly too) as the healthiest place in Kent. An example is quoted of a rector who died in 1700 at the age of ninety-six. The line-up at his funeral was a geriatrician's dream: the priests taking the service were eighty-two and eighty-seven, the sexton was eighty-six, the parish clerk was eighty-seven, and several of the mourners were centenarians. This was not just a one-off phenomenon. It is recorded that a couple of decades later 'there were in this small parish, which consisted of only fifty-eight souls, nine persons whose ages made 636 years'.

And the planners worry these days about an ageing rural population . . .

Barfrestone is still very small, just a couple of farms, a few thatched cottages, a pub, a village pond – and of

THE SPECTACULAR SOUTH DOORWAY OF BARFRESTONE'S MUCH-EMBELLISHED CHURCH.

course that church. I can ignore it no longer. From a distance I don't think it looks all that exciting – a stocky building, less than fifty feet long but quite high, with the lower half of the side walls left blank and no tower to break the line of the roof. Until you walk up the churchyard path you might wonder what all the fuss is about. Then you are confronted by the spectacular south doorway, and the marvelling begins.

The masons who built the church probably belonged to the same guild as those who built Canterbury Cathedral, less than ten miles away. It is said that some of the stone they used was taken from a chapel at Hackington. It seems the monks at Canterbury were worried that Hackington might grow into a rival to their own establishment, and

petitioned the King and the Pope to have it demolished. When they eventually succeeded they apparently had no fears about it being rebuilt at Barfrestone; perhaps they had heard of its reputation for longevity and assumed its inhabitants were more interested in staying alive than concentrating on the hereafter.

The carvings date from about 1190, and they really are quite astonishing. Over the south door Christ is seated in majesty, with his right hand raised in blessing and an open book on his knee. He is surrounded by seraphs and sovereigns, nobles and ladies, and a small squadron of the angelic host. At his feet are a couple of mermaids, a griffin and a sphinx. And, believe it or not, that is just the start.

All around the doorway are floral designs, legendary beasts, assorted gargoyles. In the arch above the door are twelve illustrations of how the medieval leisured classes spent their spare time, ranging from a love-scene to hare-coursing. Then there are fourteen carvings of servants doing household chores. The two sets of pictures thus represent an early version of 'Upstairs Downstairs'. There are decorations around the blocked-up north door and priest's door too, and surrounding the distinctive wheel-window in the east wall.

Inside are more carvings along the walls, around the windows, up the chancel arch – everywhere a mason could reach with a chisel. You might spot St Martin of Tours sharing his cloak with a beggar, or a couple of butting rams, or just a man putting a rabbit in a cooking pot. All human life, as they say, is here – plus most of the animal world and some grotesque creatures you wouldn't want to meet on a dark night.

No wonder, then, that people enthuse over Barfrestone Church. Some may decry the carvings as no more than fancy decoration, just the masons showing off, and certainly I think those masons might be a little flattered by the depth of knowledge they are supposed to have possessed regarding religious folklore and symbolism. I get the impression myself that they worked on a simple principle: if it moved, carve it. But even at that basic level the results are impressive, and if indeed the carvings have all the subtle significance the experts attribute to them, they are very impressive indeed.

Even so, the feature of Barfrestone which particularly appeals to me is not the work of a mason, but of some anonymous improviser who has left just as distinctive a legacy to the church. I mentioned it has no tower, so there is no obvious place to hang a bell. You will actually find it hanging in a yew tree in the churchyard, and it is rung by a rope which passes through the wall of the church and into the tree.

None of the reference books names the person who first devised such an ingenious and economical belfry, but in my book he rates right up there with the masons . . .

TOP: BARFRESTONE'S UNUSUAL BELFRY – A YEW TREE IN THE CHURCHYARD.
BELOW: THE PRESERVATION WORK GOES ON . . .

A VERY GRAND GRANDSTAND, THE ABBOT'S CURSE, AND A STONEMASON'S NIGHTMARE

SHERBORNE
GLOUCESTERSHIRE
15 miles east of Cheltenham

In the Church of St Mary Magdalene – which is more like a family chapel than a church because it is firmly attached to the side of Sherborne House – is the seventeenth-century memorial to John Dutton, whose family lived there for four hundred years. He is portrayed, rather alarmingly, standing up in his shroud, with a lengthy inscription setting out his many sterling qualities: 'one who was master of a large fortune and owner of a mind equal to it' is one typical tribute.

However, the memorial omits some rather interesting facets of Mr Dutton. It does not mention, for instance, that he was universally known as Crump Dutton because he was a hunchback; the erect figure in the shroud gives no hint of it. And while he was indeed 'master of a

large fortune', the epitaph does not add that he was a notorious gambler and nearly lost the family estate in a game of cards. Legend has it that he offered it as a wager at the gaming table, and it was only a vigilant butler who saved the day. When he heard the players cry 'Sherborne is up!', the devoted fellow – perhaps seeing his own job in jeopardy – picked up his master bodily and carried him out of the room.

In spite of his gambling, Crump Dutton did much to lay the foundations of what Sherborne is today, a well-preserved village of traditional Cotswold cottages with their stone-mullioned windows and stone-slate roofs, well spaced out along the Sherborne Brook, with the massive outline of Sherborne House at the centre, virtually dividing it in half. This was not the house that Crump built; a much later Dutton, the second Lord Sherborne, rebuilt it in the early 1830s. But there is one impressive building he was responsible for which still stands on the outskirts of Sherborne; it was probably the most elaborate grandstand in England.

A RATHER GRISLY DETAIL FROM ONE OF THE DUTTON MEMORIALS.

Crump Dutton's grandfather managed to acquire Sherborne after the Reformation. It was originally owned by the monks of Winchcombe Abbey, who had a grange and chapel where Sherborne House stands now. When Crump inherited the estate he enlarged the grange, and the story goes that he moved the chapel ten feet to make more room for it, thus incurring the wrath of the Abbot for building on holy ground. The Abbot, it is said, put a curse on the Duttons, which lately seems to have come home to roost.

At the same time Crump erected the building which stands on the other side of the main A40 trunk road from Oxford to South Wales. In Crump's day the route lay through Sherborne itself, but fortunately for the village a road along the ridge to the south became a turnpike in the eighteenth century, and it has been the main road

ever since. The Dutton estate extended well beyond it, and Crump decided to create a deer park there. The building, now called Lodge Park, was for the express purpose of giving his guests a grandstand view of the hunt.

It looks more like a mansion than a grandstand, and indeed it was eventually converted into living quarters, but its object was just the same as the directors' stand at White Hart Lane or the hospitality suites at Lord's. There were just two big rooms inside, each taking up the whole of one floor, where the guests refreshed themselves before hunts and had a banquet afterwards. Outside the first-floor windows was one balcony, on the roof was another, and from this two-tiered grandstand the guests had a splendid view of the park, and in particular of the long straight drive where the stag was released, just ahead of the dogs. Crump and his friends would bet on which dog caught it first.

Only a qualified expert could describe Crump's grandstand properly. In the words of one writer, 'it bursts with architecture'. French Renaissance, Italian Classicism, pediments and cornices, friezes and brackets, Crump used the lot. In due course, when staged deer hunting fell out of favour and England switched to foxes, there was no further use for it as a grandstand, and it saw more humble service as two gamekeepers' cottages. It recovered its pride a little at the turn of this century when Emma Lady Sherborne converted it into a dower house, no doubt finding it a lot more manageable than Sherborne House itself, with its staff at that time of thirty-eight servants. It has since passed to the National Trust.

The Duttons continued to live at Sherborne House until the last war, when the Army moved in. After the war it became a private school, then a variety of different study centres, until in 1981 it was converted into thirty-five luxury flats. The only part of it accessible to the public is the church, and

Sir JOHN DUTTON *Baronet* PETER
Son of Sir RALPH DUTTON, by MARY the Daughter of ~~JOHN~~ BARWICK,
Doctor of Phyfick departed this Life February the firft 1742/3

SIR JOHN DUTTON WOULD NOT LOOK SO NONCHALANT IF HE KNEW ABOUT THE STONEMASON'S BOOB BELOW.

you have to go round the stable block to reach it, but it's worth a visit, not only to see the unhunched Crump, but a rare example of a stonemason's nightmare.

The memorial to the second Baronet, Sir John Dutton, is even more imposing than Crump's. It has Sir John in a toga instead of a shroud, standing with his legs casually crossed and leaning nonchalantly on a convenient urn, with a lengthy inscription below. Unfortunately the chap who carved it put the name of Sir John's grandfather as John Barwick – and discovered too late that it should have been Peter. Apparently he had no alternative but to score out the 'John' and carve 'Peter' above it. The correction is still there, 250

years later, and wherever the stonemason is, no doubt his face is still red.

Perhaps Crump Dutton is blushing a little too, because that curse he brought on the family when he moved the chapel and enlarged his grange on holy ground seems to have been fulfilled. The Abbot forecast that the estate would not descend by direct linear succession, and the line would eventually die out. In the years that have followed the line has been broken four times, and on the last occasion, when the eighth Baron succeeded his cousin in 1982, he himself was eighty-four years old and unmarried. There is no Baron Sherborne in *Who's Who* today; the Abbot's curse is complete.

THEY SHOE THEIR MAGPIES – AND HANG OUT THEIR PONDS TO DRY

PIDDINGHOE
EAST SUSSEX
2 miles north-west of Newhaven

In the past couple of hundred years two very nice things have happened to Piddinghoe. The village lies in a valley through which the River Ouse flows down a very slight gradient, and until the end of the eighteenth century it was constantly flooded as the estuary became blocked and the water built up behind it. Then came the Lower Ouse Navigation Act. Floodbanks were constructed along the entire stretch of river, and Piddinghoe was saved from the floodwaters.

The second deliverance came in 1919 when a bypass was built for the main road which passed through the village, thus preserving it from another kind of flooding, the rising tide of traffic between Newhaven and Lewes. So, no longer beset by these two perils, Piddinghoe was able to relax and settle back into a more untroubled existence, and meditate upon its good fortune. It was, perhaps, this meditative atmosphere which produced the curious assortment of local sayings about the village, one or two of which are quite incomprehensible to the visiting stranger.

Not that many strangers do visit Piddinghoe. Mention the name to most people and the reaction will probably be 'Pidding-who?' Which, in fact, would be surprisingly accurate, because that is the way the name should be pronounced. It is confirmed by one of those local sayings, which also confirms the meditative nature of the villagers. Perhaps they had suffered too much from the attention of the press gangs in Napoleonic times, or they may have been conscientious objectors ahead of their time, but

PIDDINGHOE CHURCH AND ITS 'BEGILDED DOLPHIN' – OR IS IT A SALMON?

the saying goes: 'Englishmen fight and Frenchmen too. We don't – we live in Piddinghoe'.

That may not be entirely accurate these days, but it is not quite so far off the mark as Rudyard Kipling's reference to the village in a poem called 'Sussex', written in 1902. He must have been impressed by the weather-vane on the church, because he referred to 'where windy Piddinghoe's begilded dolphin veers'. I am afraid he only scores two out of three. Piddinghoe can still be windy, and the weather-vane is still begilded, but a dolphin? Come now, Rudyard, if that fish is a dolphin then Mowgli was a chimpanzee . . .

Unfortunately no particular story is attached to it to confirm its identity, but the locals reckon it is a salmon or a sea-trout, and I don't think they are far out. Originally the weather-vane was in the form of a pennant, but Piddinghoe is a good centre for anglers, and I suppose somebody thought a fish was more appropriate than a flag – particularly in view of the villagers' non-militaristic reputation.

Another local saying, somewhat obscure these days, is 'Piddinghoe hangs out its ponds to dry'. It goes back to the time when one of the local industries was chalk-mining. The chalk was dug out of a cliff near the old brickworks and turned into blocks of whiting which were used to make white-wash. The process involved drying the chalk slurry in big containers, which were 'hung out to dry' in the sun.

The most obscure old saw of the lot is simply: 'Piddington people shoe their magpies'. Does it mean they are considerate folk who don't like to see birds getting their feet wet? Are they particularly skilful with their needles? Or does it just add up to a load of miniature cobblers? I have found no explanation, except for the obvious one: they are just shoo-ing the wretched birds away.

The local guidebook quotes all these sayings in passing, but concentrates mainly on the church. It is one of only three in Sussex with a round tower; the others are in neighbouring Southease and in Lewes. The steeple is tiled with wooden shingles, another unusual feature for this part of the world. The cottages are mostly flint, and together with the name of the river they are reminiscent of my own part of East Anglia, but it is not nostalgia, nor a rare church tower, nor Kipling's 'dolphin' which is Piddinghoe's main asset.

You would appreciate it most if you have set out from Brighton, or Newhaven, or if you are particularly unfortunate, from Peacehaven. The contrast between these busy, crowded resorts and the peace and quiet of Piddinghoe is almost unbelievable after such a short drive. If it is still not quiet enough, then take the unclassified single-track lane to Telscombe, just a few miles away. It is worth it for the drive alone – there are magnificent views across the South Downs, and nobody is likely to toot a horn if you pull up and enjoy it. You will find Telscombe is even quieter and more isolated than Piddinghoe. There is no round tower or gilded fish to attract the tourist; not even Kipling could think of anything to say about it.

So pause for a while and relax. But beware; don't press on beyond the village, and be thankful the road peters out, because a mile or so ahead lie Saltdean and Rottingdean – and everything you have been trying to avoid . . .

A SECLUDED CORNER OF THE CHURCH.

WHERE THE HORSES GALLOPED – AND HELPED TIME STAND STILL

TELSCOMBE
EAST SUSSEX
4 miles south of Lewes

The little lane that weaves across the Downs from the old Newhaven-Lewes road is the only way in or out of Telscombe for a vehicle, and long may it stay that way. If the lane continued for another mile or two towards the coast it might finish up in the back streets of Peacehaven, and I wouldn't wish that on anybody. As it is Telscombe has managed to preserve itself almost unchanged in appearance since the 1930s, thanks not only to the lack of a road link with the coastal resorts, but also to the forethought of a generous local landowner, Ambrose Gorham, who bequeathed the entire village into the care of a charitable trust when he died in 1933. Its members include the rector, three members of Brighton Council, and some of the villagers, and they have carried out Mr Gorham's wish that the village should be spared the piecemeal development which has taken place elsewhere in that area – generally to devastating effect.

It was the final gesture of a man who had done a great deal for Telscombe during his lifetime, and didn't want his efforts to be wasted after his death. Ambrose Gorham came to the village towards the end of the last century and lived in Stud House. He was in fact a racing man, a trainer of considerable repute. His racehorses were kept in the stables next to his house, and were trained on nearby Telscombe Tye, one of the ancient Sheep Downs on which villagers used to graze their flocks.

In 1902 his Shannon Lass won the Grand National – and Telscombe's good fortune began. He celebrated the victory by restoring the church, and in the years that followed he built a recreation hall for the villagers called the Village Club, he paid for the village children to learn dancing, he gave each of them a book and a pair of Wellingtons every Christmas, and he did many other kindnesses. As the owner of most of the land thereabouts he was the principal employer, and he looked after his employees and their families

well. In fact, he filled the traditional role of the paternalistic country squire, and Telscombe has good cause to be grateful to him.

There are no racehorses there now. Telscombe Tye was ploughed up during the second World War and the gallops were never restored. Along the edge of the Tye is a track going to a modern development on the edge of Saltdean which bears the name of Telscombe Cliffs, but it is well away from Telscombe itself, which remains virtually as Ambrose Gorham left it.

One or two alterations have taken place, but they have had little effect on the appearance or character of the village. The Manor House, the oldest house in Telscombe, is now owned by the National Trust, and judges who tour the local circuit have the good fortune to use it as their lodgings. A row of flint cottages near the church has been converted into a youth hostel, the only concession the village has made to the tourist industry, but the terrace still looks much the same.

Certainly the church itself is well preserved, thanks to Ambrose Gorham's restoration work and some later improvements by Ernest Thornton-Smith, who lived in the Manor House and left it to

THE DOWNS ABOVE TELSCOMBE, LOOKING INLAND.

the National Trust. Ernest and his brother Walter concentrated on restoring the Lady Chapel. A window they gave is made up of fourteen hundred pieces of fourteenth-century glass, and they brought an altar from Verona and installed the oak screen between the chapel and the chancel.

Much of the church, however, dates back to Norman times, with its stumpy tower and tiled 'Sussex cap'. On the corner of the tower there are still two Mass dials, which registered the time of the service in the days before public clocks. It also bears a more modern guideline, a bench-mark recording the altitude above sea-level as precisely 219.2 feet.

Rather unexpectedly, this modest little village boasts a town council and a mayor, complete with mayoral chain. I would have thought the residents of such a 'villagey' village might have preferred to stay that way, but apparently in 1974 the Parish Council decided that it couldn't resist the opportunity, under the new Local Government Act, to put on the style. Actually the 'town' also takes in a bit of East Saltdean, over on the far side of the Down, so in terms of population I suppose Telscombe is officially not as small as it looks.

To the visitor, however, its loftier status makes little odds, unless he happens to bump into the mayor on one of his official outings. Telscombe remains secluded, peaceful and picturesque, just the way a village should look, and just the way that Ambrose Gorham wanted. It is also, thank goodness, just the way the Trust intends to keep it.

TELSCOMBE CHURCH, RESTORED BY THE LOCAL BENEFACTOR AMBROSE GORHAM AFTER HIS HORSE HAD WON THE GRAND NATIONAL.

HERE COME THE COKELERS –
BUT DON'T PASS THE COCOA

LOXWOOD
WEST SUSSEX
17 miles north-east of Midhurst

If you have driven through Loxwood lately – and from what I have seen of it, a great many people do – you may well wonder why it features here. It straggles along the main road from Billingshurst to Guildford, and although some nice old cottages are dotted about, it is difficult to identify any village centre – just a road junction with a Post Office and a few new shops, and an enclosed pond at the rear. There's a pub at each end of the built-up area, and a fairly modern church just outside it, and that's about it. Only the sign announcing that Loxwood has won a best-kept village award is proof that this is actually a community.

So I would not congratulate it on its cosiness, its compactness, or its calm. It was two other 'C's that attracted me there, two intriguing features of West Sussex life in the last century which have both almost vanished from view today: the Cokelers, and the Canal.

Nobody is quite sure why they are called the Cokelers. It is rather reminiscent of the Ovaltineys of happy memory, but that is quite the wrong impression, even though it is slightly preferable to the name of the sect from which they sprang, the Peculiars. The popular theory is that, being teetotal, they drank cocoa at their meetings, but in fact on those occasions they didn't drink anything at all. If, indeed, it was cocoa that gave them their nickname, it was perhaps because their founder, John Sirgood, used to visit the local inns, well ahead of the Salvation Army, and he might have had a cup, just to be sociable. Alternatively it might come from Cokkes, the name associated with some land they bought to build their Combination Stores. The Cokelers themselves much preferred their correct title of Dependent Brethren, but whatever one called them, everyone agrees that they were very good for Loxwood, and they are remembered with affection and respect.

John Sirgood arrived there from London in 1850, pushing a handcart laden with his worldly

PART OF THE OLD COKELER CO-OP, NOW MUCH ALTERED.

goods and, when she tired of walking, his wife. He set out to seek converts to his somewhat puritanical religious beliefs, and although he had a rough reception at first, he was so successful that they virtually took over the village. The Cokelers' co-op next to the pond incorporated a bakery, a butcher's, and in due course a garage, a petrol station, and even a taxi service, the first of its kind in the area. In the late 1940s they extended their commercial empire still further; a Cokeler family bought the Hilltop Stores, which confusingly is halfway down the hill, and completed their local monopoly.

Their chapel in Spy Lane was the main centre of worship in the village, they were the main employers and the main suppliers. If such a thing had happened in Italy or the States one might have suspected that some sort of Mafia had moved in, but the Cokelers were the souls of honesty and humility as well as piety, and their influence did nothing but good.

Then numbers began to decline. In 1973 the Combination Stores were sold, and closed down soon after; new shops now stand on the site. The Hilltop Stores became an antiques shop, then closed as well. The chapel where John Sirgood was buried is now used by the Ifold Evangelists. There is just one survivor of the original close-knit community, their last leader Alf Goodwin, now a very old man. Loxwood is poorer without them.

It is also the poorer, so canal enthusiasts would say, without the Wey and Arun Canal. When it was finished in 1816 it was acclaimed as completing the chain of navigable waterways from the Thames to the English Channel, London's second route to the sea. It joined the Wey and Arun Navigations, running for eighteen miles from just south of Guildford to Newbridge, and passing through twenty-three locks, over two aqueducts, under three main roads – and past Loxwood. But it closed in 1871, due largely to the arrival of the Guildford-Horsham railway (now, ironically, also defunct), and it was forgotten for a hundred years.

These days in Loxwood it takes a little spotting. You have to go round the back of the Onslow Arms, and there is the broad trench of weeds and puddles which used to be the canal. It stops abruptly at the main road; the bridge was destroyed in the early 1900s. The only reminder of its existence, apart from the Canal Bar at the pub, is the Wharf building just up the road, now a furniture workshop, which was the warehouse for goods coming off the barges. Incidentally the church-like windows came from the old Chapel of Ease, the Church of England's only competition with the Cokelers until the church was built in 1900.

However, in 1971 the Wey and Arun Canal Trust cut away the first brambles across the derelict waterway, and they have been working on it ever since. Currently they are battling with the stretch beyond the Onslow Arms (if you meet some exhausted characters with aching backs but big smiles in the bar on a Sunday lunchtime, that's who they'll be); and that gives me an excuse to mention Drungewick, which is at the other end of that stretch, and which offers all the peace and seclusion that Loxwood now only remembers.

I was tempted in fact to give Drungewick priority, but it can hardly claim to be even a hamlet these days, just a quiet country lane with one or two farms, some cottages, a manor house – and of course the canal. The Drungewick aqueduct was one of the main features of this section, built for all of £600. It is only in the last thirty years that it

finally disappeared, and now the volunteers are hoping to put it together again.

Meanwhile, Drungewick slumbers around its splendid manor house, which was bought in 1935 by an American stage and film impresario, Gilbert Miller. He only lived there for a couple of months a year, but he enormously impressed the locals by arriving in his own aeroplane, using a field near the house as a landing strip. They were impressed even more when they learned that his wife Kitty was a close friend of one Mrs Wallis Simpson. During the Abdication crisis, Drungewick Manor fairly buzzed with the latest titbits. And it is a measure of Drungewick's leisurely world that the local historian recalls: 'I used to visit Drungewick in the sixties – and it was *still* below-stairs talk!'

I don't think the Cokelers would have approved, but that's the sort of village for me.

THE REMAINS OF AN OLD LOCK ON THE DERELICT WEY AND ARUN CANAL NEAR LOXWOOD, NOW BEING RESTORED BY VOLUNTEERS.

ONCE ITS ACTIVITIES WERE BEST KEPT SECRET – NOW IT'S JUST BEST-KEPT

THURSLEY
SURREY
6 miles north of Haslemere

When you have won more awards for being the best-kept village than anywhere else in Surrey, that means you must be jolly well-kept; and when the judges actually deduct points because they say you are so pretty that you start with an unfair advantage, then you must be very well-kept indeed. By 1988 Thursley had won the competition twelve times, plus a few extra awards for having the best village hall as well, and it reached the stage where they didn't enter for a year, to give the others a chance. Since then they have been back in the fray, and in 1991 the cricket club maintained the tradition by winning the best-kept sports ground award.

The cynics might argue that Thursley has another advantage which the judges ought to allow for. It is in the heart of what used to be called London's stockbroker belt until the stockbroker image got rather frayed round the edges; its population consists largely of well-to-do commuters who can afford to lay out on fancy shrubs around their gateways and festoons of flower-baskets around their cottage doors. (A 'cottage' in this part of Surrey, I gather, is anything with less than six en-suite bedrooms.) Not too many of the residents spend their spare time throwing rubbish in the ponds or smashing the glass in the telephone kiosk.

But it could be argued the other way too. Many of them probably never see their village in daylight during the winter except at weekends, and they may work at weekends too. It must be difficult to build up the sort of community spirit which these competitions require when most of the community has disappeared up the A3. So all the more credit for keeping the pace so idyllic.

It was not, as they say, ever thus. The ponds are artificial ones, known as hammer ponds, and they were created when Thursley was a centre of the iron-smelting industry in the seventeenth and eighteenth centuries. Life must have been rather noisy in those days, and it was noisier still, according to legend, when the Norse god Thor hurled a thunderbolt on to the common, presenting Thursley with the 'Thur' in its name as well as a block of sandstone which is still known as Thor's Stone.

There is a reminder of Thursley's iron-smelting days in the churchyard. The grave of the village blacksmith, Richard Court, who died in 1791, has one of those coy epitaphs which

collectors of tombstone curiosities love to seize upon:

My sledge and hammer lie reclin'd,
My bellows too have lost their wind,
My fire is out, and forge decay'd,
And in the dust my vice is laid.

'Vice' – get it? Ho-ho . . .

Also in the churchyard is a stone with a much sadder story:

In perfect Health and in the Flower of Age
I fell a Victim to three Ruffians' Rage;
On bended Knees I mercy strove t'obtain,
Their Thirst of Blood made all Entreaties
vain.

This is the grave of an unknown sailor, who was attacked on the Portsmouth road by three assailants and flung into the Devil's Punchbowl, the local beautyspot. One version of the story says they were travellers who pretended to be in distress, and attacked him when he went to help them. Another says they were fellow sailors who met him in the Red Lion at Thursley and accompanied him on his way. However it happened, the culprits were captured near Petersfield trying to sell his stolen clothes, and were hanged on Hindhead Common. The gibbet chains were made by Richard Court, the blacksmith

THURSLEY IS A GREAT PLACE FOR TOMBSTONE CURIOSITIES.

who is buried near their victim in Thursley churchyard. The sailor was never identified, but the villagers were so touched by his fate they paid for his funeral and erected the stone.

Violence was not uncommon on the Portsmouth road in those days, and as Thursley is so close it sometimes got involved. There is supposed to be an underground passage between the road and one of the houses, where highwaymen made their escape after holding up a coach, and it has been suggested that certain Thursley vicars occasionally used it as well,

donning the black mask to augment the church funds. Perhaps it is significant of the way church finances were run in those days that the ancient parish chest has three locks, for which the keys were held by the vicar and the two churchwardens, so none could open it without the others. As one writer delicately puts it: 'By this method their honesty was never in doubt'.

Thursley was on the smuggling route too, because the iron smelting was followed by silk weaving, and the raw silk was often smuggled from France. The smugglers extended their activities to whisky as well, and about this time the village blacksmith came back into his own. After a dearth of iron-smelting, he assisted the smugglers by turning their horses' shoes back-to-front to confuse the Excisemen.

Once the highwaymen and the smugglers had departed Thursley settled down to a more peaceful existence. People like Sir Edwin Lutyens came to live there, the common is now a nature reserve populated, not by footpads and smugglers, but by twenty-six varieties of dragonfly, and the son of the village blacksmith did not follow the village tradition of smelting iron or reversing horse-shoes, but founded the company which makes Goble harpsichords and recorders, renowned throughout the musical world.

Harpsichords and recorders conjure up a pleasanter picture of the past than highway robbery and smuggling, and they fit much better into the Thursley of today, a placid place where you can enjoy strolling along The Lane or The Street (they don't go in for elaborate street names), wandering the acres of empty common or taking in the splendid view from the churchyard, across to the Hog's Back. I suppose that if the Norse god Thor reappeared and hurled another missile, Thursley's first reaction would be to enter a competition for the Best-Kept Thunderbolt . . .

IT'S BEEN MORE THAN FOUR HUNDRED YEARS, BUT THE SANDYS ARE NOT RUNNING OUT

OMBERSLEY
HEREFORD AND WORCESTERSHIRE
4 miles west of Droitwich

Twenty years ago Ombersley would not have featured here. It stood on the junction of two busy main roads, and even a local enthusiast had to admit that it was 'something of an adventure to cross the so-called village street'. He also described Ombersley as a 'show village', which is guaranteed to put me off. But mercifully a bypass has now cleared the worst of the traffic, and while the surfeit of timbered houses does put it in the picture postcard bracket, Ombersley has less obvious features which are in its favour.

The name itself has an unusual history. It started off as Ambreslege, and the theory is that Aurelius Ambrosius, whose father Constantine was King of Britain after the Romans left, set up camp here for a few days after defeating the invading Saxons. He was on his way from York to Winchester, and if you glance at a map you may wonder what he was doing here when the direct road was well to the east. Nobody can answer that, except Aurelius Ambrosius, but it is known he camped near Worcester, and 'lege' means a patch of ground that could be used as a campsite, so maybe he just decided to take the scenic route.

After being owned by the Abbots of Evesham for several centuries the village was acquired by the Sandys family in 1560. By that time Ambreslege had become Ambersley, and while Ambersley became Ambresley, then Ombresley, and finally Ombersley, the Sandys have remained there, with their spelling unchanged. They still live at Ombersley Court, having rebuilt it in 1812, and

they have played a significant role, not just in local affairs but in county and national life. Dr Edwyn Sandys, who bought the manor when he was made Bishop of Worcester, went on to become Archbishop of York. One of his sons was patron of the Pilgrim Fathers and became governor of the Virginia Company, another followed him to America and became Virginia's treasurer.

The next generation didn't fare so well. Colonel Samuel Sandys held Worcester for Charles I, but when the King was defeated he had to pay a crippling fine to Cromwell, and the Sandys family were banished from the country. The Vicar of Ombersley, who shared their views, continued to use the Prayer Book in defiance of Parliament until he was ejected too. The locals didn't take to his replacement, and one villager, Walter Moyle, was indicted 'for that one day he publicly drank the health of the devil' – presumably as a gesture of solidarity with the absent vicar and to defy the new one. The indictment adds that after the toast Walter 'fell down as one dead, to ye amazement and terrour of ye beholders', and this apparently was considered punishment enough, since no other is recorded. Happily, the collapse was not fatal; it may, in fact, have been due more to Walter's consumption of porter than heavenly retribution . . .

After the Restoration, the Sandys family returned, along with 'ye routed vicar', as he called himself, and Ombersley rejoiced. It had good cause to, because they have been great benefactors to the village over the centuries. In 1826, after the church was condemned as unsafe, Baroness Sandys offered to pay two-thirds of the cost of a new one, plus a new organ. Even so, it took the church council nearly five years to make up its mind, even though the tower and spire were a foot out of the perpendicular and likely to collapse on to the south aisle at any time. The church guidebook observes that there was 'much dissent, strife and procrastination', and judging by contemporary reports that was putting it mildly. One local historian comments wryly: 'Doubtless

the village derived no little entertainment from the conflict – and laid long odds on the leaning spire'.

Most of the old church was finally demolished, and all that remains is the chancel, which stands in the churchyard as the private mausoleum of the Sandys family. However the new building was not without its impressive features. The most obvious are the box pews, enough to seat 875 people, and divided up to accommodate the different-sized families in the village; the most imposing, of course, is the Sandys pew, complete with its own fireplace. But I prefer the marvellous Gothic stove that was installed, a cast-iron monster made in the shape of a church tower, complete with a Gothic church door opening on to the grate. It was appropriate that the sexton had to kneel reverentially to light it . . .

Although the 'new' church has now been standing for over 160 years, it is a lot younger than much of the rest of the village – which brings me

THE PLAGUE STONE, ORIGINALLY PLACED OUTSIDE THE VILLAGE TO HOLD FOOD AND SUPPLIES FOR COLLECTION.

inevitably to all those picture-book timbered houses. The most spectacular is the Dower House, once the Court House when the Abbots owned the manor, left to decay after Henry VIII had dispossessed them, then rebuilt by Sir Samuel Sandys early in the seventeenth century. It makes a splendid sight, but I am just as taken by the unusual stone which also stands in the centre of the village. When the Black Death swept through the countryside in 1348, towns and villages hit by the plague placed a hollowed-out 'plague stone' on the outskirts, and left money in it to pay for food and other supplies; Ombersley's is one of the few plague stones still left.

That kind of deal required a certain amount of honesty on both sides, and the village has not always been spotless on that score. When the foundation stone of the new church was laid, some gold and silver coins were buried where one of the chancel pillars was being built. 'Three weeks later,' says a note in the parish records, 'the Deposit was plundered.' Maybe they should have put it in the building fund instead . . .

THE MERGER THAT WORKED –
AND THEY SAY THE FLOWERS DO TOO

BRIGHTWELL-CUM-SOTWELL
OXFORDSHIRE
3 miles east of Didcot

Brightwell-cum-Sotwell, as you must have guessed, is two villages merged into one. The parish councils decided to amalgamate in 1946 – not least, I gather, because one person was clerk to both councils and got fed up writing to himself. A village meeting decided the joint name should have Brightwell in front of Sotwell, which seems logical because Brightwell has always been the larger. It also saved the local branch of the British Legion from altering its banner. . .

Actually, the two villages had grown so close together that it was impossible to see the join. As far back as 1830 it had reached the stage where a local chronicler wrote of the chapel: 'The parish of Sotwell only claims that part of the chapel that the pulpit stands in – therefore the sectarian stands in Sotwell and preaches to his hearers in Brightwell'.

So the two parishes have become one, but fortunately the same process has not taken place with their other close neighbour. The town of Wallingford is officially two miles away, but its houses have crept out along the main road to Didcot until there is now barely a glimpse of green between the last houses and the turning to Brightwell-cum-Sotwell. Many villages in this situation would have succumbed to the pressure and become just another suburb, but in spite of this close proximity to Wallingford it remains unmistakably a village.

Many of its residents, of course, are 'incomers'. With Wallingford so close, Didcot a mere three miles away and Oxford only twelve, it could hardly avoid them; some hardy souls even commute to London. But thanks to some sensible planning for a change, and no doubt because the incomers want to keep it that way, Brightwell-cum-Sotwell has

survived the influx. The narrow village street still winds between attractive thatched cottages and fine old houses, particularly at the Sotwell end, and the new developments have been slotted in discreetly without spoiling the overall impression. The village pond is actually in someone's garden, but it is still alongside the street, it still has its ducks, and it still looks like the village pond, while the Red Lion is still everyone's idea of a village pub, thatched and timbered, with a history going back to the fourteenth century.

The only obvious reminders of the village's previous dual existence are the two churches, St Agatha's in Brightwell and St James's in Sotwell.

ST JAMES'S CHURCH, SOTWELL, REBUILT UNDER ITS ORIGINAL ROOF.

The churches are very different, and the parishioners like to regard themselves as different too. I gather Brightwell considers itself very much the big brother, and it has a certain right to do so, quite apart from its size. It can claim the earlier mention in a Saxon charter: 'Beorhtanville' is referred to in AD 854, 'Suttanwille' comes a little later. In the *Domesday Book* Brightwell has a mill and a church, Sotwell only a mill. Brightwell once had its own castle, and Sotwell can't match that, though it can claim the first recorded royal visit – Henry VII's son Arthur stayed in a manor there on the way to Oxford. However, Brightwell could argue it was first to score a king – George III rode through the village after a stag-hunt. These days most of the public amenities seem to be in Brightwell, and most of the village societies have their headquarters there.

Sotwell, on the other hand, argues that the amalgamation was a merger, not a take-over, and likes to preserve its identity – and St James's provides the focal point. It is a good example of how the village has altered over the years without sacrificing its appearance, because the church is only a hundred years old, yet it fits in perfectly with the older buildings in Sotwell. Its predecessor, 'a miserable old structure', was pulled down before it fell down in 1883, but much of it was incorporated in the new building, not least its fourteenth-century roof, an elaborate and complex structure of fine old oak timbers, which was lifted bodily while the new walls were built beneath it. That sounds like a spectacular piece of engineering, but the *Abingdon Herald* did not get over-excited: 'The whole roof . . . was preserved intact, being simply raised six feet from its original height by leverage'. Some lever . . .

The builders also kept the fourteenth-century doorway, some old windows, and a couple of eight-hundred-year-old carved faces high up on the walls, but the box pews were cleared out – perhaps to the regret of one old parishioner who worshipped in the original church and lived until 1953. 'In winter,' she recalled, 'the doors of the pews were shut tight to keep out the draughts, and feet were warmed by hot bricks wrapped in flannel.' Sounds a lot cosier than modern heating.

Apart from St James's, Sotwell has one other notable institution, and Brightwell can claim no equivalent. The Bach Centre, founded by Dr Edward Bach in 1934, firmly states its address as Sotwell – none of this 'cum' business. In spite of being a 'Centre' it merges, like everything else, into the village; it is in fact a delightful old house set behind a garden of honeysuckle, cranesbill, rock roses and poppies. These are not just for decoration, they are the Centre's raw material.

Dr Bach made medicine from flowers, not to cure illnesses but various forms of emotional distress – though he did argue that if a patient felt better mentally, the illness might respond too. So he produced potions made from flowers for people who worried too much, or were too wrapped up in their own problems, or were frightened of the future, or depressed. Sceptics might try to dismiss the idea, but long after the doctor's death the Centre still gets three or four hundred letters a week asking for its remedies. They are sold in hundreds of health food shops, used in homeopathic practices, and distributed as far afield as Australia and South America.

I have to say I have not tried any myself, although I was tempted to after discovering that, having talked to Dr Bach's admirers and pronounced his name several times as 'Bark', like the composer, I should have said 'Batch'. I felt an urgent need for a spot of larch extract (for restoring self-confidence). Nobody told me my mistake at the time; they must have been having a course of chicory (for those constantly seeking to put others right). But I still can't make up my mind whether or not it would do any good. Maybe I need a good strong dose of scleranthus – for indecision . . .

DR BACH'S GRAVE IN SOTWELL CHURCHYARD.

CANTERBURY TALES – THE SEQUEL

EWELME
OXFORDSHIRE
3 miles south-west of Watlington

Thousands of English villages have churches more than five centuries old. Several hundred must have notable five-hundred-year-old tombs inside them. But not so many have five-hundred-year-old almshouses attached to them, and very few indeed have a five-hundred-year-old grammar school alongside them. Ewelme has got the lot.

The church, the almshouses and the grammar school are all fulfilling their original functions, and they all owe their existence to one person, the lady in that tomb. Together they make Ewelme a very notable village, and not even the close proximity of Benson RAF Station can take away its fifteenth-century flavour. In fact it may have helped to preserve it, because the main road is on the far side of the airfield, and the only through traffic which finds itself in Ewelme has probably got there by mistake.

A film unit did home in on it, to use the church and almshouses as a setting for John Mortimer's *Paradise Postponed*, and this no doubt stepped up the entries in the visitors' book. But the choice was not surprising because, as well as its period atmosphere, Ewelme has literary connections going back just as far. They range from Geoffrey Chaucer to Jerome K. Jerome, and I imagine the intruders were not resented too much by Mr Jerome, who lies in the churchyard, nor by the lady in the tomb, who was Chaucer's grand-daughter.

Alice Chaucer's life was beset by bereavements. She was betrothed to Sir John Phelip, who died of dysentery at the Siege of Harfleur. She married the Earl of Salisbury, who was killed by a cannon-ball at Orleans. And her second husband, William de la Pole, Earl of Suffolk, was banished to France and had his head cut off en route. But there were compensations; she did have a great deal of money to console her.

This didn't come from Grandpa Chaucer, who had to rely on his civil servant's pay to subsidise his poetry, and never earned much from the *Canterbury Tales* except a place in Westminster Abbey. It was his son Thomas who founded the family fortunes, thanks to making the right friends at court and marrying an heiress whose estates included the manor of Ewelme. When he died in 1434 he left it all to his only daughter, who by this time was thirty years old and on her second marriage, as Lady de la Pole. The de la Pole name is still well-known in Suffolk – it was a de la Pole who built Wingfield Castle and another who built the castle-like porch on Fressingfield Church, where Alice's initials are carved on one of the bench-ends. But it was when she and the Earl moved to Ewelme that they went into the building business in a really big way.

They started by enlarging her father's manor house to make it, literally, fit for a king. In later years Henry VIII was to spend a honeymoon there – which was not exactly a unique distinction, but it puts it into the top six. Alice herself entertained Henry VI's wife, Margaret of Anjou, though this may have been a mistake, since her husband is said to have been very close to the lady; Shakespeare certainly staged an affair between them. But it was through this royal connection that the Earl became a Duke and Alice became a Duchess, so maybe she knew what she was doing.

Having set the manor house to rights she turned her attention to the village. She decided the church needed smartening up, and completely rebuilt it except for the tower. And while she was sorting out the church she decided to add the almshouses and the school. In Suffolk, red brick was already used as a building material, and it was probably the de la Poles who introduced it into Oxfordshire – there are no other brick buildings in the area which date back as far.

The almshouses were designed to house thirteen poor almsmen, and there are still thirteen living there, each in two comfortable rooms with all the amenities, and looked after by a resident nurse. The school has also been in virtually continuous use for the same period. Not even the raids on church property by Henry VIII, and later Cromwell, affected Ewelme; maybe Henry cherished happy memories of his honeymoon there, and it is said that Cromwell's men were never actually able to find it. So Ewelme has the oldest church school still using its original building and still non-feepaying; it has always followed its fifteenth-century statute that the village children should be taught 'freely without exaccion of any Schole hire'. The church guidebook comments frankly that it 'escaped' being developed into a public school – the writer is obviously relieved that it didn't suffer the same grim fate as Eton, which is three years its junior.

Alice seemed to lose interest in building things after the death of her husband in 1450, but she lived on at the manor house for another twenty-five years, and when she died her son John built the splendid tomb which is the final legacy left in Ewelme by the de la Poles. A description of it fills a whole page in the guidebook, and that is called a condensed version, so I won't even attempt it here. But I must quote its helpful suggestion for

enjoying the frescoes on the roof of the tomb's lowest compartment, which stands on little arcades only a foot or so off the ground. 'On a sunny day, the frescoes can be clearly seen by anyone who lies prone on the sanctuary floor and looks up at the roof through the arcades.'

It must be quite startling to walk into the sanctuary and find a row of feet sticking out from under the tomb. But I suspect most visitors will be satisfied just to look at the copy of the frescoes on the wall.

Then the guidebook comments, a little obviously one might have thought: 'The frescoes must of course have been painted before the tomb was placed in situ'. But I'm not so sure. I prefer to think of the artist working from a hole in the floor underneath it, like a mechanic in a car bay. He might even have painted the frescoes sprawled full-length alongside it; dash it all, I used to paint the skirting-boards that way.

Perhaps they call it the de la Pole position . . .

PART OF THE FIFTEENTH-CENTURY HERITAGE LEFT TO EWELME BY ALICE DE LA POLE AND STILL IN USE – THE COURTYARD OF THE ALMSHOUSES.

'IT'S TOO OLD TO DIE!' – AND IT DIDN'T

LETCOMBE BASSETT
OXFORDSHIRE
2 miles south-west of Wantage

It happened more than forty years ago, but the older folk in Letcombe Bassett still relish the memory of their battle against the planners, which they fought and won. They still refer to 'troublous days' of 1948 and 1949 when the future of the village hung in the balance. If the planners had been successful, Letcombe Bassett would have ceased to exist as a village. In the words of the county planning officer: 'Bassett would, in effect, revert to a little group of farms with associated dwellings for stockmen, etcetera, side by side with a few houses like the Old Rectory and what might be termed cottage retreats'.

Nowadays, when county planners generally want to expand small villages rather than abolish them, and even create new ones, it is difficult to envisage an era when they were actually talking about systematically killing them off – with malice, the villagers would say, aforethought. But in the post-war years there was this extraordinary conception that a village with fewer than five hundred people was not 'a reasonable social unit', and should be merged with a larger one. One of the first of these 'under five hundred' villages to be threatened with the axe was Letcombe Bassett, where the planners' idea was to shift most of the villagers to Letcombe Regis, its big brother a mile and a quarter away. New houses would only be built at Letcombe Regis, and gradually the population of Letcombe Bassett would be transferred into them, and their old cottages left empty. It was almost reminiscent of the days when lords of the manor moved entire villages because they spoilt the view . . .

Frederick Barrett's *Letcombe Bassett Then and Now* gives a graphic account of how the villagers 'rose up in wrath' to fight back, rallying under the slogan: 'Letcombe Bassett is too old to die!' Mr Barrett himself was in the forefront of the fray, and he acquired some powerful allies, among them John Betjeman, *The Times* and the *Architects Journal*. The BBC staged a discussion about it: 'Are our small villages likely to be planned out of existence', and some of it has been preserved in the *Oxford Book of English Talk*, including Betjeman's eloquent defence of Letcombe Bassett, and an opponent who described it as 'a rural slum without redemption'.

An enquiry was held, and the result was a resounding victory for the villagers. The planners were routed and the idea of killing off the village was abandoned. As Mr Barrett put it: 'For once, village Hampdens have triumphed'. Twenty years later Letcombe Bassett was designated a conservation area; the decision was vindicated, and the victory complete.

So what sort of a village is this, which was considered dispensable by the planners, and anything but by those who lived there? It is set in a combe below Lambourn Down, a cluster of thatched cottages and farmhouses alongside the brook, with the Down stretching south-wards behind it. The parish actually extends on to the Down, which of course is not down but up, so there is

LETCOMBE REGIS – SOMETIMES REFERRED TO AS LOWER LETCOMBE.

a difference of some four hundred feet between one end of the parish and the other. The ancient Ridge Way runs across the top of it.

But this is not just another nice village. That battle cry of fifty years ago sums it up: 'too old to die'. Letcombe Bassett has a history going back beyond the *Domesday Book* to Saxon times, when Alfred the Great had a palace at Lambourn, not far away. It has survived the coming of the Normans, a succession of assorted lords of the manor until it came under Queen's College, Oxford for four hundred years, then the Enclosure Acts which changed the face of rural England, followed by the Great Western Railway, which transformed the area around it a few miles to the north, and in more recent times the M4 motorway, which had

much the same effect a few miles to the south. With a history of survival like that, maybe the county planning officer never stood a chance.

Originally Letcombe Bassett was just Bassett, situated beside the 'letecombe', the brook in the valley. By the fourteenth century it had acquired the Frankie Howerd-like title of Up Letecombe Bassett, which got shortened to Upletcombe. According to Mr Barrett some of the older inhabitants still call it Upper Letcombe, while Letcombe Regis is referred to as Lower Letcombe.

Apart from farming, Bassett divided its interest between watercress and racehorses. The water-cress beds have fallen out of fashion now, but this is still very much racehorse country. The Yew Tree Inn was one of the last hostelries still com-bined with a farrier's, and Captain Tim Forster's stables at the Old Manor produced two winners of the Grand National.

Mr Barrett makes the most of the village's rather tenuous literary links. He recalls that Dean Swift stayed at the rectory for three months, and wrote some verses there sitting under the great mulberry tree in the walled garden. Very fairly he adds that Swift seemed to find life in Letcombe Bassett singularly boring; he wrote in a letter that his host the rector was 'such a melan-choly thoughtful man that I shall soon catch the spleen from him . . . I read all day, or walk, and do not speak as many words as I have now writ'.

The other connection was through Thomas Hardy's *Jude the Obscure*, in which the village 'Cresscombe' is based on Letcombe Bassett, and a cottage which features briefly in the story still stands there by the brook. The links are nearly as obscure as Jude was, but fortunately the village doesn't have to rely on them for a place in history. Thanks to that successful battle of half a century ago, and sensible well-controlled development since, Letcombe Bassett has held its own against the sort of pressure which few ancient villages have had to face. It has proved that those campaigning villagers got it right; it's too old to die.

THE TOWER OF TWIN GABLES – AND AN EPISCOPAL GHOST

FINGEST
BUCKINGHAMSHIRE
7 miles west of High Wycombe

Here's a little literary exercise: who do you think wrote this?

Here before you stands the strange and lovely parish church of St Bartholemew. Look well at this ancient and sturdy citadel of Christianity, for there is none quite like it in all the land . . . Back, back into the haze of history this church of ours has been served continuously and faithfully until the present day . . .

Do you recognise the lyrical style, which as church literature goes might be called Decorated Gothic? No, neither did I. It was actually written by Sir William Connor, better known as Cassandra of the Daily Mirror, a columnist noted for his vitriolic prose, and not usually associated with church guidebooks. But Sir William lived in Fingest, and Fingest is the sort of village which soothes the most furrowed brow, and mellows the most acerbic pen.

I remember the village from the happy days I spent around the more remote corners of Buckinghamshire, in search of a pleasant pint in a peaceful pub. One of my discoveries was the Chequers Inn at Fingest – 'a tiny and secret place in a deep bowl in the Chilterns, the chatter of the rooks in the tall trees around the church is a raucous overlay upon the gentle undertone that drifts from hundreds of sheep high up on the meadows'. No, not Cassandra this time, just a normally staid gazetteer, but it seems to have come under its influence too.

I didn't notice much about Fingest at the time. My main interest was the Chequers, and its inner sanctum with the old box settles and the gun rack over the fireplace. On a fine day I had my pint in the garden; beyond it the lush pasture land sloping up to the beechwoods that sat astride the rolling hills. Whoops, now it's got me too . . .

The real treasure of Fingest is just across the road from the Chequers, the church that Cassandra was going on about, with its astonishing Norman tower, so spacious inside that some say it was originally used as the nave. Its distinctive

THE MASSIVE TWIN-GABLED TOWER OF FINGEST CHURCH.

feature is the twin-gabled roof that was added a couple of centuries after the Normans built it. The brickwork and the tiling on the gables were renewed about forty years ago, but the original oak beams are still there, holding it up.

The tower contains only one bell of the original peal. Officially the rest were sold off during the Reformation, but the story goes that a former rector lost them in a gambling session with a fellow priest. That sounds a little profligate, but it seems a fair reflection of how Fingest itself was shuffled about by the clergy over the centuries.

It started off under the Abbot of St Alban's, who claimed direct allegiance to the Pope, but the Bishop of Lincoln argued that St Alban's and its churches came under him. After years of argument it took Henry II and a couple of archbishops to sort out a deal whereby the Abbot retained St Alban's but handed over Fingest to the Bishop. After the Reformation, the Bishop of Lincoln kept on the right side of Edward VI by giving him Fingest, as well as other parishes. The King gave it to the Duke of Somerset, and the Duke swopped it with a prebendary of Wells Cathderal for a manor near Wells. This 'Pass the Parish' game was suspended for a few centuries, then in 1837 the dioceses were altered and Fingest found itself under the jurisdiction of Oxford.

Throughout this chopping and changing, Fingest preserved an unbroken succession of rectors, and in the early days there was frequently a bishop in the village as well. In such a vast diocese as Lincoln the bishops spent much of their time on tour, and they often stayed in Fingest's old manor house, long since demolished. One of them, Henry de Burghersh, found that his stay was unexpectedly prolonged, when he became that considerable rarity in English villages, an episcopal ghost.

Although he was a bishop, Henry de Burghersh was also 'excessively covetous and encroaching', and he took over most of the common land in the village for a hunting park. After his death in 1343 his ghost appeared, dressed as a keeper in a green jacket and carrying a bow and arrow, and announced that he was doomed to remain thus until the land was handed back to the village. The message was passed back to Lincoln, the fences and banks were duly taken down, and the land restored to the village. The bishop was able to rest in peace.

Things have been pretty quiet in Fingest ever since, but one custom lives on from the old days. It is supposed to be unlucky if a bridegroom fails to lift his bride over the church gate after the wedding – and the gate is kept locked on such occasions to make sure he does. Strangely, Sir William Connor doesn't mention this in his paean of praise to Fingest. How could a Daily Mirror man miss a story like that?

B IS FOR BEDFORDS...
BENEFACTORS...BILLS...

CHENIES
BUCKINGHAMSHIRE
2 miles north-west of Chorleywood

I have known Chenies since I took the steam train to Chorleywood with a youth club, and hiked the mile or so to the village and on into the Chess Valley. It never occurred to me that Chenies was anything special. It was just another village with just another village pub that refused to serve beer to sixteen-year-olds, and I was happy to leave it behind for the more promising delights of the riverside, where a little dalliance with a female companion was not unknown.

In later years I went back there because it was the nearest rural village to the suburban sprawl which spread out of Harrow along the Metropolitan Line, through Pinner and Northwood and Rickmansworth. On these occasions the village pub did agree to serve me, but its meal prices were high, and we only ate there on celebratory occasions. It did not occur to me to enquire why it was called the Bedford Arms; I only knew that, for a cheap supper, I had to go up the road to the Red Lion. I may have noticed the elegant 'B' above the dates on the cottages, and I certainly noticed the old manor house, though I had no idea of its history. But when I attended weddings in the church there – its picturesque surroundings are very popular with brides – I never realised it had a chapel which one expert calls 'the richest single storehouse of funeral monuments in any parish church in England'.

It was only much later that I realised the sig-

nificance of Chenies. The whole village is virtually a memorial to the good management of the Earls and Dukes of Bedford, who lived here before they moved to their more famous home at Woburn, provided the village with some of the finest estate cottages in England, and are buried, not at Woburn, but here in the Bedford Chapel.

The first Earl, John Russell, acquired the village when he married into the Cheyne family. It was originally called Isenhampstead, then the Cheynes extended the name to Isenhampstead Chenies. In view of what the Bedfords have done for the village since, they could well have made it Isenhampstead Russell, in which case, with Isenhampstead being dropped in the last century, Chenies would now be called Russell. No matter; there are plenty of reminders of the village's benefactors – the Bedford Arms of course, and the 'B' on all those cottages, and the Bedford Chapel, closed to visitors, but you can catch a glimpse of all those Earls and Dukes and their ladies.

The easiest to identify is the fourth Earl, who was involved in the draining of the Fens and gave his name to the Bedford Level. He and his wife share an altar tomb with their 'chrisom child'; the baby died within a month of baptism and was buried in its chrisom, or baptismal cloth. Among all the Bedfords you may also see their predecessors, Sir John and Lady Cheyne. The effigies are six hundred years old and Sir John's looks every day of it, but in fact it is not due to wear and tear, it was left as a rough block and for some reason never completed.

Sir John lived in the original manor house, but is was rebuilt by a later Cheyne, and when John Russell took it over in 1526 he added the south wing, still called the 'new' building. Henry VIII held a Privy Council there, and for once Queen Elizabeth really did sleep there, not just once but on three separate visits, one of them lasting four weeks. So Chenies must have been just as attractive then as it is today, but it looked rather different, because in the 1840s and 1850s the Duke rebuilt all the cottages – though he did give them Tudor chimneys, for old times' sake. The cottages were built in pairs, each with two bedrooms, and each pair costing £300, a substantial sum for a landlord to spend on his workers' accommodation at that time. In fact the Duke who built them always ploughed back twenty per cent of his gross rental in improving his estate properties; not many other landowners equalled that.

The benevolence of the Bedfords seemed to rub off on their staff. The steward to a previous Duke, William Davis, who was a tenant in the manor house, bought two cottages and a field in Chenies from him, resigned his office to help build a Baptist Chapel on the site, provided a home for the minister and gave the whole lot to the church, except for one cottage he lived in himself. In later years a son of one of the ministers, Dr Charles West, founded the Great Ormond Hospital for Children; I am sure that William Davis would have approved.

A TYPICAL CHENIES COTTAGE, WITH THE DISTINCTIVE HIGH CHIMNEYS AND THAT UBIQUITOUS 'B'. PITY ABOUT THE AERIAL . . .

The Bedfords moved out of the manor house at the time of the Civil War, and it was let to tenant farmers and stewards. One of them, a Mr Davis – surely not the same one? – converted part of it into tenements for his workers without the Bedfords knowing. When they found out, twenty-five years later, he had to reinstate the building at his own expense. This was typical of the Russell family's concern for the village; they kept out any unattractive development, and today you still can't find any ugly additions to the village. The scene around the picture-postcard green has been unchanged for nearly 150 years.

It would be difficult, in fact, to find a better example than Chenies of a 'close' village which has been controlled for centuries by benign land-lords, and it would have been nice to think that such an admirable set-up could continue. But in 1953 the twelfth Duke died, and the unlucky thirteenth found himself faced with a bill for four and a half million pounds in death duties. Chenies had to be sold to help raise it, and today the manor house is privately owned – though open to the public at times – and the village has lost its benefactors. So far it has survived unscathed, but it is very convenient for those commuter trains into London, and Metro-Land has already spread past it to affect Little Chalfont and Amersham; the pressures are going to be great.

But one thing I know, if the developers ever do move into Chenies, the first sound they'll hear will be a mighty rumbling from the Bedford Chapel. It will be all those Russells, turning in their graves . . .

SECRET WORSHIP IN THE KITCHEN – NOW WEDDINGS IN THE MAYFLOWER

JORDANS
BUCKINGHAMSHIRE
3 miles east of Beaconsfield

I used to drive past Jordans regularly and hardly notice it was there. It lies just off a lane which was a useful cut-through from the A40 Oxford road to Watford, in the days before the M25 provided a much more spectacular alternative, though not always a quicker one. Most of the village is out of sight as you drive past, and there is no hint of its considerable size or its methodical layout. I only knew that it had a special significance for Quakers, so I assumed it must take its name from the Biblical river. I also knew it had a connection with William Penn, and so did the brewers who built a new pub in Rickmansworth, his nearby birthplace, and named it after him. It was only later they realised that William would not be too happy having his name linked with licensed premises, and they hastily re-named it the Keystone – perhaps in acknowledgment that it was a fair cop.

I found I was as ignorant about Jordans' origins as the brewers were about Penn. Old Jordans was a farmstead occupied by a Quaker family, where William and other Friends worshipped illegally in the early part of the seventeenth century. The kitchen where they met is now the dining room, and the Society of Friends has converted the building into a hostel. Just as famous among Quakers is the Meeting House, built in 1688 and little changed since; William Penn is in the burial ground beside it.

But the best known building to non-Quakers is the Mayflower Barn, the original farm barn attached to Old Jordans, which may contain beams

WILLIAM PENN'S GRAVE BESIDE JORDANS MEETING HOUSE

from the *Mayflower*. Then again it may not. The debate has gone on since Rendel Harris, the Quaker antiquarian, announced in 1920 that the barn was 'as valuable as Stonehenge', and put forward eleven arguments in support of the Mayflower theory. Other experts then produced just as many arguments against. Whoever is right, it's a jolly good barn, remarkably well preserved, and used these days for wedding receptions and the suchlike.

The story of the village itself, though, is not so well known but in many ways is even more remarkable. Like Heronsgate, a few miles away across the Hertfordshire border, it started as a social experiment, and like Heronsgate it didn't work out as planned, but the aims of its Quaker founders are still being observed, and some at least of their original objectives have been achieved.

Mind you, the Quakers got the idea a lot later, seventy years after the Chartists created Heronsgate. For some time they had wanted to preserve the surroundings of Old Jordans and the Meeting House, and when a neighbouring farm was put up for sale they bought 102 acres to establish what they called a 'village estate'. It was to be based on Christian principles, and be self-sufficient with its own industries, amenities and institutions. It was not essential to be a Quaker in order to live there; you just had to be the right sort of chap.

The first bricks were laid on 15th February 1919, and in the years that followed the village prospered, but the industries didn't. 'Jordans Village Industries' found plenty to do at first, because it was building the village, using a lot of materials it made itself. But post-war inflation was too much for it, and in 1923 it went into voluntary liquidation.

However, the village continued to grow for the next sixty years, with 'Jordans Village Ltd' retaining the ownership of blocks of flats and terraces around the central green, and a number of other houses around the village. They are rented out on a monthly basis; the other properties on the estate are privately owned. Instead of a parish council, Jordans has a committee of management, all members of 'Jordans Village Ltd', and they control development, look after their properties, settle the rents from their tenants and collect amenity charges from the private owners.

In most other respects Jordans follows the pattern of the traditional English village, with a village school, a village hall, a village green, even a village lending library. There are the usual summer fairs and harvest suppers and bonfire nights and, in addition, Jordans has created a village tradition all its own. On the Friday nearest to 15 February, the date the first bricks were laid and the village was officially founded, there is always a commemorative supper in the village hall.

Inevitably, what Jordans lacks is old-world charm. Its greatest fans would not claim it was picturesque. It does of course have its Possibly-Mayflower Barn, and its old farmhouse and Meeting House, and there's another old farmhouse with its equivalent barn (definitely non-Mayflower) on the outskirts, but otherwise there isn't a building in the village which is more than seventy-odd years old. But its history and significance go back a lot further than that, to the days when William Penn and his friends risked fines or imprisonment by gathering for secret worship at Old Jordans. I suspect that, for the Quakers who come to Jordans, the fact that he happened to go off and found Pennsylvania is rather less important.

THE MAYFLOWER BARN, WHICH MAY OR MAY NOT CONTAIN TIMBERS FROM THE *MAYFLOWER*, BUT IT IS STILL A JOLLY GOOD BARN.

AND I THOUGHT WELL-DRESSING WAS JUST A PRETTY BUNCH OF FLOWERS . . .

YOULGREAVE
DERBYSHIRE
3 miles south of Bakewell

Fifty years ago there were only about fourteen Derbyshire villages which dressed their wells. Today there are twice that number, to the delight of the tourist trade, and they are dressing not only wells but pumps and taps and even where pumps and taps used to be. At Youlgreave they also dress the singularly ugly stone tank in the middle of the village where the first piped water was stored in 1829. They make it sound rather romantic by calling it The Fountain instead of The Tank, but that's what it was, a reservoir for fifteen hundred gallons of soft water which came through iron pipes from a spring outside the village. Another water system was introduced in 1869, involving

WELL-DRESSING IS NOT ONLY FOR WELLS; THIS IS YOULGREAVE'S 'FOUNTAIN' – ACTUALLY A STORE TANK.

public taps along the main street, and these got decorated too. Today there are five 'wells' in Youlgreave which are dressed on the Saturday nearest to St John the Baptist Day – which you will instantly recollect is June 24th.

Nobody is quite clear how this well-dressing business began. It probably had something to do with pagan offerings to the water gods, but it only happens in Derbyshire, where you might think, judging by the weather, there was plenty of water about without making sacrifices to the gods for it. It may well have had Celtic origins, and one theory is that there were Celts tucked away in the heart of the Peak District who preserved their identity and their customs while Romans, Saxons, Danes and Normans came and went. A more mundane argument is that these villages stand on porous limestone which soon dries out, so springs and wells are particularly vital.

The Church turned this pagan rite into a religious festival, so the wells are blessed as well as dressed, and most of the decorations have a religious theme. In Youlgreave at the turn of the century, there were prizes for the best-dressed wells, and when the prizes ran out the dressers put collecting boxes beside their work and split the takings between them. These days the boxes are still there, but the money goes to charity.

You may still be thinking, as I did, that well-dressing is just a simple form of floral decoration, somewhere betweeen a bunch of flowers and a wreath. Don't dare suggest that in Derbyshire! These are works of art in natural materials, built up berry by berry, seed by seed, petal by petal. They are created on big wooden frames which are filled with clay. The design is drawn on paper first, then transferred on to the clay by pricking it through the paper with a spike. Then berries or beans are set in the clay along the lines of the holes, to make the design stand out more clearly. Still with me?

The picture is filled in with different coloured materials, the larger and plainer areas with mosses or lichens or pieces of bark, the more delicate areas with petals, pressed onto the clay one at a time, each one overlapping the one below like tiny slates, so rain will run off. The dressers in one village worked out that they used 10,000 petals, 3,800 bits of corn, 3,500 leaves, 80 yards of cones, 7 jars of seeds and 3 buckets of parsley. It took 80 people 400 hours of work – and at the end of it all the pictures would only survive for three or four days, certainly not more than a week. In terms of labour efficiency, well-dressing is a nonsense; in terms of job satisfaction it must be difficult to equal.

Jim Shimwell, member of a Youlgreave family which has been well-dressing for generations, explains its attraction more elegantly. 'For people with the creative urge but no great ability, it offers a chance to achieve aesthetic satisfaction.' I'm not sure we'd all agree with him about 'no great ability', but I can see his point. I've also seen some of the pictures that he has helped to create, and the design and detail and colours are quite astonishing. They range from an African village scene called Kumbaya to Biblical stories like Daniel in the lion's den, and the wedding at Cana. If you're not around on the Saturday nearest to St John the Baptist Day, you can still get an idea of the work of Youlgreave's well-dressers from the colour photographs in Roy Christian's *Well-Dressing in Derbyshire* – the only way these minor floral masterpieces can be preserved for more than a week.

But what about Youlgreave during the other fifty-one weeks of the year? A village can't live by well-dressing alone, and Youlgreave has plenty to commend it in its own right, perched on its ridge in the heart of the National Park. Just behind that hideous 'Fountain', for instance, is Thimble Cottage, which is very tiny, and Thimble Hall, which is half the size of Thimble Cottage and very tiny indeed. It is not much bigger, in fact, than a two-storey store cupboard, and from what I could see through the windows, that is all it is used for, but if it ever functioned as a meeting hall, those who met there must have been the size of Thomas Cockayne's effigy in Youlgreave Church.

Thomas lies on an alabaster tomb in the centre of the chancel, a diminutive figure about three feet tall but clad elaborately in full armour and chain mail. He died in a fight over a family marriage settlement, and judging by the size of his effigy it's no wonder he lost. But Thomas was not as tiny as that, and indeed he would take a poor view of one reference book that suggests he was a midget. The church guide explains that it was the practice in the fifteenth century to make a smaller effigy if a son died before his father.

The guide also clears up a query in another tourist book which says that the twelfth-century font has a tiny bowl on the side of it, 'projecting from the mouth of a strange animal'. The animal is in fact a salamander, symbol of baptism, and the little bowl was probably used for oil. The tourist book calls it 'unusual'; the church guide says firmly it is 'unique'. But it also admits that the font doesn't really belong to Youlgreave at all; it came from the daughter church at Elton, which discarded it during rebuilding. Later the parishioners of Elton asked whether they could have their font back, and offered the sum of £5 to Youlgreave to make itself a replica. Youlgreave made the replica all right – then gave it to Elton, and kept the original.

I doubt that Youlgreave would get away with such bare-faced cheek in these liberated times, but in those days, I imagine, daughters didn't argue . . .

TWO YOULGREAVE 'MINIATURES' – THIMBLE HALL, AND THE EFFIGY OF THOMAS COCKAYNE.

No Stockings, But Still Well-Dressed – And It Hasn't Lost Its Marbles

ASHFORD-IN-THE-WATER
DERBYSHIRE
2 miles north-west of Bakewell

ASHFORD is not actually in-the-Water, but it must be very grateful for its close presence. The River Wye provides a protective line of defence between the village and the heavy traffic using the A6 trunk road between Bakewell and Buxton. The three ancient bridges which used to link Ashford and the main road provided an additional deterrent. All three were so narrow they had to be negotiated with care; one used to bear a plaque recalling how a vicar of Bakewell, perhaps trying to cross it too hastily, was thrown from his horse, fell over the parapet and was drowned. These days the pack-horse bridge is closed to vehicles, and the other two, which crossed the Wye and a tributary in quick succession on the other road, have been replaced by two new ones, much safer but a lot less picturesque.

Whether you enter Ashford-in-the-Water by this route, or walk over the old pack-horse bridge further along the river, which still has the stone pen beside it where sheep were brought to be washed, you will find yourself in a place which was uncommonly rich in old country customs – and had its fair share of traditional crafts and industries too. Well-dressing and wakes, sheep-washing and funeral garlands, a path through the churchyard called the Corpse Road, the 8 p.m. curfew bell which on Shrove Tuesday became the 11 a.m. pancake bell, even a famous dwarf, Mollie Bray, who was only a metre high but lived till she was eighty-one – Ashford-in-the-Water has had the lot.

It also had the earliest men's Friendly Society in the country, founded in 1769 and surviving for over two hundred years, and the nearly-as-old and

rather rarer Female Friendly Society. Then there was the marble works which produced anything from tables and memorials to brooches and tortoiseshell combs. There were the eighty-odd cottages with stocking frames which supplied the local stocking mill, and the candle-maker and the corn mill, and the eight beerhouses and inns – if you want to sample a pot-pourri of Olde England, then take a sniff around Ashford-in-the-Water . . .

None of the industries, alas, has survived. The marble works, for instance, where Henry Watson built a water-wheel in 1748 to cut and polish the local black limestone known as Ashford Marble, is now a depot for the North Derbyshire Water Board. It was closed in 1905 because of the increasing competition from overseas, but there are still plenty of its products in the church, including Watson's own memorial. It records that he was 'the first who formed into ornaments the Fluors and other Fossils of this county'. The inlaid marble table in the church was made rather later; it won a silver medal at an exhibition in Derby in 1882, and the medal is still there too.

Also in the church are four funeral garlands or virgin crants, white paper rosettes attached to a rush or wooden frame which used to be carried at the funerals of unmarried women. Afterwards they were hung above the pews used by the bereaved families – which must have cheered them up no end. There are various theories about how the practice originated. I favour the idea that it started in Scandinavian countries, where it is still the custom at traditional weddings for the bride to wear an elaborate crown. The thought is that girls who died unmarried were given the virgin crant to make up for the crown they missed out on.

Until 1936 there were five of these garlands in the church, then one fell down and for some reason was not replaced. These days they are suspended more securely and preserved with greater care – each one is inside a perspex dust-cover.

TOP: AN ORIGINAL GARLANDS IN THE ROOF. BELOW: A MORE RECENT COPY, FOR VISITORS TO INSPECT.

The curfew bell is still there too, but it no longer rings at 8 p.m.; the custom died out a few years ago. Well-dressing died out as well after the last war, but perhaps with an eye to the tourist trade it was revived in 1954. On Trinity Sunday, the church's patronal festival, the village wells are decorated as a thanksgiving for the water. For good measure the parish pump is decorated too. Originally the celebrations went on all week, a traditional wake with a fair in the main street, but the Tourist Board may have felt that was too much to hope for.

Now all this is very charming, but not unique to Ashford-in-the-Water. Other villages have had curfews, and well-dressing, and even virgin crants. I had to turn to the little village of Sheldon, up in the hills on the other side of the A6, to find something really unlikely. It involved a duck . . .

Sheldon was commended to me by the Archdeacon of Chesterfield, the delightfully named Venerable Phizackerley, formerly of Ashford. He is currently editing a diary of Maria Gyte, a farmer's wife who ran the village pub, the Devonshire Arms, during the first World War, and it promises to be fascinating reading. Meanwhile the Devonshire Arms is a pub no longer, but just outside is the site of an ash known as the Sheldon Duck Tree, and although the Archdeacon did not in fact mention it, the story of the Sheldon Duck was just what I was looking for.

In 1601 – the story is as precise as that – a duck flew into the ash tree and mysteriously disappeared. Two hundred years later the tree was felled and sawn into planks – and in two of the central planks they found the exact outline of a full-size duck.

Is it possible, I wonder, that the bird dematerialised on touching the ash tree and was absorbed into it? Or, more likely, did the unfortunate creature somehow get wedged inside, and its corpse merged with the trunk as the years went by? Either way, it's a nice story; pity about the duck . . .

NOT EXACTLY TIMELESS – WITH SIXTY-THREE MINUTES TO THE HOUR

OLD BRAMPTON
DERBYSHIRE
3 miles west of Chesterfield

As you drive into Old Brampton on its only sizeable road, you might well believe you were in Surbiton or Potter's Bar. Nice detached houses, nice well-kept gardens, nice big garages containing nice big cars. It is only when you catch a glimpse between the houses that you realise you are on a ridge between two deep valleys, and just beyond the nice back gardens there is a steep drop on either side down into open farmland. From Old Brampton you can't see any sign of Chesterfield, technically three miles away, but the suburbs are edging nearer and nearer. Nor can you see the vast jungle of housing estates to the north, a great rash of red brick spreading over the green Derbyshire hillsides. You can't even see the

Linacre reservoirs, created in the valley a century ago to provide Chesterfield's water supply, but well concealed by the woodlands that were planted at the time.

On the face of it, judging by those pleasant modern houses, Old Brampton is an up-market dormitory suburb in Chesterfield's equivalent of the stockbroker belt. The gazetteers, of course, describe it rather differently. 'One of the most attractive villages in the county,' says one. 'A mellow place in which ancient houses and their gardens are a timeless mixture of past and present,' says another. Well, I have seen dozens of Derbyshire villages more attractive than this, the 'ancient' houses are few and far between, and the

mixture of past and present is in the ratio of about one to ten. As for timeless – we'll see.

Nevertheless I have included Old Brampton because, in spite of all the pressures around it, the original part of the village near the church has still managed to retain its rural character, and I think it deserves encouragement to keep the developers at bay. You have to go much further away from Chesterfield to find another corner like this. Opposite the church is the fine old seventeenth-century Hall, complete with mullioned windows, part of it probably medieval. The stables and cowsheds in the farmyard used to be labourers' cottages in the early nineteenth century, until it was found more convenient to have the farm stock near the house, so the workers were moved down the road into the old farm buildings.

The village inn and some old cottages are nearby, and as the road was closed in one direction

THE 63-MINUTE CLOCK FACE ON OLD BRAMPTON CHURCH.

when I was there, preventing through traffic, this little oasis was particularly peaceful. Mysteriously the inn was closed at lunch-time too, perhaps in sympathy with the road, but happily the church was open, and this is where the real flavour of Old Brampton lives on, beyond the two thatched lych-gates.

Strangely, the folk who tend the church don't seem anxious to make the most of its more interesting features. In one instance they even admit as much themselves, in the church guide. There is an alabaster slab in the north aisle, a memorial to one of the earlier vicars of Old Brampton, Thomas Ball. It is nearly six hundred years old, and one might think it was of more than passing interest, but the guide comments laconically: 'It is partly covered by the cupboards there, but is still visible'. Only until they need another cupboard, perhaps, judging by what has happened to the most historic and rare memorial in the church, the thirteenth-century tombstone of Matilda Le Caus.

Matilda's head and shoulders are carved into the stone in bas-relief, which gave quite a shock to the grave diggers who accidentally unearthed it in

1801. It gives the impression that she is actually inside the stone, and that effect is heightened when you see that her feet appear to be sticking out of the bottom. Her hands are uncovered too, and they are holding her heart. The inscription is amazingly clear, considering she died in 1224.

The Le Caus family were Lords of the Manor until the fifteenth century, and the name lives on in Caus Farm. So it is quite something to have such an important relic of the village's earliest years. Yet Matilda is propped up against a wall, with a notice-board hard up along-side her on one side, and a cabi-net containing church literature partially obscuring the stone on the other. It all seems rather un-dignified for a lady who probably had the power of life and death over the predecessors of those who arranged the furniture in this way.

What intrigued me most, how-ever, was that the guide makes no mention at all of quite the most fascinating feature of the church, its sixty-three minute clock. If you look at the clock face on the south side of the tower you will see that the number of divisions between the Roman numerals varies considerably. There are seven between the I and the II, only four between the IV and the V, an extra one between the VII and the VIII, and another extra one between the X and the XI.

The story goes that, many years ago, the workman responsible imbibed too heartily at the inn across the road, and returned in mellow mood. As one version puts it, 'his concentration was severely affected'. Perhaps he just miscounted, or did he think he'd have a spot of fun and see if anyone noticed? Presumably nobody did at first, or he would surely have been told to do the job again. When it was eventually discovered, I suppose the churchwardens thought it was a bit of a laugh too, and left it at that. So I must say it seems a little odd that the church guide, which goes into some detail about the architecture, the memorials, and all the routine features of the church, totally ignores this touch of whimsy. Could it be, perhaps, that these days the residents of Old Brampton, in all those nice houses, find it rather embarrassing?

SEVEN HUNDRED YEARS ON THE SAME CYCLE – YES, IT *IS* A RECORD

LAXTON
NOTTINGHAMSHIRE
10 miles north-west of Newark

If you happen to live in Norfolk, the three large fields that surround Laxton in Nottinghamshire don't look all that large. Norfolk went through a period of 'prairie-isation' after the war, a process as unfortunate as its name. Farmers were paid a subsidy to pull up their hedges and combine small fields into big ones, so they could increase production. These days production is too high and they are being paid a subsidy to put the hedges back again – such are the idiosyncrasies of British agriculture. But in Laxton those three big fields are not amalgamations of smaller ones; in fact, originally they were much bigger. Their significance is that they are the only fields in England where the medieval system of open-field farming has survived for more than seven hundred years.

While the rest of the English countryside was being divided up and enclosed by the big landowners in the eighteenth century, somehow Laxton remained unaffected. Portions of the great fields were whittled away over the years, and from nearly two thousand acres they were reduced to just 483, but they are still divided into strips, and each strip is still allocated and administered by the Court Leet, acting on behalf of the Lord of the Manor – nowadays the Crown Estate Commissioners.

The medieval three-year cycle of cropping was to plant winter wheat one year, then a spring-sown crop like barley or peas the second year, then to leave the land fallow in the third year, so it had a rest and provided grazing for sheep. These days, in many cases, the original strips have been amalgamated into larger ones so that tractors and combine harvesters can be used, and the field lying fallow is made more use of, but the basic cycle remains unchanged. A jury appointed by the Court Leet still inspects the fields once a year, to make sure the boundary posts are in the right place, and nobody has encroached on a neighbour's strip or on to the cart-roads which run through the fields, and the Court still has the power to impose fines for any transgressions into neighbouring territory.

Every resident of Laxton is on a list called the Suit Roll, and anyone on the list can be ordered to attend the Court's annual meeting at the Dovecote Inn; in theory they can be fined two pence if they don't turn up. That particular penalty isn't taken too seriously these days, but on the whole the Court continues to function as it did in medieval times – the only one in the country still to do so.

I expect a lot of all this is only of interest to historically-minded farmers, and indeed to a casual visitor there is little to indicate how Mill Field, West Field and South Field at Laxton are any different from many other big fields in rural England, but there is another medieval feature of the village which is much more obvious. Most of the buildings along the main street seem to be either farmhouses, or barns, or both. In a lot of cases they stand end-on to the road, and they date back to the days when each farmer had a narrow strip of land extending back from the village street. This layout has remained virtually unchanged since the first official map of Laxton was

ONE OF THE CART TRACKS WHICH THE COURT LEET INSPECTS TO ENSURE NO FARMER HAS ENCROACHED.

drawn in the 1630s, and it could date back even before those three big fields were brought into cultivation.

Most English villages in this book are mainly devoted to farming, but not many give the impression that the farming is actually going on in the village itself. Instead of the usual assortment of shops and houses and cottages, Laxton has all these farmyards in the heart of the main street. Even the parish church is geared up to its predominantly farmyard setting: a notice on the door says, 'Welcome – but please, no muddy boots'.

Once you have scraped off the mud, it is worth going in, if only to see the fourteenth-century effigy of Margery de Everingham, the only wooden medieval effigy left in Nottinghamshire. It survived the complete remodelling of the church in 1854, when the original building was 'unhappily in a

state of neglect and decay'. Earl Manvers, the Lord of the Manor, paid for one end of the nave to be removed, the aisles to be made narrower, and the tower to be taken down and rebuilt in a new position adjoining the shortened nave. The Earl also spent a great deal of money building Thoresby Hall, and this may have helped Laxton to preserve its old system of farming, because he had plans for 'improving' it, but ran out of funds before he could do so. His successors never got around to it either, and the sixth Earl finally sold the three open fields to the Ministry of Agriculture in 1952. The Government has kept them going on the original system ever since.

Laxton has another surviving link with the past, the motte and bailey of a twelfth-century castle just to the north of the village. The castle itself has long since disappeared, and so has the manor house which was built on the site four centuries later, but the man-made mound on which they stood is still there, one of the best preserved and certainly the highest such mound in Nottinghamshire, and there are some fine views towards Sherwood Forest and, of course, across those famous open Laxton fields.

Famous? Well, so it would seem, even though to the layman they just look like pretty average fields. They are famous enough for Laxton to have its own visitors' centre, an unexpected amenity to find in a village which seems to consist almost entirely of farmyards. There are walking tours from the centre which take in the three fields, as well as the church and the castle site, and even on a cold and damp February morning I came upon a little group of walkers on one of these tours, knowledgeably discussing the almost indiscernible strips of land in the West Field. But even without its importance as England's last open-field village, Laxton has some of the best attributes of an English village; it is unassuming, it is peaceful – and it is used to muddy boots.

A WELCOME TO WAYFARERS, BUT A CURSE ON THE CORBETS

MORETON CORBET
SHROPSHIRE
9 miles north of Shrewsbury

It was the sign at the entrance to the church which immediately endeared Moreton Corbet to me. It had obviously been there a long time, and it said cheerfully: 'Welfarers Welcome – from an open road to an open church'. I have so often travelled long distances to see churches which prove inaccessible that this was a most refreshing change, and here's one wayfarer who felt very welcome indeed.

I had already been disappointed twice that day. First I had been to High Ercall, where I understood there were impressive remains of a Royalist stronghold, but the impressive remains turned out to be covered in scaffolding and surrounded by barbed wire, the village pub's 'mid-nineteenth-century façade', as the gazetteer put it, was just boring Victorian, and High Ercall itself was on a junction of two busy main roads. So I tried a village called Knockin, which was credited with a ruined castle on a grassy mound, an old sheep-dip and a black-and-white Tudor mansion which was Knockin's crowning glory. Alas, Knockin was on an even busier road, so busy I couldn't pause to inspect the sheep-dip, I never did find the ruined castle or even the grassy mound, and the black-and-white 'crowning glory' was, well, black-and-white. The only consolation was the name of the village store; its waggish proprietor had christened it The Knockin Shop . . .

Slightly hysterical, I left the main roads and tried my luck around the Shropshire byways. I found one signposted to Moreton Corbet, a name unknown to me, but it sounded vaguely promising. And so it proved, because what the signpost didn't mention was Moreton Corbet Castle, a really splendid ruin in a quiet, secluded little village, with

some marvellous tales to tell. What with that and the welcome to wayfarers, my cup was full.

Moreton Corbet was the seat for many centuries of the Corbets, one of the most ancient and distinguished families in Shropshire – they really did come over with the Conqueror. Sir Richard Corbet acquired it in about 1239 when he married into the Toret family, and the village's name was changed as a result. The Torets were a Saxon family who had managed to hang on to their estate after the Conquest, and the village was called Moreton Toret. Actually it was still Moreton Toret until at least 1516, so the Corbets were not too assertive about their name, but they owned so many estates in Shropshire that they hardly needed to push it.

Parts of their earlier medieval castle still stand, but in the sixteenth century Sir Andrew Corbet started to rebuild it. He died half-way through, and his son Robert had a go. Robert was 'carried away with the affectionate delights of architecture', but he too died before the work was finished. In fact the Corbets were still getting around to completing it when the Civil War broke out. The castle was defended by Sir Vincent Corbet, but he didn't stand much chance when a Parliamentary force turned up from Shrewsbury, because the castle wasn't really a castle at all, more of a lightly fortified manor house. The Roundheads captured it, causing a fair amount of damage in the process, then set fire to it – and that just about put an end to it. After the war the Corbets decided they might as well live in one of their other stately homes, and the castle was allowed to fall into ruins. English Heritage looks after Moreton Corbet Castle these days, but it is still owned by the Corbets, as it has been for over 750 years.

During that period some delightful legends have been passed down about the family. It is said, for instance, that during the Crusades the Corbet heir was away so long at the wars that it was assumed he was dead. His younger brother succeeded to the estate and decided to get married on the strength of it. According to Charlotte Burns' *Shropshire Folklore*: 'On the wedding day, in the midst of the feasting and rejoicing, a pilgrim came to the gate asking for hospitality and alms. He was bidden to sit down to the board and share the feast. Scarcely was the banquet ended, when the pilgrim revealed himself.'

You can guess the rest. Well, perhaps you can't, because the bridegroom, far from being put out by his elder brother's return, immediately offered to hand over the inheritance and retire with his wife into poverty. Then his brother, far from demanding his rightful inheritance, said he was happy to end his days in obscurity in a house on the estate, and leave the bride and groom to live happily ever after (much to the relief of the

THE PLEASANT APPROACH TO MORETON CORBET CHURCH.

bride, saved at the last minute from a sudden reversal). So they must have been awfully decent chaps, these Corbets.

That still seemed to apply many years later, when a Puritan called Paul Holmyard was taken under the protection of Sir Vincent Corbet during the period before the Civil War. At that stage the Puritans were having a rough time under King Charles, but Sir Vincent was obviously a very tolerant fellow, even though a keen Royalist – he was the one who later fought the Roundheads at the castle. However, it seems that his tolerance ran out when Holmyard kept on preaching inflammatory sermons, and he threatened to denounce him. It is not clear whether he actually did, but Holmyard was denounced by somebody and assumed it was Sir Vincent.

He managed to escape capture, and after suffering considerable privations he reappeared at the castle one day, where Sir Vincent was still trying to get the building work finished. 'Woe to thee, hard-hearted man,' cried Paul Holmyard, or words to that effect. 'The Lord has hardened thy heart, but rejoice not in thy riches, for neither thou, nor thy children, nor they children's children, shall inhabit these halls. They shall be given up to desolation; snakes, vipers and unclean beasts shall make it their refuge, and thy house shall be abandoned to them.'

Extravagant stuff, but he was absolutely right. I can't vouch for the vipers, but the castle was never completed and no other Corbet has lived there since. As curses go, that must have been a real humdinger . . .

PARLIAMENT IN THE BARN, AND LUNCH UP A TREE

ACTON BURNELL
SHROPSHIRE
7 miles south of Shrewsbury

I came upon Acton Burnell in a search for maiden garlands, once a feature of virgins' funerals. The best-known collection in Shropshire is at Minsterley, but Minsterley lies on a busy roundabout at the junction of three main roads, and doesn't quite fit my picture of an English village. As well as the garlands, however, the church had a helpful note about other places they might be found, and one such place was Acton Burnell, a dozen miles away through a maze of country lanes. Alas, it no longer has any garlands – I eventually found some at Ashford-in-the-Water, featured on other pages – but it does have just about everything else.

Like Minsterley it lies on a crossroads, but the roads are mere lanes and one of them is a dead-end. It takes you into an impressive cluster of historic listed buildings: the ruins of the oldest fortified manor house in England, the remains of a massive tithe barn where Edward I is said to have held the first really representative Parliament in English history, a church which apart from its tower remains unaltered since the thirteenth century, a tomb in the church with the best brass in Shropshire, and a magnificent Georgian mansion. Throw in the finest timber-framed house in the county, also in the parish, add the good taste of a nineteenth-century squire who 'rurified' the

ACTON BURNELL CHURCH, STILL STANDING JUST AS ROBERT BURNELL BUILT IT IN THE THIRTEENTH CENTURY.

plain façades of his estate cottages with rustic porches and decorative mantles over the windows, and Acton Burnell makes my picture of an English village just about complete.

The chap who laid the foundations of it all, seven hundred years ago, was Robert Burnell, whose family gave the village its name. Robert was one of those medieval masterminds who combined high office at court with high office in the church – a predecessor of Tybald, Wolsey, Cranmer and the like, though he came to a happier end. He got a foot in the door with the Royals when he became chaplain to Prince Edward, son of Henry III. When

Edward became King he promoted Burnell to Bishop of Bath and Wells, and as a bonus made him Lord Chancellor of England as well.

On his double salary, and with the perks from both jobs, the chancellor-bishop started building on a grand scale, both at his workplace in Wells – parts of his palace still stand – and back home at Acton Burnell. First he built the church, then his fortified house, known incorrectly but under-standably as Acton Burnell Castle. The great Tithe Barn was close by, and it was renamed Parliament Barn when his friend the King came to stay with him and called Parliament to meet there. What the

ROBERT BURNELL'S 'CASTLE' – ACTUALLY A FORTIFIED MANOR HOUSE, BUT THE WORD HAS STUCK.

MPs thought of having to traipse up to Shropshire, just so that he didn't have to break into his weekend, is not recorded, but I imagine in those days one didn't argue with the King.

The church still stands just as Burnell built it, except for its Victorian tower. He doesn't feature in it himself – he was buried in Wells Cathedral, as befitted his station – but another Burnell, Sir Nicholas, has a tomb in it with a splendid brass portraying him in his armour, which is much admired by the experts. Rather more elaborate, though, is the monument to Sir Richard Lee, whose family took over from the Burnells in the sixteenth century. He is surrounded by effigies of his wife, their three sons and nine daughters, and for good measure their pet dog, which is un-accountably crawling out of its master's gauntlet.

The Lee family were succeeded in their turn by the Smythes, two centuries later, and it was they who built the Georgian mansion, now a college for overseas students. The Lees, however, did not lose interest in their home village, even though they went to America and became somewhat involved in local politics. Richard Henry Lee was one of the signatories of the Declaration of Independence, and General Robert E. Lee got into the history books too. The family remained in Virginia, but when Acton Burnell Church needed substantial restoration work in 1960 they came to the rescue. I wonder if it should be renamed Acton Burnell-Lee . . .

Curiously, there is a feature missing in what is otherwise an archetypal conservation village: it has no pub. There used to be the Stag's Head, but it became a private house in the 1870s and now it is the village shop. Perhaps as compensation the parish boundaries were extended in recent years to include the hamlet of Pitchford, and that includes the spectacular Pitchford Hall, 'a riot of exotic carpentry' as one expert called it, the

SIR RICHARD LEE'S DOG LURKING IN HIS GAUNTLET ON THE FAMILY TOMB.

ultimate in timber-framed country houses. It has not changed hands for money since it was built in the reign of Henry VIII, and it is still privately owned and occupied, though opened regularly to the public. Architects eulogise about its lozenge and chevron framing, its decorated cable moulding, its carved bressummers and barge-boards, but to me the most intriguing feature is not the hall itself, but its tiny counterpart, a little house apparently made of timber and stonework, with arched doors and windows and a tiled roof – built in the branches of a tree!

It dates back to the seventeenth century, but the 'stonework' – actually plaster – and the other trimmings were added a hundred years later, and it came into its own during the present century, when it was constantly used by the highly eccentric Lady Sybil Grant. Lady Sybil was the daughter of a former Prime Minister, Lord Rosebery, who by all accounts was a fairly normal sort of chap for a politician, but when she married General Sir Charles Grant, the squire of Pitchford Hall, she decided the place was haunted and spent much of her time in the Tree House, where she insisted on having her meals. I would love to have seen the unfortunate butler struggling up the tree, balancing her lunch on a silver salver, let alone Lady Sybil herself scrambling into her lofty retreat – she was a large lady, prone to dying her hair orange and wearing flowing, flamboyant dresses. The local bird population must have been in a permanent state of shock.

The General, I gather, took it all very calmly and spent his time in the west wing, communicating with his wife via the butler or by battery telephone. When he entertained guests to lunch he was liable to suggest, as a little post-prandial outing: 'Like to take a look at old Sybil, what?'

They don't come like that any more.

TALES OF MAD JACK MYTTON – AND THE FIRE HE WOULDN'T HAVE FAKED

HABBERLEY
SHROPSHIRE
9 miles south-west of Shrewsbury

It was a sheer fluke that I came upon Habberley – and it made my day.

I had been to Minsterley in search of maiden's garlands, hoping that the church they were in, and the village itself, would prove as fascinating as this early tradition of carrying decorated crowns at the funerals of unmarried girls. The garlands were there all right, but the church was a solid red-brick affair, more like a village hall inside than a church, and Minsterley turned out to be on two busy main roads, complete with a large roundabout in the

middle. So I headed off into the hills along a tiny lane, hoping for the best.

It was a marvellous contrast to the main roads I had left behind, and the views across the Rea Valley were already making me feel better when I came down a hill to a tiny crossroads, again the greatest contrast to that Minsterley roundabout, and there was Habberley, a handful of farms and cottages round a little church, in the middle of nowhere. The hills rose on all sides. In fact the parish of Habberley itself rises nearly three hundred feet from one end to the other. The farms are concentrated in the village because most of the surrounding area was common land, so this increases its isolation.

The church is fairly modest, and indeed at one time it was so unassuming that the villagers weren't even sure of its name. In 1885 a cleric called Drinkwater told Shropshire Archaeological Society: 'It is said by some to be dedicated to St Mary, by others to St James. In the parish books nothing is said about the dedication.' His own theory was that its patron saint was St Lawrence, because the local annual holiday was held near his festival day. But Mr Drinkwater lost out, and so did St James: these days it is called St Mary's.

Apart from the church Habberley has sixty-nine people, twenty-six houses, a village hall, a pub, and one bus a week, and that seemed about it. Then the name of the pub rang a bell:

the Mytton Arms. Hadn't I heard of a Shropshire squire called Mad Jack Mytton, a reckless hell-raiser who once rode a bear into the dining-room to startle his guests, drank eight bottles of port every evening, went shooting wild duck stark naked, and eventually gambled away the family fortune, to die in a debtor's prison? By sheer chance I had come upon the village where the Mytton family were squires at Habberley Hall for over three hundred years.

The locals are probably rather prouder of Mad Jack's relation, William Mytton, a noted and highly respectable eighteenth-century historian, and indeed there is some doubt as to whether Habberley was actually Jack's permanent home. One reference book says he lived at Whittington, near Oswestry, and another says his father left him 'the family seat at Halston Hall, near Shrewsbury'. But there were certainly Myttons at Habberley, it is not that far from Shrewsbury, and I can't find a road atlas which shows a place called Halston anywhere in Shropshire. The locals seem quite sure that he lived at the Hall, and they even tell how he kept bears in the barns, and how one part of the village where a house now stands was called the bear-pit, which seems to tally with the story of the after-dinner bear-ride.

So for my money Habberley is the place, and I can quite picture Mad Jack up at the splendid old sixteenth-century Hall, knocking back his eighth bottle of port before mounting another bear, or driving around these country lanes in his gig, terrifying other road users and unnerving his passengers. On one outing he asked his companion if he'd ever turned over in a gig. His friend confessed he had not, whereupon Mad Jack cried: 'What a damned slow fellow you must have been all your life', and promptly drove up the bank and ran one wheel into a rabbit-hole . . .

Another Mytton story seems to fit in with Habberley, like the bear. There are remnants of old mines up in the hills, lead, silver and copper, and according to the story it was a miner who tried to upset the hounds while Mad Jack was out hunting. The Squire got off his horse, challenged the man to a bout of fisticuffs, and fought twenty rounds with him until the miner admitted defeat – whereupon Mad Jack gave him half a sovereign for putting up a decent fight, got back on his horse and rejoined the hunt.

On a cold hunting day he would take his one-eyed hunter Baronet into any convenient cottage and dry him off by the fire; he probably owned all the cottages, so nobody argued. But he took less care of his own health. His method of curing himself of hiccups was to set fire to his nightshirt. His friends had to put out the blaze and treat his burns, but his only comment was: 'Well, the

hiccups is gone, by God'. Mad Jack went himself, in 1834, aged only thirty-eight; more than three thousand mourners attended his funeral.

So Habberley has its own striking example of one aspect of English rural life, the eccentric squire, and as I say, it made my day. But I was not the first to come upon the village and discover that Habberley Hall offered just the right kind of background – and in the other case, that is literally what it was used for. A film crew found that it provided the ideal setting to shoot Josephine Tey's novel, *The Franchise Affair*. The villagers were fascinated when they found out, and they couldn't wait for the final scene, when the plot required that the Hall was burnt down. They were much impressed, if perhaps a little disappointed, when the technicians devised a complex set-up for faking the fire. But I have a suspicion that Mad Jack Mytton wouldn't have settled for that. He'd have struck the match himself, and burned the place to the ground . . .

TAKE YOUR ANTLERS FOR THE NEXT DANCE, PLEASE

ABBOTS BROMLEY
STAFFORDSHIRE
6 miles south of Uttoxeter

I hesitated about Abbots Bromley, not just because it is rather larger than I like and it sits on two main roads, but its claim to fame is perhaps too obvious. On the other hand it is not as large as it was, the roads are fairly quiet except for one day of the year, and I just couldn't resist those chaps dancing about the streets with horns on their shoulders, accompanied by a hobby horse, a bowman, a male Maid Marian and a character known as the Fool, though he is surely no dottier than all the rest. Yes, this is the home of the famous Horn Dance, a tradition so quaint (did I hear, ridiculous?) that it could only be found in an English village, and a lot more endearing to my mind than those husky stick-clashing morris dancers in their bells and ribbons.

Actually, Abbots Bromley qualifies in its own right. It has a name, for instance, which has changed three times, first from Bromleah to Bromley Abbatus when an abbey was founded at Burton-on-Trent, then to Pagets Bromley when Henry VIII took it off the abbot and gave it to Thomas Paget, then back to the Anglicised version of the original when the Pagets sold it in the 1800s, even though the abbot had long since disappeared.

It has an old house where Mary Queen of Scots is supposed to have spent the night on her way to imprisonment and eventual execution. It has an ancient family, the Bagots, still living in Blithfield Hall after six hundred years, though

THE HORN DANCERS OF ABBOTS BROMLEY – AND COULD THAT BE MAID MARIAN?

THE VILLAGE GREEN DECKED OUT WITH STALLS ON THE DAY OF THE HORN DANCE.

their view has been somewhat altered by the Blithfield Reservoir, and it has a picturesque butter cross where Samuel Johnson is said to have sold books from a market stall. Enough ingredients there for any historic English village, but it is still the Horn Dance which brings the crowds, and if you don't like crowds and you're not turned on by men in reindeer antlers, then keep clear of Abbots Bromley on the Monday following the first Sunday after the 4th September – a formula which sounds almost as obscure as the Horn Dance itself, but it matches the date of the old Barthelmy Fair on St Bartholemew's Day.

You may still be blinking at that mention of reindeer antlers, because it would be more logical to find deer horns in a village surrounded by traditional deer-hunting country. In fact Richard II used to stay with the Bagot family and go hunting in Needwood Forest, and it was he who gave them the herd of what are still known as Bagot goats.

But the horns in the Horn Dance don't come from deer, nor indeed from goats. One eighteenth-century writer refers to them as 'elks heads', but he got it wrong too. These are unmistakably reindeer antlers, and they have been carbon-dated as nearly a thousand years old. Through the marvel of modern science they have been identified as coming from tame reindeer – though quite how they know this, I can't imagine . . .

This presents something of a puzzle, because reindeer became extinct in Britain much more than a thousand years ago. Mr E.R. Shipman, who has written a whole book about the Horn Dance, reckons that the Vikings must have brought them across the North Sea and up the River Trent, though why they should have included half a dozen pairs of reindeer antlers in their luggage rather baffles me. I can't imagine they danced about in them, the way they do in Abbots Bromley today – Vikings have never struck me as great dancers. Maybe the antlers arrived still attached to the reindeer, but that must have made life very uncomfortable aboard ship.

However, there they are in Abbots Bromley, carefully preserved for nearly ten centuries. On the 364 other days of the year they are kept in the parish church – or rather, they always used to be – I last heard there were increasing worries about vandalism and theft. In an era when medieval panels can be cut out of rood-screens to sell to unscrupulous collectors, I suppose there may well be a market for old antlers, though being rather large, they could hardly be smuggled out under your jacket.

There is a replica set as well, which the dancers use when they are invited to perform outside the village, and this is a wise precaution too, because legend has it that many years ago the dancing team visited Burton-on-Trent, became helplessly drunk (as Mr Shipman observes, that's not too difficult in Burton), and dropped the horns into the Trent on the way home. Fortunately those were replicas too.

The Dance may not be as old as the horns.

'MEET MY FRIEND . . .'

Nobody really knows when it started or why, and indeed one contributor to the *Birmingham Post* in the 1930s suggested the dance was a Victorian invention – 'illiterate and corrupt jack-pudding nonsense' – but don't try to tell them that in Abbots Bromley. It may have pagan origins like the American Indian buffalo dance; it may have originally marked certain hunting rights in Needwood Forest – in which case, why reindeer horns? – or it may have been dreamed up by some medieval merry-maker who wanted to cheer things up a bit at the Barthelmy Fair.

There is a more suggestive theory that it was some sort of fertility dance, and the horns were an emblem of male virility – that's why the Norsemen had ox-horns on their helmets. One historian notes that in rural France there was a similar tradition where men with cattle-horns chased the village maidens – but even a Frenchman would have problems chasing a maiden while wearing twenty-pound reindeer antlers on his shoulders, and even greater problems if he caught her.

William Shakespeare included a horn dance in *As You Like It*, and I suspect he rather favoured the virility theory, because he wrote a song to go with it which ends: 'The horn, the horn, the lusty horn, is not a thing to laugh to scorn'. I don't think you'll hear that song in Abbots Bromley though, because two much-respected families, the Bentleys and the Fowells, have been responsible for the Horn Dance for generations, and I doubt that they'd stand for any of that. But on second thoughts, maybe those rape-and-pillage Vikings did go in for horn-dancing after all . . .

A VILLAGE BY ANY OTHER NAME – TWENTY-FOUR OF THEM

ALSTONEFIELD
STAFFORDSHIRE
7 miles north of Ashbourne

You wouldn't really think that Alstonefield was in the running for any sort of record. It is tucked away in the southern part of the Peak District, just a mile inside the Staffordshire boundary, and although it is near the Dove it is mercifully well clear of the much-trodden tourist route through Dovedale. Two or three minor roads converge on it, but it's not really on the way to anywhere of any size. So no record attendance figures here to challenge Chatsworth or Haddon Hall, and although the churchyard does contain one old lady of 107, and a headstone dated 1518 is among the oldest churchyard memorials in the country, it is not these which give it the chance to enter the record books.

Alstonefield's most un-usual feature, in fact, is the number of ways it has spelt its name. All English villages have varied in their spelling over the centuries, and you will rarely find one spelt the same as it was in the *Domesday Book,* let alone the earlier variations. But Alstonefield can claim no fewer than twenty-four different spellings, starting with Aenestanefelt, meaning Aelfstans Feld, the land of Aelston free from woodland, and progressing through different combinations of Austons and Alstons with Feilds and Felts, until it finally settled on the current version. Is there another village that can beat it?

The present inhabitants can hardly claim any credit for this record, if record it is, but they deserve high commendation

THE OLDEST GRAVESTONE IN THE CHURCHYARD DATES FROM 1518.

for the state of their church. The first impression when you enter it is the smell of polish; the pews are positively gleaming, and so are the brass fitments on them. My wife was particularly impressed, because she copes with our own village church and knows what's involved.

In contrast, the least commendable feature in the church must surely be that pea-green pew of the Cotton family, which is beyond the help of any polish, and sticks out like a thumb which is not merely sore but positively gangrenous. Even the church guide admits that it is painted 'what many people think is a most unsuitable colour'; the local history society contents itself, more discreetly, with 'strangely painted'. It was built at the same time and by the same person as the very handsome oak pulpit and the other pews, back in the 1630s, so why did it acquire this bilious appearance? Presumably the Cottons liked it that way, but they have long since gone and Beresford Hall, where they lived, no longer exists. It would be depressing if this were the only reminder of the family.

Fortunately they have another claim to fame, albeit an indirect one. Charles Cotton was a good friend of Izaak Walton, author of *The Compleat Angler*, (or so I had thought), who regularly visited Alstonefield. Clutching at this straw, the church guide observes: 'No doubt, being a devout Christian, he worshipped in this pew'. There is a closer link than that, however, which the history society's booklet

THE 'STRANGELY PAINTED' COTTON FAMILY PEW IN ALSTONEFIELD CHURCH.

mentions in a surprisingly causal throw-away line. 'Izaak Walton's book, *The Compleat Angler*, first published in 1653, is famous throughout the world,' it says, 'but those who have not actually read it may not realise that the second part was written by Charles Cotton.'

Too right I didn't realise it. Nor did the compiler of my encyclopedia, who says that, if you dip into *The Compleat Angler*, 'everywhere you will find Walton's sentences flowing as smoothly, sweetly and clearly as the English rivers into

which he was wont to cast his angler's line'. Poor old Cotton doesn't get a mention. How many other people have failed to cotton on, as it were, that the Compleat Angler was not the Compleat Author?

Another family connected with Alstonefield doesn't need any famous angling friends to earn a place in history. Until 1957 the village had an inn called the Crewe and Harpur, a name which must have been quite baffling to strangers. It had nothing to do with sailors or railway junctions, it derived from the Harpur-Crewe family, Lords of the Manor and patrons of the church for four hundred years. For much of that time they lived hidden away from the village at Calke Abbey, now billed by the National Trust as 'The House that Time Forgot'.

It was Sir Henry Harpur who first displayed the 'congenital unsociability', as the National Trust calls it, which became the family trait. His son George was more extrovert, and must have made a greater impact on Alstonefield, because the church has a stained-glass window in his memory, albeit 'of very inferior glass', according to the church guide. But his son Vauncey was another recluse who wrote letters to his daughters rather than speak to them, even though they shared the same roof. His successors made no changes to Calke Abbey, and when it went to the National Trust because of death duties the rooms had remained virtually unaltered for a hundred years.

The family seemed to adjust its name almost as often as Alstonefield itself. Sir John Harpur married a daughter of Lord Crewe, and his descendant Sir Henry changed his name to Crewe in the hope of reviving the title. After he failed the family compromised by calling itself Harpur Crewe, and the hypen followed later. The pub at Alstonefield, perhaps to make sure it trod on no illustrious toes, switched the names round (the Crewes were barons, the Harpurs were baronets), and settled for the Crewe and Harpur Arms.

Alstonefield was one of the few places where Sir Vauncey Harpur Crewe appeared in public – he spent most of his time catching butterflies and shooting birds. On one occasion, when he opened a garden fete in the village, the nursemaid at the vicarage, Hannah Hudson, bought him a pound of tomatoes from one of the stalls. It must have been a rather daring move in those days, but Sir Vauncey, it seems, was profusely grateful. Her comment afterwards sums up the lonely life he had chosen for himself. 'You see,' she said, 'everybody thinks that Sir Vauncey has everything, so nobody bothers to give him anything.' They're perceptive folk in Alstonefield . . .

DIRTY WASHING, A BISHOP'S PALACE, AND AN ORDER TO ALTER THE ALTAR

LYDDINGTON
LEICESTERSHIRE
14 miles north-east of Market Harborough

Lyddington is only a small village in terms of population, never more than eight hundred people and down to four hundred today, but it has offered a remarkable range of incentives for other people to visit it. Until early this century, for instance, servants from Uppingham School used to visit it regularly to bring the boys' washing; there were four laundries in the village solely for their benefit. On a loftier plane, Bishops of Lincoln used to visit it because it was a handy staging post on their travels around the vast diocese, which stretched from the Humber to the Thames.

Rather than doss down at the local pub, the bishops built themselves a palace next to the parish church, and while they were in residence the village priests in the neighbourhood would come to Lyddington, to crave a boon, or receive promotion, or be put on the carpet.

These days most people still come to Lyddington to visit the palace, but it is now owned by English Heritage and they have come to see the splendid hall on the first floor where the bishops held audience, and the not-so-splendid room next door where the suitors waited their turn. There are

THE LOOK-OUT TOWER IN THE WALL SURROUNDING THE OLD BISHOP'S PALACE, LATER LYDDINGTON BEDE HOUSE.

INSIDE THE BEDE HOUSE, WHERE INMATES WERE 'BEDEN' TO PRAY FOR THEIR BENEFACTORS.

two identical nail-studded doors at the top of the stairs. If a priest was ushered into the one on the right, he went straight into the presence of the bishop, and could expect something very nice, or very nasty. If he was shunted into the one on the left, he found himself in the waiting-room, which meant either nothing very urgent would happen to him, or it was going to be very nasty indeed . . .

There is another group of visitors these days who go to Lyddington to eat. Again, I have to say this is not a pub or hotel guide, but if you want a rather up-market pub lunch then the Old White Hart offers, for about a fiver, a standard of cuisine which you'd be lucky to find elsewhere for a tenner.

If you are interested in early rural architecture, Lyddington has something to offer you too. You can stroll along its main street, nearly a mile from end to end, and admire the ironstone cottages, ranging from orange to brown to purple; the colours can positively glow in the sunshine. One house even has mullioned windows of ironstone; another has a row of white limestone across the

middle. Some of the names are distinctive too; I still wonder why a little old cottage at the end of a terrace is called 'Annette' – it's not just a passing fad because the name is carved permanently into the stone lintel . . .

It was a mixture of all these attractions that took me to Lyddington, but none of them, not even the steak and mushroom pie at the White Hart, was more fascinating than the unique feature I found in the church. I have seen no mention of it in the reference books – they all seem too occupied with the bishop's palace next door. By the time they have explained how it was seized by Henry VIII, given to the Cecils of Burghley House, turned into an almshouse for ten poor men and renamed Bede House (because the men were 'beden' to pray for their benefactors), there is only room for a quick mention of the church's lofty nave, the faded wall-paintings and the old stone coffin-lids by the door. What struck me, though, was the curious situation of the altar. It stands well forward from the usual position against the east wall, and it is completely surrounded by a wooden rail; I suppose about forty communicants could kneel around it at a time.

The story behind this unusual arrangement goes back to the days of Charles I, and a dispute between William Laud, Archbishop of Canterbury, and John Williams, Bishop of Lincoln. For decades there had been an argument between High Churchmen and Reformers over the siting of altars. The High Churchmen wanted to retain them against the east wall, the Reformers and later the Puritans preferred them to be in the middle of the chancel, so they could be used as Communion tables.

Sometimes an altar was shifted into the chancel or even the nave for Communion, then put back against the wall between services. That involved a lot of wear and tear on the altar, let alone on the chaps who had to shift it. It was all very confusing and unsatisfactory, and in 1634 Archbishop Laud decided to settle the matter by decreeing that an altar must stay at the east end of the church, with a rail between it and the chancel.

Bishop Williams disagreed with Laud's views – they had never really hit it off anyway. He could hardly defy the Archbishop altogether, but as a compromise he told his parish priests that they should move the altar away from the wall, but put a rail all round four sides of it. He seems to have got away with it, because he finished up as Archbishop of York.

Other churches in the diocese must have carried out his instructions too, but when the Victorians came along they altered the layout in their case to the more orthodox pattern of a raised chancel with a single rail across it. They tried to do this at Lyddington too. The chancel was raised, the altar moved nearer the wall and the rails taken away, but there was such an outcry among the populace that they were put back in place. As the church guide puts it: 'We like to think that no other church in England has quite the same arrangement. If any visitor can quote a parallel, we should be interested to hear of it.'

Since the guide was written Lyddington Church has achieved a new distinction. In December 1991, to celebrate the 450th anniversary of the Diocese of Peterborough (which Lyddington only joined in 1881, but no matter), two new 'grotesques' or gargoyles were added to the pillars in the nave. One is the traditional 'Green Man', which seems to have become a symbol of the new concern over the environment, and the other depicts the present Bishop of Peterborough, the Rt Revd Dr William Westwood. I confess I found it difficult to recognise the gargoyle as the Bill Westwood who used to sit opposite me in the 'Today' studio to present his 'Thought for the Day', but then none of us looked our best at that time of the morning. Anyway, what a nice idea to honour the Bishop in this way – and I am sure it must tickle him that he now features as a gargoyle in one of his own churches!

THE ALTAR SURROUNDED BY NAILS – 'NO OTHER CHURCH IN ENGLAND HAS QUITE THE SAME'.

MY KINGDOM FOR A HORSE? NO, MAKE IT FOUR...

GADDESBY
LEICESTERSHIRE
6 miles south-west of Melton Mowbray

If you are driving along the B674 road between Rearsby and Ashby Folville you won't think much of Gaddesby. I didn't myself. There are some fairly nondescript houses scattered along it, and a store and a school, and that's about it. You might well prefer the look of Ashby Folville – a tree-lined cricket ground, some old houses, a pleasant river. But it does have that main road going through the heart of it, and although it is only a B-road it provides a handy cut-through from Loughborough to Oakham, avoiding Melton Mowbray, and it has been widened accordingly for all the traffic. Gaddesby's good fortune is that its main street is a turning off this road, and this central part of the village retains much of the peaceful atmosphere and character that it had when Gaddesby Hall was built in 1744.

The Hall was the home of Colonel Edward Hawkins Cheney, generally regarded as Gaddesby's most famous son, though in fact he wasn't even a Leicestershire man. He came to the village when he married Eliza, the daughter of the man who lived at the Hall and whose family built it, John Ayre. It may stand on the site of the moated Grange which was occupied by the Knights Templar when they were given the village by Henry II. Certainly the cedars which still stand in what used to be its park are said to have grown from seeds they brought back from the Holy Land.

The Knights Templar were suppressed by the Pope in 1312 and Gaddesby passed to the Knights Hospitalers, who in turn were suppressed at the Reformation. With their going the fortunes of the village slumped; they had looked after the villagers and the splendid church, one of the largest in the county. It only became a parish church in its own right in 1874. There was also an exodus from the village as more profitable work became available in the coal-mines and quarries. From being a centre of population in one of the most prosperous rural areas in England, Gaddesby dwindled in importance and size. In fact nothing much seems to have happened there between the departure of the

Knights Hospitalers and the arrival of the Ayre family a couple of hundred years later, followed by the Cheneys.

The Ayres have been rather overshadowed by their successors, primarily because of the exploits of Colonel Edward Cheney. Otherwise the Cheney Arms might have been called the Ayre Arms, and indeed there was good reason to do so, because it was built at the same time as the Hall, and it is said to have been the Ayres' dower house. I stress the 'said to have been' because one gazetteer says very firmly that it is 'a purpose-built inn of circa 1750 and quite unaltered'. A local historian, however, prefers the dower house theory. He says it had stables and other outbuildings in the past, which would have been appropriate for a dower house, and he adds, just as firmly as the gazetteer but in complete contradiction: 'Where one enters now is, in fact, the rear of the original house since the road has been re-routed'. I couldn't enquire myself because it was shut at the time, so take your pick.

The church was shut too, always a frustrating experience; one has to go back to the stores on the main road for the key. But there is no dispute about the most striking feature inside it, and this for me is the main attraction of Gaddesby. In the chancel is a very large, almost overwhelming monument, a nearly life-size marble sculpture depicting Colonel Edward Cheney, astride one of the four horses that were shot from under him at the Battle of Waterloo.

Four? All shot from under him? In one battle? It sounds unlikely, but this time the gazetteer and the local historian both agree, and so do all the other reference books. The accident-prone colonel was serving in the Royal Scots Greys, which either issued its officers with a great many spare horses or else approved of them commandeering somebody else's if they lost their own. One gets this mental picture of our hero surrounded by deceased livestock, while three or four unmounted junior officers are running like mad for cover . . .

Colonel Cheney lived on until 1848, and the

story of his amazing survival at Waterloo lived on too, because that was how it was decided to commemorate him. The sculpture was originally at the Hall, then put into the church when the estate was sold in 1917. Not everyone thought it was a good idea. The great church authority Pevsner reckoned it ought to have gone to Westminster Abbey, which was the right size for that sort of thing. Gaddesby Historical Society observes, more discreetly, that 'its site is not particularly well-chosen'. But it is a source of great fascination to visitors, and the marble colonel is after all the only Cheney left in the village – the family ended its connection when his eldest son died in 1878.

His marble mount, however, is not the only horse left in Gaddesby. Somewhere near the church, on private land so I can't say exactly where, is the grave of Bendigo, a racehorse which won the first Eclipse Stakes in 1886. But if you prefer live horses, then you have only to check which days the Quorn is hunting, because Gaddesby is in the heart of Quorn country, and its stables and kennels are nearby.

The Quorn's royal connections, which came into the limelight during the Hunt's period of bad publicity in 1991, included the late Duke of Windsor, who often rode with them when he was Prince of Wales, and was entertained by the local gentry. It was during one of these visits that he first met a Mrs Simpson and her husband; the rest, as they say, is history.

There was also an occasion during that era when all four royal brothers visited the village; they were entertained to lunch at the Hermitage, which still stands in the main street. So Gaddesby has a tale of four lunching princes as well as four luckless horses – but I know which story I prefer . . .

COLONEL EDWARD CHENEY ON ONE OF THE FOUR HORSES SHOT UNDER HIM AT THE BATTLE OF WATERLOO – HIS MONUMENT IN GADDESBY CHURCH.

WATER, WATER EVERYWHERE – AND LOTS OF IT TO DRINK

UPPER HAMBLETON
LEICESTERSHIRE
3 miles east of Oakham

Upper Hambleton must be very relieved that it is Upper. All that's left of Middle Hambleton is the Old Hall, which used to be surrounded by parkland but now has water on two sides; and there is no sign of a Lower Hambleton at all. Upper Hambleton is the only village to survive on a narrow peninsula of land which juts out into Rutland Water, now covering more than three thousand acres of what used to be fields and farms and cottages – the largest man-made lake in western Europe.

It was only because Upper Hambleton stands on quite a substantial hill that it survives. It now occupies a uniquely remote position, cut off on three sides by water in what is otherwise a landlocked county. Three lanes still meet in the centre of the village, but two of them are signposted 'No Through Road' – and indeed the third one, which links the village with the main road two miles away, has a similar sign as it enters

the peninsula, as a further discouragement to traffic. Upper Hambleton, in fact, is one of the least accessible places in the Midland counties, thanks entirely to Anglian Water.

The transformation happened in the 1970s. At about the same time that the Boundary Commission officially wiped out the county of Rutland and made it part of Leicestershire (though nobody in Rutland has ever taken any notice), Anglian Water decided it needed an enormous new reservoir to satisfy the increasing demand in seven developing towns in the East Midlands: Northampton, Bedford, Peterborough, Corby, Milton Keynes, Daventry and Wellingborough. It already had Grafham Water and Pitsford Water; somebody looked at the contour lines on the land that was left, and stuck a flag in the low-lying area of farmland to the east of Oakham, along the valley of the awkwardly-named River Gwash. They may have liked the idea of Rutland anyway, because it provided a convenient syllable when they linked up the three Waters and called them the 'Ruthamford' water supply system . . .

They built a dam across the Gwash Valley near Empingham, twelve hundred metres long and forty metres high, and very soon Gwash was awash. More water was pumped in from the Nene and Welland rivers through more than twelve miles of pipelines and tunnels, and today it is up to a hundred feet deep. Just one more statistic, then I'm done. Rutland Water contains, at full capacity, twenty-seven thousand million gallons of water, enough I reckon, for every inhabitant of those seven towns to take 543 baths or go to the toilet 3,829 times.

It must have been very strange to live in Upper Hambleton at that time, seeing the waters rise all around you, and the homes and farms of your neighbours disappear. Just one prominent landmark remains from the abandoned parishes, the church on the Normanton manor estate, just across the water. The Victorians built it in the same style as St John's Church in Smith Square, Westminster, with a flat balustraded roof and an ornate pineapple on top of the columns that form its tower. It stands on the site of the original medieval church, and fortunately those early builders selected slightly higher ground than the surrounding area. Even so, it could have been completely cut off or partially submerged if Anglian Water and a local Trust had not decided to preserve it.

They built a bank with a causeway to link it to the shore, raised the floor level and damp-proofed the masonry, and it still stands there unscathed. Alas, it no longer serves as a church, because all

that remains of Normanton is the coach-house and stable block of the manor house, now converted into a waterside hotel. The church has no grave-yard or lych-gate or rooftop cross to indicate its original purpose, and at first sight you might mistake it for one of those elaborate disguises which some water companies liked to give their pumping stations to make them more decorative, but it is actually used as a museum, and at night it is floodlit, an impressive sight from the Hambleton peninsula across the water.

Upper Hambleton has its own parish church of St Andrew but, unfortunately, it is not as access-ible to the public as the Normanton church museum. Even though it is in the centre of the village and could hardly be pillaged unnoticed, I found it locked, with not even the usual faded directions for collecting the key. It was winter, and maybe the church council is more hospitable during the holiday months, but a locked church is not merely exasperating, but a contradiction in terms – particularly when there is sometimes a sign like 'My house shall be called the House of Prayer' outside the locked door.

No matter. There is plenty of hospitality to be had at the Finch's Arms, just round the corner, and also, if you can afford it, just up the lane at Hambleton Hall Hotel. Or you can wander round the village and admire the ornate metal shield on the cottage opposite the church, inscribed 'Hambleton Post and Telegraph Office' – although only the telephone kiosk remains.

For the rest, Upper Hambleton consists of a few handsome old houses and some pleasant little cottages, and some tolerable new development on the outskirts. It is not, in fact, very different from many other secluded villages in Rutland – sorry, Leicestershire – until you walk out of it along those 'No Through Roads' and find yourself in what seems like a flatter version of the Lake District. All around you on Rutland Water in the summertime are the sailing boats, the wind-surfers, the trout fishermen, the bird-watchers; there is even the *Rutland Belle*, providing a forty-five minute cruise around the lake. There are no fell-walkers of course, but there are plenty of cyclists instead, riding along the twenty-five mile track around the lake where motor traffic is banned; for cyclists who want extra togetherness, at least one hotel hires out tandems.

So Upper Hambleton is a remote rural com-munity which has suddenly found itself in the heart of a holiday playground, but mercifully more remote than ever from the ordinary outside world. Only the picnickers and anglers drive through it; most of the holiday activity is based across the water. In many ways, therefore, the village has benefited from the astonishing transformation all around it – it's certainly fared better than its neighbours. Even so, I'm glad it hasn't happened around mine . . .

A LONE FISHERMAN AND HIS DOG, WHERE MIDDLE HAMBLETON USED TO BE. ONLY THE OLD HALL REMAINS ABOVE WATER.

THE TRAFFIC-CLOGGED VILLAGE THAT GOT TWO BYPASSES – AND TIXOVER

DUDDINGTON
NORTHAMPTONSHIRE
5 miles south-west of Stamford

The sign off the main road says 'Village Only'. That isn't strictly true, because you can still drive into Duddington and out the other side, but what a good idea of some benevolent soul in the county surveyor's office to preserve the newly-won peace of a village which must surely have earned it, after enduring for years the four-way traffic on two busy trunk roads.

If you stroll through Duddington today, along the narrow winding streets between the old limestone cottages with their stone-slate roofs, it's difficult to visualise that until 1972 they had to carry all the traffic between the Midlands and East Anglia on the A47, and between Northampton and the Great North Road on the A43. It must have been quite appalling. But since the two bypasses were built the traffic has disappeared; the village took a long, deep breath of relief and settled back into the way of life it enjoyed before the invention of internal combustion. Now it is once again the most peaceful, as well as the most attractive, village in the Welland Valley.

You can still hear a distant rumble from the bypasses, but as you get closer to the river the rumble is lost behind the more rustic sound of the wind in the trees and the gurgling of the water. One writer has described Duddington as 'weirdly quiet', but I find nothing weird about a community which is obviously revelling in its restored tranquillity, and wishes to do nothing to disturb it.

The building of the bypasses was not the first time the map has been altered in Duddington's history. Back in 1664 the local squire, Nicholas Jackson, decided to change the course of the Welland. It meandered gently through the water meadows by the

village, doubling back on itself and forming zig-zag curves between the higher ground on each side. Mr Jackson wanted more water-power for the flour mill he had built near the old bridge, so he cut a straight new channel to increase the force of the flow. The mill is still there, though it no longer functions, and the Jackson family still occupies the seventeenth-century manor house in the village.

There are nearly a score of memorials and tombs in Duddington Church bearing a Jackson name, which must be something of a record for a little village church. Among them are Captain Christopher Jackson, killed in the Boer War at the age of twenty-seven, and second Lieutenant William Jackson, who was only twenty when he died in France in 1916. The Vicar of Duddington, the Revd William Cheese, went to war too as an Army chaplain; he died at Rouen on 7 November 1918, just four days before the Armistice was signed and the war ended.

The church has other notable features, not least the prominent sign outside the porch saying 'Church Open' – a refreshing contrast to all those parishes which like to keep their churches to themselves. The church door would be well capable of keeping you out if Duddington followed that unfortunate trend; it is still reinforced with the original massive ironwork of the thirteenth century, a reminder of the days when there were even greater threats to life and limb in the village than two trunk roads. Nearby Rockingham Forest was the home of bandits and outlaws who had never heard of the chivalrous Robin Hood, so when they came on a rape-and-pillage expedition the villagers retreated inside the church. That door was able to withstand the blows of

THE CHANCEL OF ST MARY'S CHURCH– NOT QUITE IN LINE WITH THE NAVE.

the raiders' axes until, with luck, some help arrived.

Inside the church is another relic of those hazardous times, when the villagers were threatened by witchcraft as well as axecraft. When I was last there the Christmas decorations were in place, but under the splendid arrangement of candles and chrysanthemums on the font I could still see the hasp which was used to padlock the cover, so the holy water could not be stolen and used for black magic.

If you look down the length of the church you might think a little black magic had been at work here too. You will find that the altar is not straight ahead of you down the central aisle; the whole chancel veers off to the right. This is not as sinister as it may sound. Apparently the Norman chancel was rebuilt in the fourteenth century, and the chancel arch was blocked off while the work was

going on, so the nave could still be used. That meant the masons couldn't line up the new chancel visually, so they did it by compass, and built the chancel pointing towards the magnetic east.

The Normans, however, had followed the line of the original Saxon church, and the Saxons, who were not too handy with compasses, had built towards the 'true' east. So it must have been quite a jolt for the masons when they opened up the arch and found they had built the chancel at an angle of about five degrees to the rest of the church. Understandably they decided not to knock it down and start again, so St Mary's, Duddington, remains slightly bent in the middle.

These days the parish is combined with the little hamlet on the far side of the river, and I think its name goes well with Duddington, now the village has resumed a more leisurely way of life – no traffic, no revving engines, just – Tixover.

A Funeral, A Pageant – And A Vicar's Definition Of Stress

GEDDINGTON
NORTHAMPTONSHIRE
3 miles north-east of Kettering

Here's your starter for ten: who introduced the first carpet into England? Was it a Roman governor, fed up with getting his feet cold on all that marble in his villa? Was it a serving wench in some baronial castle who kept tripping over the rushes and decided to weave them together to keep them flat? Or was it a medieval travelling salesman who toured the country in an unmarked wagon loaded with bankrupt stock, and held sales in the village halls?

Actually, it was Princess Eleanor of Castile, bride of Henry III's son Edward and later to become Queen Consort of England. The Spanish got the idea of carpets from the Moors, and the Princess brought them to London. Her quarters, we are told, were hung with palls of silk and tapestry, and the floor was covered with an arras. Until then an arras was something to hang on the wall for sinister people to lurk behind; Eleanor and her Castilian entourage perhaps preferred not to take any chances, and put it on the floor instead – and the idea caught on. Really she ought to have been canonised by the English carpet-making industry and become the patron saint of Kidderminster. As it happens monuments did get erected to her memory in various parts of the Midlands and Home Counties, but it was not the carpetmen who put them up, it was her husband King Edward. Three still remain, and the best-preserved stands in Geddington.

The King's devotion to his wife was surprising in the circumstances. The marriage was a political arrangement to persuade Spain to give up its claims to Gascony. Edward was fifteen and Eleanor was only about ten; it was hardly the sound basis for a successful marriage. But in fact they became inseparable, and after Eleanor died of pneumonia in 1290, still in her mid-forties, Edward 'bewailed the loss of her all the days of his life'.

She was taken fatally ill at Harby in Nottinghamshire while travelling with him to Scotland on one of his famous hammering expeditions. The King decided to carry the body to London by a circuitous route which would take in the places they had spent happy times together, and to erect a monument at each stopping-place. These were the famous Eleanor Crosses, twelve of them altogether, but the one at Geddington was different from all the others. It is triangular, with three statues of the Queen instead of six, and it is thought to be the only one designed by Spanish architects. It stands in the village square, the statues facing the three roads that run into it.

Nearby is the site of the royal hunting lodge, the reason for Edward including it on the funeral route. He had developed it into a fair-sized palace, and he and his Queen spent many a jolly weekend there, but there is no sign of it now. It has disappeared under new development, and Geddington has grown into a substantial modern community. Apart from the Cross, the parish church with the 'King's Door' which led to the hunting lodge, and the medieval bridge across the River Ise, there is not a lot around which the royal couple would recognise. Little Newton Manor, home of the fifteenth-century Tresham family, has disappeared too; only its dovecote remains. It was Francis Tresham who betrayed Guy Fawkes and his Gunpowder Plot.

RUSHTON'S UNIQUE TRIANGULAR LODGE.

GEDDINGTON'S ELEANOR CROSS, WITH ITS THREE STATUES OF THE QUEEN FACING THE THREE ROADS THAT RUN INTO THE VILLAGE SQUARE.

There is, however, a curious memorial to his father, Sir Thomas 'The Builder' Tresham, in the nearby village of Rushton.

Sir Thomas was a devoted Roman Catholic who was frequently imprisoned for his faith. It was perhaps his obsession with the Trinity, and thus the figure three, which drove him to build Rushton's Triangular Lodge. Each of its three sides is thirty-three feet long, it has three floors with three triangular windows in each, and on the roof are three-by-three pinnacles. It bears Latin inscriptions in double-three couplets, and each line has thirty-three letters. Only the bricks are four-square.

The other famous Geddington character, Sir Robert Dallington, who became Master of Charter-house, left a charity which still distributes money to the poor of the village, but that is rather an intangible attraction for the casual visitor, who is more likely to be struck – I hope not literally – by the traffic on the A43; it is much too close to be comfortable. However, Geddington does have another intangible asset which could well be the envy of some villages; its community spirit.

You get a hint of it in the very substantial magazine which covers all its activities; even the licensees of the three local pubs contribute. But that community spirit took a more material form when a pageant was staged in 1990 to mark the seven hundredth anniversary of Queen Eleanor's funeral. It was not quite a cast of thousands, but about two hundred people were involved in it in some way or other, and that isn't bad for a village of fourteen hundred. No doubt the other twelve hundred were in the audiences; so were visitors from as far away as Norfolk and Sussex, and one man cycled to see it from Leicester – in the middle of December! I didn't see it myself, but the reports were ecstatic; even King Edward, I think, would have been impressed.

The pageant was the inspiration of the vicar, Richard Dorrington, who deserves the last word. He was thrilled by the support he received: 'I feel like climbing on to the church roof and shouting out "Yippee, I feel so proud of you all!"' But the production had its traumas, and I must quote his definition of stress – it's having a horse and an archdeacon in the church at the same time . . .

WE DON'T QUITE KNOW ABOUT INIGO – BUT YOU CAN'T DISREGARD THE BARD

BARTON-ON-THE-HEATH
WARWICKSHIRE
4 miles east of Moreton-in-Marsh

The only reference to Barton-on-the-Heath that I could find in the standard gazetteers was actually in an entry about Birmingham. 'Birmingham,' it said, 'is not the place you would choose for your summer holidays, yet in *The Domesday Book* the place was as rural as Barton-on-the-Heath.' It goes on about the number of ploughs Birmingham had, and a wood half a mile long and four furlongs broad, but there is no further mention of Barton-on-the-Heath, and it doesn't crop up anywhere else in the book.

So why should it be singled out as typifying the traditional rural English village, the complete antithesis of an industrial city? I think the answer is that, on the face of it, there is nothing very special about it, so it remains virtually undiscovered, undisturbed and unspoilt. It lies on the edge of the Cotswolds, only a few miles from the Oxfordshire border, and about as far as you can get from Birmingham, without leaving Warwickshire. All around it are well-known tourist centres – Chipping Norton, Moreton-in-Marsh, Stow-on-the-Wold. There is the famous Tudor mansion at Compton Wynyates, and the world-renowned Rollright Stones, on a par with Stonehenge and Avebury. But somehow Barton-on-the-Heath has

escaped all this. It is tucked away beneath Barton Hill, midway between the two main roads used by all the tourists, the A34 from Oxford to Stratford-upon-Avon and the A44 to Broadway and Evesham, and they all seem to go straight past. So as well as sharing the attractive appearance of the better-known Cotswold villages nearby, it has the priceless bonus of tranquillity and peace.

You will find in Barton the same mellow stone cottages with slate or stone-tiled roofs, 'seemingly created by nature as part of the landscape rather than built by men,' as one enthusiast puts it. You will find those typical features of Cotswold villages, a grand eighteenth-century rectory (which, typically, is no longer used as such), and a much grander manor house (which, typically, still is). You will find a sturdy little Norman church, with a side chapel which looks too big for it and a saddle-bowed tower which looks too small. And you will find a little triangular green, very similar to many others except for its ornate stone well-house, and a little village Post Office situated, as so many are, in the back room of one of the cottages.

So, nothing spectacular there, but for the visitor in search of peace and quiet in a typical English village, all these offer pleasures enough. As one such visitor observed: 'A week in this village has the same curative properties as a whole course of valium tablets'. But there is more to Barton-on-the-Heath, and its church and manor house, than just providing a backdrop for a nice long snooze. There are stories, and one or two puzzles, tucked away here which are worth exploring.

Barton House, for example, has an Oak Room with some of the finest panelling in Warwickshire, and this is probably by the architect Inigo Jones, who is supposed to have built the house for James Overbury in 1612. But this is where the first puzzle comes in. The manor wasn't acquired by the Overburys until 1625, and then it was William Overbury who rebuilt the house. Only two other Overburys succeeded him, his son Nicholas and his grandson Thomas, who died childless; there was no one in the family called James. According to the Warwickshire archives, nobody is quite sure how old the house is, or how much of it is attributable to Inigo Jones, but whoever it was did a pretty good job; it is still a very

splendid house with very splendid panelling.

While the Overburys were Lords of the Manor they gave the church most of its communion plate, and they were its patrons until Thomas Overbury handed the responsibility over to Holy Trinity College, Oxford in 1704. His tombstone with the family crest is set in the floor, but to spot something rather more unusual I suggest you look up, rather than down. A curious carved animal is running up the chancel arch; it looks like a very large horned pig or a very small rhinoceros. Nobody knows what it is or why it is there, but it provides another little puzzle to ponder in Barton-on-the-Heath.

The Old Rectory next door was once the home of Olivia Wilmot, who left another unsolved puzzle behind. She spent her childhood there in the late eighteenth century with her uncle, the rector, and she was married in the church, but in later years, after separating from her husband and becoming landscape painter to the Prince of Wales, she called herself Princess Olive and claimed to be the daughter of the Duke of Cumberland. This caused quite a stir at court, but nobody seemed too impressed – least of all, I imagine, the Duke of Cumberland – and the relationship was never established.

The other famous resident of Barton-on-the-Heath was Robert Dover, a seventeenth-century attorney who founded the Cotswold Games, held on Dover's Hill near Chipping Campden. For me, however, he is much more memorable as one of those rare mortals, a lawyer who actually encouraged his clients to find a compromise solution in order to avoid lengthy and expensive litigation. Perhaps Barton-on-the-Heath had its tranquillising effect on him too.

Barton has one other attribute which no self-respecting Warwickshire village can be without – a Shakespearian connection. It cannot claim to be the birthplace of the bard, or of his wife, or even his mother or father, but it was the home of his cousins the Lamberts, and perhaps because of his visits there it can actually boast a mention in his works. The Prologue to *The Taming of the Shrew* contains the line: 'Am I not Christopher Sly, old Sly's son of Burtonheath?'

Barton-on-the-Heath – which is Burtonheath, as near as dammit – can rest content.

VENDALE, YES. AMERDALE, OK. BUT EMMERDALE? NO THANKS...

ARNCLIFFE
NORTH YORKSHIRE
11 miles north-east of Settle

I suppose it is considered a mark of distinction when a village is selected as the setting for a television series. In my view, though, what gives Arncliffe much greater kudos is that, having been selected, it politely told the television people what they could do with their cameras. Thus they avoided, not only all the hassle that television involves, but the glare of publicity which has destroyed the atmosphere and seclusion of less strong-minded communities, intoxicated perhaps by the thought of summer wine . . .

It was not the first time that Arncliffe has attracted literary attention. Charles Kingsley frequently visited the village while he was dreaming

up *The Water Babies*, and he renamed Littondale, the valley it lies in, Vendale; Wordsworth called it Amerdale. So it was not too far a jump from Amerdale to Emmerdale, but mercifully the filmic farm was diverted to another location. Wordsworth's version is preserved by Amerdale House Hotel, once the manor house, now a very civilised hotel run by the delightfully named Mr and Mrs Crapper.

The hotel is the only acknowledgment Arncliffe makes that it is in the heart of marvellous holiday country. It is only a few miles from Grassington, with its National Park centre, its shops full of anoraks and walking boots, and its streets full of people wearing them. But Arncliffe is discreetly tucked away up two little lanes which wander up Littondale on either side of the Skirfare River. When they reach the village, one continues alongside the river to the top of the valley, then round the flank of the much-climbed Pen-y-Ghent to the main road at Stainforth; the other goes over the fells to Malham Tarn, an awesome drive where a swerve off the road could send you toppling down the hillside. I have walked up the valley road and driven up the other, and the contrast between placid riverside and hilltop drama is quite remarkable.

Arncliffe itself definitely favours placidity. The last drama it experienced was when the young men of the village marched off behind Lord Henry Clifford to fight the Scots on Flodden Field, carrying longbows fashioned from the yew trees above Cowside Beck. It followed years of harassment by Scottish raiders; the village green was regularly turned into a stockade, where the sheep and cattle were driven for protection; the villagers defended them inside the square of cottages in much the same way that American settlers formed a circle with their wagons to fight off the Indians. At Flodden the Scots lost their king and ten thousand men, and Arncliffe hasn't been bothered by them since.

The names of the dalesmen who fought in that battle in 1513 are preserved in St Oswalds Church, but the present building is much later than that. The first stone church was there in the twelfth century, then a new one was built about the time of Flodden, and lasted nearly three hundred years. But in the eighteenth century, thanks to one long-serving vicar, it was completely transformed, and in the nineteenth, thanks to another, it was transformed again. The vicars were very different in character, and so was their taste in churches.

Dr George Croft came to the village in 1779 and demolished the entire church except for its tower. He replaced it in a style which is described rather scathingly these days as 'churchwarden Gothic'. One critic called his church 'a plain, oblong, ill-constructed building', another considered it 'a hideous structure of oblong shape, with modern-looking sash windows and a flat ceiling'.

Maybe Dr Croft built it that way just to annoy his parishioners, because he had endless disputes with them, and spent most of his thirty years as vicar well away from the parish, in his other capacities as headmaster of a school in the Midlands and a lecturer in Birmingham. He said quite frankly that he was glad of the excuse 'to live far away from those who were far from agreeable'. I wonder how many incumbents are muttering, 'He should be so lucky'?

Arncliffe's religious life faded to such an extent that when young William Boyd applied for the living, the Archbishop of York told him he had never heard of the place. 'I have no such living in my diocese, Sir,' he said firmly. The registrar had to point it out to him on the map, whereupon, one imagines, the archbishop shook his head sadly, wished Boyd the best of luck, and probably forgot it again.

It did not remain forgotten for long, and nor did the new vicar. He set himself first, as he put it, 'to recover for the church somewhat of a more ecclesiastical and religious character'. About a third of Dr Croft's 'hideous structure' was taken down, a chancel was added, buttresses built to replace some of the sash windows, and the ceiling was removed to reveal the roof timbers.

The parishioners took a little time to get used to their revamped church and to a vicar who actually spent his time in the parish, but he soon got them behind him. He persuaded local landowners to contribute to a new schoolroom and built another one in neighbouring Litton; he instructed the teachers and gave 'cottage lectures' himself.

All this activity did not pass unnoticed. He was

made rural dean, then archdeacon, which involved travelling as far afield as Wakefield, Huddersfield and Halifax, but he still spent plenty of time and energy in Arncliffe, and even in his eighties he was still active enough to get the churchyard enlarged. He remained there for fifty-eight years, and became universally known as 'the Patriarch of the Dales'.

His successor in 1893, Canon Suffrey, was vicar for another thirty-eight – the last of the long-stayers. He was a notable local historian, and much of this information originated from him, but he also went in for a little scientific research, and I must record one of his more curious discoveries which may be of consolation to residents and visitors alike who, perhaps, find Arncliffe's winters a little gruelling: during its not infrequent snow-storms it experiences no fewer than thirty different types of snowflake!

Unfortunately all of them make you wet . . .

FEW CHURCHES CAN HAVE A BETTER SETTING THAN THIS.

'BROTHERS, WE ARE TREADING WHERE THE SAINTS HAVE TROD'

LASTINGHAM
NORTH YORKSHIRE
6 miles north-west of Pickering

I hesitate to draw attention to Lastingham, because for years it has been a haven from the rest of the world, where we have escaped to enjoy the vast emptiness of the North Yorkshire moors, the unhurried remoteness of Lastingham itself, and the gentle cosseting at what has been called,

with some justification, the most peaceful hotel in Britain. If it gets named too often it may not stay that way, and in any case this is not a hotel guide, so I shall just say it was converted from a seventeenth-century farmhouse, and the parents of the present proprietor started running it as a hotel

in the 1950s. It stands right on the edge of the moors, so you can walk out of its courtyard, down the drive and on to the moor, and you may not see another soul until you reach Rosedale, five miles away.

But that is not why Lastingham is such a special village. There are many others which give access to the moors, and some of them have suffered as a result. Just a mile or so away, for instance, is Hutton-le-Hole, featured in every guidebook, with its pleasant stone cottages scattered along each side of Hutton Beck, and sheep grazing on its common. Once it must have been idyllic; now there is a folk museum and folk park, a souvenir shop and a café, and in spite of the car park which the village had to provide for visitors, the main street is constantly clogged during the summer months. I would not want to divert any of these motorists to Lastingham, but they are actually missing, not only in my view a more picturesque village, but one of the most ancient and historic little churches in Britain.

HOPEFULLY, PEACEFUL LASTINGHAM WILL REMAIN AN UNDISCOVERED TREASURE.

It stands on the hill in the centre of Lastingham, opposite the two-hundred-and-fifty-year-old Blacksmith's Arms, where we sometimes adjourn after Sunday morning service – and it was not unknown to meet the vicar there too. He was, of course, just a fellow-customer, but some two hundred years ago we would have found him serving behind the bar. The landlord of the Blacksmith's Arms was also curate of St Mary's, and managed to combine both sets of duties without too many problems. Indeed, in some ways it must have been quite convenient; at least he was in constant touch with his parishioners. He also found time to produce thirteen children, and it was to keep this substantial family fed that he needed, as it were, the day-job. According to one reference book, he explained to the Archbishop of York when he was questioned about the double life he

was leading: 'Your Grace, my stipend is but £30 yearly, and my children go hungry without the inn. Give me but £20 more and I will eschew the alehouse and my children will bless you'. I don't know how the Archbishop reacted, but if the Church's finances were anything like they are today, I suspect the curate had to keep on pulling the pints . . .

That was in the early days of the Blacksmith's Arms, but a very late stage in the history of the establishment across the road. The actual church dates back to 1078, which makes it historic in its own right, but its site was a centre of worship and devotion for four hundred years before that.

The first hint you get of its antiquity is an inscription on the well in the street outside: 'Cedd: Abbie Lastinga Fundator 654'. And you soon notice something exceptional when you enter the church; a flight of steps descends through the centre of the floor. Down these steps and through the door at the bottom you find the real glory of Lastingham, a perfectly preserved Norman crypt on the spot where St Cedd worshipped in the days of King Oswald of Northumbria, and where his body is buried.

You immediately sense the atmosphere of serenity and calm in this ancient holy place. The guidebook quotes the line from 'Onward, Christian Soldiers': 'Brothers, we are treading where the saints have trod', and that is exactly how it feels. You are taken back through thirteen centuries, to the time when a Saxon bishop called Cedd was invited to set up a religious community on the lines of the famous monastery already established at Lindisfarne.

Cedd was one of a priestly quartet of brothers, bearing the euphonious names of Cedd, Cynebill, Caelin and Chad. They were all educated by the monks at Lindisfarne, where a bishop from Iona had established his See, and where the boys' parents established, as it were, their four 'C's. They all grew up to be priests, and two of them, Cedd and Chad, became bishops.

The Venerable Bede, author of the earliest and greatest of all church guidebooks, tells how Cedd found a site for his monastery 'among some high and remote hills, which seemed more suitable for the dens of robbers and haunts of wild beasts than for human habitation'. There is nothing much wilder than a bullock roaming those hills now, but a cave was discovered a few miles away at St Gregory's Minster, which Cedd also founded, that contained the bones of a veritable Noah's Ark of assorted wildlife, from lion and tiger to reindeer and rhino. Not all of them were around in Cedd's day, but if his builders were faced with only a small selection of them, they might well have cried 'Enough, Cedd!'

However, the monastery was duly established,

and it was not wild animals but the plague that finally disposed of the bishop. His brother Chad took over, and built a stone church dedicated to St Mary, where Cedd's body was interred; that is where the present St Mary's stands today.

So it is not surprising that you feel you are stepping back in time as you enter the crypt, built by a Norman abbot on the site of a Saxon church as a shrine to a seventh-century Bishop. As the vicar puts it: 'In this holy place, the spirits of Cedd and Chad move on the stones of the floor and in the air you breathe'. And perhaps this atmosphere of timelessness, of unchanging tranquillity over the years, has welled out from the ancient crypt to affect the pace and quality of life in Lastingham itself. It would certainly not surprise me if some of it has been absorbed by that converted seven-teenth-century farmhouse on the edge of the moor, the name of which still quite escapes me . . .

THEY'LL ALWAYS REMEMBER THE LORD'S DAY THAT FELL ON A SATURDAY

HAROME AND SALTON
NORTH YORKSHIRE
10 miles west of Pickering

Iassumed it must rhyme with Salome, or perhaps Laramie, or even as a long shot Jerome, but I was wrong on all three. Harome dates back to a twelfth-century Steward of Helmsley Castle, Drew de Harum, who built a stone Hall in the village, and his name gives a clue to the pronunciation. It is Harome as in harum-scarum – and my word, didn't Harome do just that when they met St Fagans in the final of the 'Cricketer' Village Cricket Championship in 1991! It was their finest hour, and they talk about it still. In the bar of the thatched and timbered Star Inn, one of Yorkshire's cosiest pubs, the newspaper reports of the great day are still displayed on the walls, and I have the parish magazine which wrote it up under the heading, 'The Lord's Day'.

A lot of villages have reached Lord's in this championship over the years, but few are so genuinely villagey as Harome. Their opponents, for instance, came from a 'village' on the outskirts of Cardiff, where most of the players lived in Cardiff itself but joined the cricket club for its social attractions – they play on the Earl of Plymouth's estate. St Fagans' resident population only just comes below the official maximum of 2,500, whereas Harome has only 300 people, and the team was drawn entirely from that number. It was very much a rural affair – nine of the players

were farmers or earned their living on the land, and they included three pairs of brothers, of whom two pairs were cousins. Most of the three hundred are in fact related to each other – 'even if they don't know it', as one villager commented.

It was probably the only time that Harome received national Press coverage, but it has seen the odd excitement over the centuries. The Harums who lived at the Hall were quite a lively lot: Sir William Harum defended Helmsley Castle against King John, another Sir William was noted for what one reference book calls his 'somewhat aggressive love affairs' – alas, it doesn't go into detail – and Robert de Harum became Lord Mayor of York and was a local ringleader in the 1381 Peasants Revolt.

After the Harums left Harome the Hall was replaced in the fifteenth century by a barn and sheepfold, but it was rebuilt a century later, using great wooden crucks as the main supports. Manor courts were held there, then in 1907 it became a dissenters' meeting house, and in this century it was the headquarters of the Women's Institute. More recently, however, the conservationists decided to take it over, and it was transplanted to the Ryedale Folk Museum – cruck, stock and barrel.

HOWZAT IN HAROME!

Happily they left the rest of Harome's old buildings behind, and there is still plenty of thatch, a smattering of Regency and Georgian, and some reasonable modern houses. The effect, with the broad main street and the central square, is of a much bigger place, a reminder that it was once a centre for weaving, dyeing and fulling cloth, until 150 years ago. In Victorian times it was big enough to have its own brass band, and there were Quaker and Calvinist meeting houses and a Methodist Chapel as well as the church, which at that time was brand-new – it was built for the Earl of Faversham to replace the thirteenth-century chapel. Lord Faversham built the school too, and a house for the master.

Things are a lot quieter in Harome now, largely because it lies on the wrong side of the A170, the road from Thirsk to Pickering which skirts the edge of the North Yorkshire Moors. Most tourists turn off north to the moors; very few turn south into the less scenic Vale of York. Nevertheless it is good farming country with some attractive secluded villages, and there are rivers everywhere – small ones on the whole, but they give an extra dimension to the landscape. Harome, for instance, has the River Riccal, which wanders off to join the Dove and the Rye near Salton, just a few miles away.

Salton itself is quite different from Harome, just a cluster of houses and a church around a little green, and a few scattered farmhouses; its population is well under a hundred. However, it has a much more eventful history, and a much older church. It dates back to the Normans, and it was twice set on fire by marauding Scots, first in 1138 and again, just when they were feeling fairly safe, nearly two hundred years later. There are supposed to be red marks left by the raiders on the walls, but I didn't spot them. I did find evidence of a rather different fire, however, an incongruous little fireplace set in the wall near the priest's chair, with a chimney poking out of the roof. I suppose the Victorians added it for his benefit when they restored the church in 1881, but it was not perhaps their most inspired thought . . .

The Scots may have taken such a dislike to this remote little village because it belonged to Hexham Priory, and the Prebendary Prior had a hall there which he used on his visits – no doubt offering rich pickings. It was a substantial building with its own chapel and brewery, stables and fish-ponds. Today only the fish-ponds remain. Salton itself used to be much bigger too, with a couple of alehouses, the odd shop or two, and in Victorian times the inevitable brass band. It also had a butcher called Bishop Dowker, who wrote the immortal lines:

Wilt th'a be hay? Nay.
Wilt th'a be fodder? Ah'll be nowther.
Wilt th'a be muck? Aye.
That's me luck.

And that, I am afraid, was more or less the luck of Harome's cricket team at Lord's. St Fagans made 169 off their forty overs, and after a some-what shaky start Harome began to catch up, and needed to score thirty off the last three overs – whereupon St Fagans posted nine men on the boundary, allowing Harome only to score in singles. They were still seventeen runs short at the close, and St Fagans took the trophy back to Wales for the third time. Nevertheless the Harome team returned home to a hero's welcome; the honour of Yorkshire cricket had remained unsullied, and Harome was anyway the premier cricketing village in England – a fitting accolade for a genuine English village.

DID MARAUDING SCOTS REALLY LEAVE TRACES OF THEIR ARSON ATTACK ON SALTON CHURCH?

THE WEAVING WENT, THE CLOTH WAS CAPPED – BUT HARTLEY KEPT COINING IT IN

HEPTONSTALL
WEST YORKSHIRE
1 mile north-west of Hebden Bridge

If it hadn't been for the Rochdale Canal, Heptonstall might be as big as Hebden Bridge today, if not quite as unattractive. Only a mile separates the two in distance, but they could have been created in different worlds.

Heptonstall, up on its hilltop, was a weaving town of some four thousand people, with its own Cloth Hall, its rows of weavers' cottages, and a thriving business community. In due course the cloth trade began to switch to the more accessible town of Halifax, but the big transformation to the area took place in 1804, when the Rochdale Canal came through the valley below, and the little hamlet of Hebden Bridge developed into a mill town, with steam-powered mills and those tiered terraces of workers' cottages up the hillside, not back-to-back but bottom-to-top. The canal which made all this possible has long since ceased to function, but its weaving legacy remains.

Heptonstall's population dwindled to two thousand, and although they still produced cloth – the last handloom weaver only died in 1902 – the town declined into a village and let the Industrial Revolution pass it by. Some of the weavers' cottages are still there, but Weavers' Square is a modern creation, a 'museum of stone' using different varieties of cobbles and setts and flags, and the weavers who used to live on the site would think it very odd indeed.

However, it is not Heptonstall's weaving history which is its special feature – there are many ex-weaving communities in the north, though they may not be on such a pleasant hilltop.

It is not the reason either why so many Methodists visit the village. They are all heading for the Octagon, completed in 1764, and the oldest Methodist Chapel in the world in continuous use. John Wesley himself laid the foundation stone, and the roof was brought by pack-horse over Mount Skip and escorted into Heptonstall by hundreds of hymn-singing supporters. The chapel has been extended since then, but it retains its octagonal shape; Wesley liked his 'preaching houses' that way so they did not imitate the traditional churches, and the idea was that the congregation worshipped first at the church, then moved on to the Octagon for the Methodist version. They obviously had more stamina in Wesley's day . . .

What interests me more than the Octagon, though, is back at the church, or rather the churches, because Heptonstall has two. John Wesley, not a man to pull his punches, described the earlier one as the ugliest he had ever known, and he would doubtless have approved when a storm blew most of it down in 1847. Instead of demolishing the rest and building on the same site, they decided to put the new one beside, perhaps hoping that in due course another storm would finish off the job more cheaply. But the ruins still stand there, and for all I know will outlive the new one.

It is not the churches themselves that attract me; the ruins are just ruins, and the new one has an even newer interior, which I think John Wesley would really have had a go at – even the official guide admits it is 'ultra-modern and somewhat controversial'. No, it is the gravestones and the graveyard which I would head for. The graveyard is reputed to contain a hundred thousand bodies, which is surprising enough in itself – with a maximum population of four thousand at any one time it must contain a great many generations of Heptonstallions (and Heptonmares?). But I would single out just a couple of them.

If you stand in the porch of the ruined church, walk twelve slabs forward and two to the left you will find the tombstone of David Hartley, the King of the Cragg Coiners. An entry in the church register sums up how he got there: '1770, May 1st: David Hartley . . . hanged by the neck near York for unlawfully stamping and clipping a public coin'.

That sounds a pretty drastic punishment for a rather childish offence – did you never put a penny on a railway line, I wonder, so it would be 'stamped and clipped' by the train wheels? But the Cragg Coiners did a lot more than that. At their headquarters in Cragg Vale, two miles out of Heptonstall, they went into stamping and clipping on a production line basis, chipping the edges off gold sovereigns and making forged coins out of the scraps. It became such a large-scale operation that it got close to devaluing the national coinage, and the Customs and Excise moved in.

They did not find it easy. One inspector was murdered, and anyone suspected of spying for them was brutally tortured. A labourer who

THE OCTAGON, THE OLDEST METHODIST CHAPEL IN THE WORLD STILL IN USE; ITS FOUNDATION STONE WAS LAID BY JOHN WESLEY.

HEPTONSTALL CHURCHYARD, REPUTED TO CONTAIN A HUNDRED THOUSAND BODIES.

boasted in a Heptonstall inn that he knew where to find the forgers was overheard by members of the gang, and they held him round the neck with heated fire-tongs and plunged his face into the fire. For good measure, they tipped burning coals down his trousers.

The Cragg Coiners were not a jolly Yorkshire version of the Lavender Hill Mob; they were a very unpleasant bunch indeed. Small wonder that when their leader, John Hartley, was captured, he was sentenced to death. The only surprise is that he was buried in consecrated ground – but amongst a hundred thousand others, maybe nobody noticed.

I can't leave Heptonstall on such an unsavoury note. There is another hanged man buried there, with a much worthier record. Mark Saltonstall was only nineteen when he was hanged at Halifax in 1783 for taking a leading part in the Corn Riots, a protest against the exorbitant price of bread. When his body was brought back to the village a huge crowd of mourners turned out to escort the coffin, and he is considered a martyr. His gravestone used to be in the same graveyard as Hartley's; now it lies near the font inside the new church.

So there they are, a clear-cut villain and a clear-cut hero, one out in the graveyard, the other brought in from the cold. But where, I wonder, would you put Thomas Spencer, another local man who also died on the gallows. He was one of the Cragg Coiners, but he must have evaded the Excisemen when Hartley was captured. Thirteen years later he was with Saltonstall at the head of the Corn Riots; he was arrested and hanged alongside him.

Villain or hero, then? I'll be hanged if I know...

FOUR WINNERS, TEN DUCKS, AND THIRTY PIECES OF SILVER

BISHOP BURTON
HUMBERSIDE
3 miles west of Beverley

J. B. Priestley caught 'a most entrancing glimpse of a pond, old walls and red roofs'. It was adjudged to be 'one of the twelve loveliest villages in England'. And a gazetteer describes it as 'an unforgettable village, cupped in a hollow with a large wayside pond reflecting the scene – a place of white-walled red-roofed houses, trees, and a grey stone village church'.

But Priestley caught his entrancing glimpse of Bishop Burton back in 1933. It was placed among the twelve loveliest villages in 1939. And the gazetteer, being a gazetteer, fails to mention that the main trunk road which goes slap through the middle of it carries such heavy traffic these days that, if Priestley slowed down for a moment to catch that entrancing glimpse, he would probably have caught a bumper up his boot as well.

Nevertheless, Bishop Burton tries hard to preserve its original charm. It has more than once won the 'Best-Kept Village' competition in recent years, and if you turn your back on the main road, and perhaps insert a pair of earplugs, you can still picture it in the days when Burton-by-Beverley was elevated to the episcopacy. It must have been very peaceful indeed when the Archbishop of York built his manor house there in the thirteenth century, and it must still have been fairly peaceful when John Wesley preached on the village green. Even in the last century, when four stage-coaches passed through the village each day between Beverley and York, the traffic was not enough to distract the local stables from producing four winners of the St Leger.

So, what was good enough for an archbishop, for John Wesley, and for a string of successful racehorses is good enough for me – particularly as they have all left an unusual mark on the village, which still exist today.

The archbishop, of course, left it with the Bishop in its name, which has survived long after his manor house and deer park have disappeared.

If Henry VIII hadn't commandeered the Bishop Burton estate when he was having his vendetta with the Church, it might have been Archbishop Burton by now . . .

One of the St Leger winners also gave a name to the village. The local pub, once the Horse and Jockey, was renamed the Altisidora to mark the horse's victory in 1813. All these winners were owned by the squire, Richard Watt, whose great-uncle bought the estate in 1783. Uncle Richard was a stable-boy in Liverpool before going to the West Indies and making his fortune, and maybe young Richard inherited his early knowledge of horse-flesh as well as his estate. His stables also produced Blacklock, founder of one of the most successful dynasties of racehorses in Britain.

While on the subject of memorable names, I must record that at one time Bishop Burton cricket team rarely played a match without ten Ducks; they were a family of joiners and

BISHOP BURTON IS A WELL KNOWN NAME IN BEST KEPT VILLAGE CIRCLES.

wheelwrights. The only non-Duck in the side was the village schoolmaster – whose name was Swann. The team was supported by other 'feathered friends' who lived in Bishop Burton, the Birds, Cockerills, Sparrows and Drakes. I wonder if the Ducks were ever joined for lunch by a couple from the Hall, Green the gardener and Pease the agent. Mr Stuffin, alas, was unavailable; you can find him in the churchyard . . .

But the most notable name associated with Bishop Burton is that of John Wesley, and he is commemorated in a most unusual way. When he came to the village he preached on the green under an ancient elm tree known as the Wych Elm. One might well ask which Wych Elm, because the parish records note that in 1679 'by tempest ye grate Elmetree was broken down', and it seems strange that it could survive for another

THE ROW OF COTTAGES LEADING UP TOWARDS THE CHURCH

THE VILLAGE GREEN WHERE JOHN WESLEY PREACHED
(IS THERE A VILLAGE GREEN WHERE HE DIDN'T?)

hundred years. There is no doubt however about the demise of Wesley's elm; it was struck by lightning in 1836, and Richard Watt, perhaps feeling benevolent after his fourth St Leger win, had a bust of Wesley carved from the wood and presented it to the newly-built Wesleyan Chapel.

That is not where you will find it today. Bishop Burton must be one of the few villages in England where a bust of the great founder of Methodism is installed in the Anglican parish church. At about the turn of the century the chapel fell into disrepair, and to raise money to restore it some of the contents were sold, including the bust. It was purchased by the rector, the Revd William Pearman, a man with perhaps an unfortunate sense of humour, because he paid for it with thirty silver threepenny bits, then taunted the Methodists for selling their Master for thirty pieces of silver . . .

However, he did the right thing by Wesley's memory. The bust had become somewhat dilapi-

dated, and the rector sent it to Beverley to be restored. It came back in due course with a bill which read: 'To inoculating John Wesley and curing him of worms, 7/6'.

About fifteen years ago, at a joint service with the Methodists, the bust was brought out of obscurity in the vestry and installed in its present place of honour on the wall of the south aisle. One reference book reports that an open-air service is held on the green every third Sunday in July to commemorate Wesley's visit, but the local historian tells me it hasn't happened for many years; with all that traffic thundering by, it is just as well.

However, all is not lost; I am told there is talk of a bypass. Alternatively, there used to be a toll-bar across the road at the entrance to the village; maybe somebody knows where it went . . .

DING-DONG FAR TOO MERRILY ON HIGH . . .

BLANCHLAND
NORTHUMBERLAND
9 miles south of Hexham

One enterprising writer has likened Blanchland to an Italian village transplanted to Northumberland, because the houses are laid out around an L-shaped square (he suggests 'piazza'), and there is a castellated gatehouse at the entrance; but surely those sturdy-looking rows of grey stone cottages could only be English, and the Lord Crewe Arms is very English indeed. What does make it very different from most English villages, though, is that it didn't just grow over the centuries, it was built about 250 years ago on the site of a medieval monastery, using the same layout and incorporating the remains of the original buildings. The Lord Crewe Arms, for instance, was partly the Abbot's lodge, partly the guest-house, and partly the abbey kitchen – the vast fireplace in the lounge was used by the monks to smoke their meat. The gatehouse, now the village Post Office, was the entrance for lay workers into the abbey precinct. One of the rows of cottages lining the square includes part of the monks' dormitory, another incorporates the original walls of their refectory, and the square itself was the abbey courtyard.

There were other complete villages built in the eighteenth century, but mostly by Lords of the Manor who didn't like the look of the old ones. For instance, when Sir Robert Walpole moved into Houghton Hall in Norfolk he thought the village made his park look untidy, so he knocked it down and built a new one outside the gates – a double row of cottages with just enough room between them for two carriages to pass. That was a couple of hundred years ago, but it is still called New Houghton.

Blanchland is very different, a picturesque cluster of cottages set in a remote corner of the Derwent Valley, with the fells rising steeply on each side, and not a stately home in sight. And although its existence is due to one very rich man, it was not built until some years after his death.

Its name goes back much further, to the White Monks who came over from Germany in the twelfth century. They were called, somewhat clumsily, Premonstratensians, which sounds like a female ailment, but the name actually comes from Premontre, where the Order was founded. They built Blanchland Abbey in 1165, and lived there for nearly four hundred years until Henry VIII sent his commissioners to throw them out and sack the abbey.

The story of how the commissioners found their way to Blanchland is part of local folklore. While they were riding across the fells a heavy mist came down and they became hopelessly lost. The monks, believing perhaps that they had been saved by heavenly intervention, rang the monastery bells in thanksgiving – and kept on ringing until the commissioners, who had heard the bells through the mist, followed the sound all the way back to the monastery. The modern moral, I suppose, is that if you're in danger of a sacking, don't draw attention to yourself . . .

That was the end of the Premonstratensians, and the estate finished up with the local Forster family. In 1699 Dorothy Forster married Lord Crewe, the last of the 'prince-bishops' of Durham Cathedral, and the man whose money was eventually responsible for creating Blanchland as it looks today.

It was an unusual courtship. The bishop was nearly forty years older than Dorothy, and when he first proposed it could hardly have surprised him that she turned him down. He married elsewhere, but when his wife died nine years later he proposed again, and this time, perhaps impressed by his tenacity, she accepted. She inherited half the Blanchland estate and Lord Crewe bought the rest.

In spite of being so wealthy he doesn't seem to have done much to look after the cottages on his land, and when he died in 1721 the village that had grown up at Blanchland was in a pretty tumbledown condition. The estate was taken over by the Lord Crewe Trustees, who have run it ever since, and it was they who rebuilt Blanchland in its

BLANCHLAND IS TUCKED INTO A REMOTE CORNER OF THE DERWENT VALLEY.

present form. The finishing touch was to create a parish church from the ruins of the abbey choir. The writer I quoted earlier calls Blanchland 'a memorial of medieval piety and eighteenth-century beneficence', and this time I can't fault him.

The story of the village itself is unusual enough, but there is another tale attached to it which adds to its romance. Inside the great fireplace at the Lord Crewe Arms there is a priesthole where Dorothy Forster's nephew Thomas, a general in the Jacobite army, is said to have hidden from government troops after the 1715 rebellion. He was captured and taken to Newgate Prison to await trial for treason, and the story of his escape would have done credit to the Scarlet Pimpernel – indeed there is a novel based upon it.

In this case the heroic and ingenious rescuer was his sister, another Dorothy Forster, who disguised herself as a servant, rode to London sharing a horse with the village blacksmith, acquired the keys of her brother's quarters at Newgate, had duplicates made, and smuggled them in to his servant. Thomas invited the prison governor to join him for a drink – he was that sort of prisoner – then excused himself for a call of nature, locked the door behind him, and made tracks for France. He stayed there, at the court of the exiled Old Pretender, until his death, while Dorothy married a local squire in Northumberland and, presumably, lived happily ever after. Barbara Cartland, I am sure, would have loved it; personally, I think she should have married the blacksmith . . .

THE LORD CREWE ARMS HAS JACOBITE CONNECTIONS.

BEAUTY AND THE BIGAMIST – PLUS GOOSE-GATE, WHITTLE-GATE, CLOG-SHOES AND HARDEN-SARK

BUTTERMERE
CUMBRIA
13 miles south-west of Keswick

It is not easy to select a village in the Lake District which has not been affected in some way by the holiday industry, even if it is only the permanent traffic jams. Somehow Buttermere has just about managed to survive unscathed – a little cluster of cottages, a pub and a church, tucked away on the hillside between Crummock Water and Buttermere Lake, two of the prettiest stretches of water in Cumbria. The main centres for tourism in that area are Cockermouth, birthplace of William Wordsworth, and Keswick, home of Coleridge and Southey, and favourite haunt of Shelley, Tennyson and the rest. Buttermere is well away from both of them, a tricky drive from Keswick over Newlands Pass, or a longer haul from Cockermouth alongside the River Cocker and Crummock Water.

Nevertheless, Wordsworth and his friends knew all about this obscure little village, thanks to a young lady whom they have immortalised in prose and poetry, and who has become known as the Beauty of Buttermere. They have told her story with such eloquence and feeling that it would be impertinent to compete, so I will just set out the facts. If you wish to see them wrapped up more stylishly, try Wordsworth's *Prelude*, the passage that goes:

> *From our own ground; the Maid of Buttermere,*
> *And how, unfaithful to a virtuous wife*
> *Deserted and deceived, the spoiler came,*
> *And woo'd the artless daughter of the hills . . .*

The Maid was Mary Robinson, eighteen-year-old daughter of the village innkeeper at the Fish Inn. The spoiler was a visitor calling himself the Hon Augustus Hope MP. When he 'woo'd the artless daughter' – a somewhat euphemistic way of putting it, I gather – she proved not to be as artless as all that, and insisted on marriage. The wedding duly took place amid great celebrations, but within a few weeks it transpired that the Hon Augustus Hope MP was not a Member of Parliament, his name was actually John Hatfield, and he was anything but honourable; he was married with a family, and had a number of other 'wives' already.

Hatfield was not just charged with bigamy, but the much more serious offence of defrauding the Post Office, since he was in the habit of franking his own letters. The Post Office was even touchier about such things then than it is today, and the penalty was death. He was hanged at Carlisle on 3 September 1803.

Mary returned to Buttermere, bringing with her a wave of sympathy and a host of curious visitors. Business boomed at the Fish Inn, which made her father very happy, and in due course she married a local farmer, which made her very happy too. Even John Hatfield, it seems, was not all that depressed; when he was taken to the gallows he is supposed to have said: 'A happy sight – I see it with pleasure'. Maybe life with Mary had not been too idyllic – and indeed the cynics suggest that she only married him for what she expected to get out of him. Wordsworth and his friends took a more romantic view, so let's give her the benefit of the doubt. Certainly they do at the Fish Inn, now much restored and altered, but still enjoying the benefit of her memory.

For a lot of people this tale is Buttermere's only claim to fame, apart from its splendid location. But there was another character associated with the village who is less well-remembered than Mary, and who never brought much business to the Fish Inn – quite the reverse – but he enjoyed some much more curious benefits than being picked up by a handsome stranger. His name was Robert 'Wonderful' Walker, and he was the reader in charge of the church at Buttermere, in the days when it came under the priest at Brigham, on the far side of Cockermouth.

His home was at Seathwaite, and when I looked at the map I thought Robert must indeed have been a Wonderful Walker, because a village

ST JAMES' CHURCH, OVERLOOKING THE VILLAGE AND BUTTERMERE LAKE, AND AT ONE TIME IN THE CARE OF ROBERT 'WONDERFUL' WALKER.

of that name lies about twenty miles from Buttermere, with the slight obstacle of Scafell in between. But there is another Seathwaite in Borrowdale, which is much more handy, and in fact he was probably quite happy to walk a few miles to work to get away from it, because this Seathwaite holds the unenviable record of having the highest average rainfall in England.

As well as fulfilling his church duties so ably that they called him Wonderful Walker, he augmented his tiny stipend by doing a bit of ploughing and cloth-spinning, but what really helped him were four local customs which present-day lay readers might well appreciate – or at any rate the first three. They had the delightful names of clog-shoes, harden-sark, whittle-gate and goose-gate, and they entitled him to receive from the parish free shoes and clothing, free food and board if he didn't fancy the trip back to Seathwaite, and free grazing for his goose. He was looked after so well, in fact, that he lived to the age of ninety-three and left the very tidy sum of two thousand pounds.

I have to say that I much prefer this tale to Mary Robinson and her ill-fated romance. It is finding out about clog-shoes, harden-sark, whittle-gate and goose-gate which to me is the real Beauty of Buttermere.

ACROSS THE LAKE TO WORDSWORTH'S – AND WAINWRIGHT'S – FELLS.

NOT JUST A PRETTY RAILWAY – THERE'S A VILLAGE THERE TOO

RAVENGLASS
CUMBRIA
18 miles south-east of Whitehaven

I first went to Ravenglass for the same reason as most other visitors, to have a ride on the Ravenglass and Eskdale Railway. But unlike most of the others I went into the village first, which lies beyond the station, and I am very glad I did. 'Seaside backwater' sounds a contradiction in terms, but it makes a very attractive combination. The only road into the village goes alongside the estuary, then runs into what used to be the market square, and just peters out at the far end, on the edge of the beach. Thus there is no through traffic and, since most people get no further than the station, there is very little traffic at all.

The delights of Ravenglass were first discovered by the Romans, but they appreciated it for quite a different reason. This is the meeting place of the Esk, the Irt and the Mite, three little rivers with even smaller names – the Mite is particularly apt – but together they create what used to be a substantial harbour. It was an ideal site for a fort, and the Romans duly built one. A small portion of it still exists, the bath house tucked away in the trees just outside the village. It is publicised as one of the highest Roman remains in Britain, but to be honest it has been so neatly restored and trimmed and smartened up that it could have been built last year. No matter; the Romans would probably still recognise it, and as it is Ravenglass' only tourist attraction, apart from the railway, I can't blame them for making the most of it.

Later the Vikings used it for the usual spot of rape and pillage, but once that was all over and things had settled down it was granted a market charter in 1209, and started its heyday as a market town and port. However, the silting up of the estuary ended its main port activities, and the main line railway took away the trade from its market. A

A CONVENIENT SPOT TO PARK THE BOAT – THE HOUSES BACK ON TO THE BEACH . . .

little fishing still went on, and after the last war one could still see Neptune-like figures wading about in the estuary – fishermen with three-pronged forks searching for flounder. Cynics might say that now it is Ravenglass itself which has been left floundering, without a market, any sea trade, or even a flounder, but I am sure its present residents prefer it the way it is, and so do the holiday boating folk who now sail into the wide, sandy estuary.

Although it has little else to lose in terms of industry or amenities, it does still face the perennial hazard of being lost itself. It may be convenient for cars to drive straight off the end of the road on to the beach to park, but it is not quite so handy when the sea returns the compliment and comes up into the village. In recent times flood defence works have been erected along the side of the estuary, and floodgates have been installed at the end of the street. The cottages along one side back directly on to the sand, but they have substantial walls behind them as protection. Looking back at Ravenglass from anywhere on the vast area which is left bare when the tide is out, there is almost a continental flavour about those high walls rising out of the sand. But you shouldn't hang about too long with your back to the sea; the tide comes in extremely fast.

One early rector discovered that, to his cost, on his way from a service at nearby Waberthwaite to another at Muncaster Church, which serves Ravenglass. He had to cross the Esk on stepping-stones, but failed to time it right. The tide swept up the river, bowled him off the stepping-stones, and drowned him.

Another tragedy which affected the parish is commemorated in the church. For nearly eight hundred years Muncaster Castle, a mile from the village, has been the home of the Penningtons, though these days it is open to the public. In 1870 the head of the family, Josslyn Lord Muncaster, took his wife and some friends on a European tour. In Greece they visited Marathon and were ambushed by bandits. The women and children were released but the men were held for ransom; only Lord Muncaster was allowed to go, taking their demand for a £5,000 ransom and an amnesty. The Greek government agreed to the ransom but refused the amnesty. They sent troops to surround the kidnappers' camp, and as a result the hostages were murdered.

One can imagine Lord Muncaster's feelings as he returned home. In Muncaster Church he installed four windows in memory of his friends, then restored the whole building, adding the

... BUT WITH QUITE A HIGH WALL IN BETWEEN

transept and vestry and installing a new organ. The most dramatic feature is the 'Doom' west window, one of the very few of its kind in the country, but this was paid for, not by him, but by the parishioners. It was intended as a recognition of his generosity, but it can hardly have cheered him up.

In the castle itself is 'The Luck of Muncaster', a glass goblet given to Sir John Pennington by Henry VI for sheltering him after his defeat at the Battle of Hexham. The family is supposed to be lucky as long as the goblet is preserved in the castle. It didn't do Josslyn much good, but nevertheless it is guarded with great care; when a similar lucky goblet at Eden Hall was given away to a museum, the hall was demolished soon after . . . Muncaster Castle is open to the public.

So much for Ravenglass village, the castle and the church. But I did eventually get back to the Ravenglass and Eskdale Railway, known locally as 'La'l Ratty', and in due course reached the village of Boot, at the other end of the line. It turned out to be as delightful as its name, which is why there is a separate section devoted to Boot, to boot . . .

THE ESTUARY WAS POPULAR WITH SMUGGLERS IN THE SEVENTEENTH AND EIGHTEENTH CENTURIES.

THE END OF THE LINE THAT REACHED THE END OF THE LINE

BOOT
CUMBRIA
6 miles east of Ravenglass

If you were mentally picturing a site for a railway terminus, you would hardly think of Boot. It is a tiny white-painted village tucked away down a dead-end in the hills of the Lake District, a couple of hundred feet above sea level, with just an old watermill, a couple of pubs, a little church half a mile away, and no obvious reason for a railway at all. But 115 years ago it was the terminus for the three-foot gauge Ravenglass and Eskdale Railway, and the station was the loading point for thousands of tons of iron ore from the Nab Ghyll mines just above the village. The line ran over the saddle of the hill – if the owners had shown a touch of whimsy they could have called it the Boot and Saddle Railway – and down Eskdale to Ravenglass on the coast, where the ore was transferred to the main line.

The remains of the station are still there, along a stony track out of the village which continues where the lane leaves off. You can just make out the platform and the chutes where the ore was tipped into the wagons. The ruins of the mine offices and stores are there too, and the derelict mine workings are all about you – and very dangerous to explore. This desolate scene was a hive of activity from 1875, when the line was opened, until the mining company collapsed in 1882. The railway maintained a spasmodic service for another twenty-five years until it became too unsafe to operate. Then a new company was formed and tried to revive it, but in 1912 the Nab Ghyll mines were completely flooded, and it closed for good.

The story of how W. J. Bassett-Lowke discovered the derelict railway and laid a new fifteen-inch gauge track on the old track-bed to test-run his miniature locomotives, how it was developed into a regular passenger and goods service, how it faded again and was put up for auction in 1960, and how railway preservationists bought it and restored it into a major tourist attraction, is a constant succession of ups and downs, just like the railway itself. However, it has very little to do with Boot. Bassett-Lowke did lay his new line to Boot station, but the final climb proved too much for his little engines, so he took up that section and re-laid it along a former branch line to its present terminus at Dalegarth. Boot station was left to crumble into the hillside, and Boot village was left to resume its pre-railway peace.

Nevertheless, the railway is still the most civilised way to reach it. There is a marvellous ride up Eskdale, and Dalegarth station is only a short walk from Boot. More energetic passengers will strike off on foot across the fells to Wastwater and Wasdale Head, or head for the Roman fort on the Hardknott Pass, but if you are looking for a place with a special character then this Boot will fit you.

As you walk from Dalegarth along the main road it lies down a lane to the left, but for the church you have to turn right and go half a mile before you find it in its delightful setting beside the River Esk. If a church was that far distant from its village in East Anglia it would probably be due to the Black Death, which caused many stricken communities to build new homes well away from the contaminated area, leaving just the church still standing, but I have found no mention of the Black Death here. Interestingly, the information sheet which is supplied to schools visiting the area asks the same question, but gives no answer, while the church guide just says, resignedly: 'All the many authorities agree on one point at least – little is known about the history of St Catherine's Church, Eskdale'. Perhaps by calling it Eskdale Church, rather than Boot Church, it gives us the answer – it was built to serve all that area of the dale, not just the village. Or maybe the monks who built the first chapel here just preferred the view . . .

It is thought to be one of four dale chapels founded in the twelfth century by the Prior of St Bees, but details of what happened then are rather vague, and as the church was virtually rebuilt in 1881 it doesn't offer many clues. The oldest piece of evidence you will find there is the treble bell which now sits on a window-ledge by the door, but used to hang in the belfry. It is dedicated to Blessed St Catherine, and it is assumed to date back to 1445, when the chapel was given the status of a parish church. That was in response to a petition from the villagers, who were fed up with trekking ten miles across country to St Bees for baptisms, funerals and the like.

However, it did not solve the problem for the residents of Wasdale, on the far side of Burnmoor, who still had a gruelling scramble over the old pack-horse route to Boot. It was even trickier for funerals, along what came to be known as the Corpse Road. At least one pack-horse is said to have rebelled against the arduous journey; it reared up, broke away from the funeral procession and disappeared across the fell, with the coffin still strapped to its back.

In Boot itself is Eskdale Mill, with a history going back nearly as far as the church. It was working until the 1920s, and when the milling stopped, the wheel was kept turning to generate electricity for the mill cottage. Now the machinery has been restored by the County Council, and the mill has become a popular tourist attraction in its own right.

What attracts me about Boot, however, is not so much the village itself, delightful though it is, but that lonely mining site on the hill beyond if and the station that not even Bassett-Lowke could save. The railway itself, 'La'l Ratty' as they still call it after the engineer Ratcliff who originally built it, has been restored into a thriving concern, thanks to a devoted band of volunteers, and thousands of holiday-makers travel on it each year. But here on this bleak hillside is a graphic reminder of what the line was built for, and what happened when these mines flooded and Boot became, in effect, La'l Ratty's Boot Hill.

ONE OF THE REMOTE FARMS ON THE TOE-TIP, AS IT WERE, OF BOOT, NEAR THE START OF THE HARDKNOTT PASS.

FROM ASHTON-UNDER-LYNE TO ASSHETONS UNDER PENDLE HILL – AND LOOK, NO WIRES!

DOWNHAM
LANCASHIRE
3 miles north-east of Clitheroe

So far as Quakers are concerned, Downham lies in what they call 'The 1652 Country', an area in the north-west bounded by Preston to the south, Skipton to the east, Kendal to the north and Barrow-in-Furness to the west (or rather, where Barrow-in-Furness is now – it didn't exist in 1652). This was where Quakerism was born and originally flourished, and the name they have always associated with 'The 1652 Country' is George Fox, who in that year 'felt moved of the Lord' to climb Pendle Hill, and there had a vision which sent him off preaching and converting in the dales and fells. The Society of Friends was formed as a result.

For the villagers of Downham, however, it is another name which always comes to mind, and it has done so for a century longer than George Fox. Ashton-under-Lyne, near Manchester, was Assheton-under-Lyne until the railways came – maybe they couldn't fit the longer version onto a ticket. In Downham Hall you will find direct descendants of the man who acquired the town as part of his dowry in the twelfth century, and adopted its name. The family have retained the original spelling, regardless of the railways; you might call them the Asshetons under Pendle Hill. The present occupants of the Hall are the twenty-sixth generation of the line.

Richard Assheton bought the Manor of Downham three months before Queen Elizabeth came to the throne in 1558, and it has been in the family ever since. For the first couple of centuries it was not their main residence, but in 1835 William Assheton rebuilt Downham Hall and moved in. For the past five generations the family have looked after the village as squires, landlords, preservationists and protectors.

The most obvious evidence of their presence is in the church. The Assheton Chapel above the family vault is full of their memorials, from Lady Dorothy in 1635 to the first Lord Clitheroe, who died in 1984. But the evidence doesn't stop there. The church itself was rebuilt by Ralph Cockayne Assheton early this century, and he gave

PENDLE HILL FROM THE VILLAGE GREEN.

the organ too. The east window was not only given by Ralph and his brother Richard, they also designed it, stained the glass, and installed it with their own hands.

The elaborate brass cross was given by Mildred Lady Assheton, and of the five bells, one was given by Ralph to celebrate the coming of age of his son, Sir Ralph, and another was presented by Sir Ralph to celebrate his own golden wedding. There is even an annual Assheton sermon, endowed by an earlier Sir Ralph and preached each year on the Sunday nearest the date of his death in 1680.

The inscription on the late Lord Clitheroe's memorial suggests that 'if any memorial is needed, look around you', and that doesn't just mean the church. When the Asshetons moved into the Hall they already owned much of the village, and they set about buying up the rest, together with the surrounding farms and land. In particular they acquired the farmland between them and the neighbouring village of Chatburn, which was industrial rather than rural and showed ominous signs of spreading towards Downham.

As well as maintaining the village in excellent repair, the Asshetons ensured that it escaped the less attractive features of modern development. If indeed you look around you, as his memorial suggests, it is what you don't see as much as what you see which illustrates what Lord Clitheroe achieved. For instance, there are no overhead electricity cables; when the supply reached Downham in 1934 he paid for the wires to be laid underground. When the telephone arrived he did the same thing, and the public telephone box in the village, instead of being the usual bright red, was painted grey to blend with the stone cottages around it. That rather ignored the point of the Post Office's colour policy, since boxes were painted red to be easily spotted by strangers. The Asshetons, I assume, had more interest in the appearance of the village than the problems of visitors. These days practicality has overcome aesthetic appeal, and the box is a standard red one.

This protective attitude has continued. You will not see any cottages with those ugly white satellite dishes on the walls. When satellite television arrived, the old aerials were removed and a communal aerial was set up, complete with communal dish. There can be few villages in England which have so little technical clutter in the streets or on the buildings, and as a result Downham can genuinely qualify for that much-abused description, 'unspoilt'.

NO WIRES, NO AERIALS, NO SATELLITE DISHES – DOWNHAM HAS DOWNED 'EM.

George Fox would probably still feel quite at home in Downham, especially as the old stocks are still in place opposite the church, but he would hardly recognise the Hall, which was given an expensive new frontage by William Assheton, with nine bays and a portico of Tuscan columns. It must have been quite a dramatic conversion in 1835, but now it looks as though it has always been there, a handsome feature of the scenery.

Even so, it is not just the man-made features, or indeed the lack of them so far as wires, television aerials and satellite dishes are concerned, which leave the greatest impression in Downham – and I have the authority of the late Queen Mary for saying so. When she visited the church she said very firmly – as she said most things – that it had the most beautiful view from any church porch in the land; and if you stand where she did, you will understand her point of view.

There ahead of you is the vast whale-back of Pendle Hill, rising 1,800 feet above the village, once the haunt of witches and devil worshippers, then the source of inspiration for George Fox, and always dominating everything else around it. From the rough cairn that marks the summit, not far from the spring where George Fox is said to have quenched his thirst nearly 350 years ago, you can see northward to the Lakeland hills and westward as far as the Lancashire coast.

Pendle Hill, in fact, is really something. Not even the Asshetons can equal that.

EXTRA WINDOWS IN ODD PLACES – EVEN IN THE CHURCH

RIBCHESTER
LANCASHIRE
5 miles north of Blackburn

First, a warning. It's as well to avoid Ribchester on a summer Sunday. That's when the trippers pour in to see the Roman remains, and you won't be able to enjoy the other things which the village has to offer, and which many visitors never even notice. It's easier to see the Roman remains too on a quieter day, but quite honestly, apart from what's in the Roman museum, which is rather like what's in other Roman museums, there are not a lot of remains to see. The present church now stands where the Roman fort was, and there are just the remains of the Roman granaries and some of the less exciting features of a bath-house – notably, the furnace room and three heating flues.

Personally I am more interested in Ribchester as it is today, not what's left of *Bremetennacum Veteranorum* except, of course, for that Latin name the Romans gave it, which is lovely to wrap your tongue around. The village is in fact the only one in the Ribble Valley actually on the river, which provides a very pleasant setting for visitors, though it has caused problems for those who lived there because of flooding and erosion. The Romans only built their fort on that site because it was an important river crossing; their successors would probably have preferred to be further away. That would certainly have benefited one of Ribchesters earlier rectors, called Drogo, who was drowned while crossing the Ribble to visit his flock – even though there is a medieval wall-painting of St Christopher in the church, which ought to have protected him on his travels.

In the eighteenth century the low-lying situation of the village caused a different kind of problem, when hand-loom weaving became the main occupation. It was literally a cottage industry, with each cottage having a weaving room, or loom-shop. These loom-shops needed a humid atmosphere, because the protective paste on the yarn had to be kept damp, and the obvious place to locate them was in cellars below ground. But in Ribchester a lot of the cellars turned out to be not merely damp but full of water. A few proved usable, and one or two can still be spotted by the windows at pavement level, but mostly the loom-shops were built on to the cottages at the back, so you can't see them. What you can sometimes see are the extra windows in the top storeys, where the yarn was prepared. They all add up to an unusual jumble of unexpected window-levels as you walk round the village.

You'll also find a pair of 'matching' pubs, the Black Bull and the White Bull, which, perhaps wisely, are kept well apart. The White Bull is in the ancient centre of the village, with the remains of the Roman bath house behind it, a couple of those cellar loom-shops opposite, and a combination of both periods outside its front door – four columns which might just be of Roman origin, and a stone mounting block from stage-coach days. A rather magnificent white bull presides over it all, perched on a platform at first-floor level

St Wilfred's Church is not far away, and it continues the theme of unlikely windows. It has the usual variety of styles and sizes that you would expect to find in a church which was originally built in the thirteenth century, and has been added to and altered ever since, but now look up at the roof. Some time in the eighteenth century it was decided that not enough light was getting into the church, and they inserted a row of dormer windows, the sort you might find in a mock-Tudor country house. They give St Wilfred's a very distinctive flavour; descriptions have ranged from 'an irregular pile' to 'architecturally confusing'. However, I think it was rather a brave solution to a problem which many old churches just have to live with – and anyway I don't expect the locals even notice those dormer windows any more.

If you prefer a church which hasn't had any extras tacked on to it – and which is well away from Roman ruins – there is one about half a mile

RIBCHESTER CHURCH WITH ITS UNLIKELY DORMER WINDOWS – 'ARCHITECTURALLY CONFUSING'.

away, the oldest church in the Ribble Valley, which has never even been given a tower, let alone dormer windows. Stydd Chapel was built in 1136 for the Knights of St John, who had a hospital on the site. Inside it is the burial place of Francis Petre, who died in 1775 'full of days and good deeds, after bestowing many alms'. Nothing unusual about that, except that Francis Petre was a Roman Catholic Bishop, and you don't find many of them buried in Anglican churches. As one of the local booklets comments: 'It must surely be unique . . . an interesting example of religious toleration at a time when persecution was well within living memory'.

There is a fascinating theory about how Stydd Chapel got its name. In the local dialect Stydd is pronounced 'Stood', and the story goes that this was the only building which remained standing after a great earthquake. I don't know how many earthquakes they used to have in the Ribble Valley, but it's a nice story – even though it is likely to be greeted locally with Ribbled laughter . . .

SWEET EMILY SAILED IN, THE WALLABIES BALED OUT

WINCLE
CHESHIRE
8 miles south-west of Buxton

'As I go out of my gate each morning I still think, after eight years here, "Fancy being paid to live here"!'

The Revd Peter Barratt is Vicar of Wincle, and he still can't believe his luck. I understand how he feels, because Wincle is set as snugly into the hillside as its near-namesake is inside its shell, and if I were paid to live there, it would take a lot to winkle me out. It lies in the centre of the square formed by Congleton, Macclesfield, Buxton and Leek, which are all only eight miles or so away, and the main road from Congleton to Buxton is just a mile to the north, but from the front gate of the vicarage you would never believe it. This is a remote corner of Cheshire where the hills of the Peak District National Park adjoin the rolling countryside of the Cheshire Plain, so Wincle enjoys the best of both worlds, and the views from its hillside, particularly from the vicarage, are something to behold. The only reminder of the busy outside world – and admittedly it is quite a prominent one – is the Telecom tower which stands within the parish. It is 225 feet high, so you can hardly miss it . . .

The vicarage faces southwards towards the River Dane, only half a mile away, which marks the boundary of the parish, the county, the diocese and the province. The vicar looks after three other parishes, but they are all on his side of the river. 'To visit "over there" I am supposed to ask the Archbishop of Canterbury, the Bishop of Lichfield and the vicar of the next village. But actually the community ignores the boundary and people think of themselves as living in Wincle even if they live "over there".'

Without them Wincle would be very tiny indeed. The village centre, if you can call it that, consists of the church, which has the date 1647 over the door but was actually rebuilt a hun dred years ago, the little Victorian village school, a farm, three houses and the vicarage. You have to head off down the lanes or 'over there' to find the rest of it.

IVY IS MAKING A TAKE-OVER BID FOR THE CHURCH.

Until 1860 there wasn't even a vicarage – previous clergy lived in Leek or Macclesfield, and their visits to Wincle could be spasmodic and brief. One bishop complained at one stage that there had been no sermons preached in the church for six months, though no complaints are recorded from the parishioners.

The present vicar has a benefactor called Thomas Daintry to thank for his rather splendid home, with its even more splendid view. Mr Daintry's memorial in the church records that, 'warm in his attachment to the people of Wincle', he gave the site for the vicarage and £267 towards building it, 'to afford them the blessings of a resident ministry within the township'. He died

before it was finished, but his widow provided another £230 to finish it off. She also endowed the village school, in accordance with the generous Mr Daintry's last request.

The other name which is revered locally is Brocklehurst. The family lived at Swythamley Hall, which is 'over there', as the vicar would say, but they worshipped in Wincle and did a lot for the village – not least in the naming of its pub, the Ship Inn, an unlikely name to find so far from the sea. Two generations of Brocklehursts were involved.

In the middle of the last century Sir Philip Brocklehurst had a ship-owner friend in Liverpool who named one of his ships *Swythamley*, after Sir Philip's home. *Swythamley* was too much of a mouthful for the men who manned her, and they boiled it down to *Sweet Emily*. The ship was wrecked off the Cape in 1862, and it was commemorated in Wincle by the Ship Inn, which had a painting of *Sweet Emily* on its sign. But in 1907 Sir Philip's son, another Sir Philip, sailed to the Antarctic with Shackleton on board *Nimrod* and in his honour *Nimrod* replaced *Sweet Emily* on the sign.

It was another member of the family, however, who made the biggest impact on the neighbourhood, though its full effect was not felt until many years later. Lieutenant-Colonel Courtney Brocklehurst, who was born at Swythamley in 1888, spent some time as a game warden in the Sudan, and when he returned he created a private zoo in the park around the Hall. It was still there when the second World War broke out, and there are two versions of what happened next. One is that animals from Whipsnade were brought there to escape the bombing, and some got out during a fire, including deer and wallabies. The other is that the animals at Swythamley were sent to other zoos when the last Sir Philip

Brocklehurst went off to the war – all except the deer and the wallabies, which were turned loose.

Whichever version is correct, the result was the same. Fifty years later the descendants of the animals which baled out, aided or not, are still roaming the countryside. Which is why the vicar was once able to count thirty-four deer from the door of his vicarage, and why a climber in the hills around neighbouring Wildboarclough is likely to meet, not a wild boar (the last of them disappeared a long time ago) but almost as unnerving, a wild wallaby. Enough to make both of them jump . . .

IMAGINE BEING PAID TO LIVE IN WINCLE . . .

A 'GREAT' PARISH THAT REALLY WAS PRETTY BIG

GREAT BUDWORTH
CHESHIRE
2 miles north of Northwich

It is not always clear why a village is called Great; I know of a number which are actually smaller than their 'Little' counterparts. But in this case there is no sign of any 'Little' in the vicinity, and the comparison doesn't apply. Great Budworth is called great because at one time it really was. It stretched for twenty miles from Holmes Chapel in the south to Warrington in the north, and claimed the title of the biggest parish in Cheshire. Within it were thirty-five smaller villages or 'townships', all now independent but then just subsidiaries.

Where this kind of situation has existed elsewhere, the principal village has sometimes made the position clearer by including a more

specific reference in its name. I am thinking of Ruyton-of-the-Eleven-Towns in Shropshire, or Ruyton-XI-Towns for short, which was the senior of eleven neighbouring townships united into one manor in the fourteenth century. Budworth however just prefers to remain great.

Unlike Ruyton-XI-Towns, which is strung out for about a mile along a busy main road, Great Budworth is reasonably compact, clustered beneath its splendid church on a hillside overlooking the Cheshire Plain. One gazetteer waxes quite lyrical about it: 'an almost unbelievable story-book village of brownish brick, gables, brick and stone mullions, pargeting, angled chimneys, and a mixture of Victorian and restored older work. Once you get to 'Victorian and restored older work' doubts may set in, but there are some very picturesque cottages, and the church at the top of the main street is perhaps the biggest, and certainly one of the finest, village churches in Cheshire, thanks to the parish's original importance.

In the days of Great Budworth's real greatness there was plenty of money about for building and extending its church, and they seem to have kept at it for a century or two, then added more touches later. The Lady Chapel, for instance, is one of the earliest parts, built in the fourteenth century, but its windows are only about twenty-five years old, made of Whitefriars glass for an anonymous donor. Inside it is buried Sir Peter Leycester, who wrote a famous history of Cheshire in 1673, and it is thanks to him that we know how the chapel, originally dedicated to the Virgin Mary, was altered after the Reformation: 'The image of the Virgin, cut in wood, curiously trimmed and decked, her shoes gilded and hair fastened upon her head ... was taken down, hewed in pieces and burned in the Vicar's oven about 1559 by command of Queen Elizabeth'.

The Leycesters were one of the principal local families and lived at nearby Nether Tabley, which was presumably part of the original parish. The Lords of the Manor, the Warburtons and later the Egerton-Warburtons, also lived away from the village itself at Arley Hall, some three miles to the north. These days Tabley Old Hall is in ruins, but Arley Hall and its gardens are still there, and open to the public during the summer months.

The Warburton chapel was added to the church in the fifteenth century, and in the centre of it is the rather battered effigy of Sir John Warburton, a distinguished Elizabethan knight. He is elegantly clad in full armour, but unfortunately legless. His nineteenth-century descendant, Rowland Egerton-Warburton, is credited with the carved exhortations on the fence outside the George and Dragon Inn, just opposite the church, presumably put there to catch the eye of departing

VILLAGE STOCKS FOR VILLAGE VILLAINS . . .

GREAT BUDWORTH HAS SOME STUNNING EXAMPLES OF CHESHIRE 'BLACK AND WHITE'.

drinkers. They range from 'Beware ye Beelzebub' to 'God speed the plough', though the plough probably slowed down a bit after a lunch at the George and Dragon.

At the end of the churchyard is the Jacobean schoolhouse, built in 1600 with money donated by John Dean of London. Who Mr Dean was, and why he should have been keen on educating the children of a distant Cheshire village, I never discovered, but they went on using it for more than 250 years, so he made a good investment. These days it is a craft shop.

The church possesses two venerable wooden chests, one with the date 1680 and the other much older, which is made of thick oak planks held together with iron bands and fitted with five locks. The keys were distributed between the priest and churchwardens, and the chest could only be opened by all of them together. However, the huge wooden beam across the entrance to the chapel was rather too big to be locked in the chest, and early in the nineteenth century it found its way from the roof of the nave into the roof timbers of a nearby farm. The farmer maintained that the beam had been thrown out as unwanted, and indeed I think it was, but presumably the vicar disagreed, and said in effect: 'Please can we have our beam back'. It was duly returned and placed in its present position – without, I trust, causing the collapse of the confused farmer's roof . . .

A Tale Of Two Panels –
And An Overcrowded Oak

WITHAM-ON-THE-HILL
LINCOLNSHIRE
6 miles north of Stamford

Just to be called anything 'on-the-hill' in certain parts of Lincolnshire would be unusual enough in itself. Lincolnshire includes that part of the Fens which you have to cross if you are entering East Anglia from the north-west, and perhaps Noel Coward assumed that it extended all the way to the east coast when he made that much-quoted comment: 'Very flat, Norfolk!' Witham-on-the-Hill is just outside the Fens, but only just. If you continue eastwards for a few miles you enter that rather eerie hinterland of featureless flat fields and danger-ously deep dykes – so dangerous that if you dozed off at the wheel from boredom on the dead-straight roads, you really would be dead.

But Witham is also not too far from the undulating hunting country of Leicestershire, and it really is set on quite an impressive hill. Hereward the Wake is supposed to have owned the village at one time, and it must have made a pleasantly lofty haven after his watery forays through the Fens.

In later years offenders against the Crown found Witham less relaxing; the old stocks still stand by the road on the village green, a tiled canopy making them look from a distance like a wooden seat in a bus shelter. I suspect they strike no chord of terror in the hearts of the prep school boys across the road, in what used to be the old manor house, Witham Hall.

Witham-on-the-Hill has three factors to its credit, so far as visitors are concerned. It has the fattest oak tree in the country, the church has a curious story of what sounds to me like ecclesiastical hanky-panky, and the church itself remains open for visitors, which all churches should, but far too many don't. One can therefore see the actual items the story is about, and the memorial to one of the central

NOT A SEAT IN A BUS SHELTER, BUT THE VILLAGE STOCKS.

characters, the hero of the story.

It seems that at some time between 1835 and 1877, during the incumbency of the Revd W.H. Johnson, the church was restored and two fifteenth-century panels were removed from the rood-screen. They bore paintings of St Stephen and St Laurence, holding the emblems of their martyr-dom – Stephen had stones, Laurence a gridiron. The panels were appa-rently stowed away instead of being replaced, until the Archdeacon of Lincoln made one of his regular visitations. He saw the panels and 'asked to have them as curios'.

This is where the rules seem to have been slightly bent. It was a bit naughty of the Archdeacon to ask for them in the first place, and it was just as naughty of the Vicar to hand them over, though in the circum-stances it was probably difficult to say no. But what happened was that the Archdeacon took them back with him to Lincoln, and nothing more was heard of them until they came to light again in 1940. This followed the death of the Archdeacon's son, Canon Kaye. The panels were found in his effects by the Sub-Dean. Fortunately they had been clearly labelled where they came from, and the Sub-Dean forthwith notified the Vicar of Witham-on-the-Hill at that time, Canon Leonard Cooley. Canon Cooley did not mess about; 'he went at once to Lincoln and brought them back'. He had them restored, and they are on show again in Witham Church – not in the rood-screen, which is a new one this century, but on the wall by the church door. The panel of St Stephen still has the small grill in it which was used by the priest to hear confessions while sitting behind the screen in his stall.

Canon Cooley, who was much loved in the parish quite apart from his speedy rescue operation, was Vicar of Witham for forty-five years, even longer than his over-generous predecessor. When he died in 1953, at the age of eighty-four, a handsome full-length brass was made depicting him in his robes – a rare memorial these days for a village parson – and it was placed in the central aisle of the chancel, the most prominent position in the church.

Few people outside the village know about the odd little panel game involving the Victorian Vicar and the acquisitive Archdeacon; I didn't know it myself until I visited the church. But everybody with a *Guinness Book of Records* knows about Witham's other claim to fame. Outside the village, but within the ecclesiastical parish, in a field behind a venerable farmhouse, stands an even more venerable tree. The Bowthorpe Oak, as it is called, has the largest girth of any living oak in Britain. When it was measured in 1973 the trunk was thirty-nine feet and one inch in circumference, and give or take the odd

inch it is much the same today.

The trunk was hollowed out in the seventeenth century, and there are optimistic reports in some reference books that thirty-nine people have stood in it all at once. On another occasion sixteen people are supposed to have sat down inside it to take afternoon tea. I have stood inside the Bowthorpe Oak myself, and I don't fancy the chances of sharing it with thirty-eight others, even if I lost a few stone. I think a dozen would be the maximum, even by London Underground standards. And if sixteen people sat in it, they must have been on each other's laps.

Never mind. There's no doubt about it, the Bowthorpe Oak is a jolly big tree, and well worth a bob or two in the collection box by the farmhouse gate, in aid of the church. It is one of the parish's great heirlooms – and the Vicar can have the encouraging thought that not even an Archdeacon can cart it away.

THE BOWTHORPE OAK – SIXTEEN PEOPLE ARE SUPPOSED TO HAVE SAT DOWN TO TEA INSIDE IT.

STONE RABBITS AMONG THE TREES, ON THE EAST-WEST DIVIDE

FRAMPTON
LINCOLNSHIRE
3 miles south of Boston

They call it a Fen village, but I know of no other village in the Fens quite like it. I reached it through the usual South Lincolnshire scenery, flat fields of cabbages, flat fields of carrots, flat fields of sugar beet. Then there was this interruption in the straight line of the horizon, and I drove into a different world of open parkland and fine old buildings, even that rare sight in the Fens, a thatched cottage – and best of all, trees!

That is the most obvious difference between Frampton and its Fenland neighbours – it has lots of trees. I have not been the only one to be impressed by them; a venerable Lincolnshire guidebook I came across goes on about them too – 'no other village around the Wash can boast so many'.

But there are other differences too, once you start looking around. Set in a field just outside the village is a big round stone, rather like the imitation millstones which some counties used to mark the boundaries of parishes or national parks, but this one may be unique. The circular plaque on it features a map with a vertical line down the middle, and around it are the words: 'Greenwich Meridian: Longitude Zero'. Frampton parish does indeed lie on the same longitude line that passes through Greenwich, so part of it is in longitude east and part in longitude west. That must apply to a lot of the places in England which are due north or south of Greenwich, including Boston some three miles away, but it was nice to find that Frampton Parish Council had taken the trouble to mark it in this way.

The other unusual feature of Frampton is its rabbits. Of course

with all those fields of cabbages and carrots stretching to the horizon – one even comes up to the churchyard wall – you must think that rabbits hardly rate as unusual, but these are rather special ones, carved in stone or wrought in iron, which bob up on certain buildings and gateposts in the village. One of them even swings on the chandelier in St Mary's Church. They were the pets, if you like, of Coney Tunnard, a member of the principal family in the village, who used the rabbit as his rebus, his pictorial signature. If you get saddled with an odd name like Coney you can't be blamed for making the best of it, and when Coney Tunnard built a house, or erected a gatepost, or presented a chandelier to the church, he 'signed' it with a rabbit.

It was he who built Frampton Hall in the park in 1725, complete with a third storey, which I gather was unusual for that period, and of course all the rabbits. Later in the same century another Tunnard built Frampton House, at the other end of

WHEN EAST MEETS WEST – ON THE GREENWICH MERIDIAN AT FRAMPTON.

the village, and later still another Tunnard took a step which made Coney's rabbits look rather small fry. My venerable guidebook records it laconically enough: 'The poor road conditions from Frampton House to the parish church, and the distance involved, resulted in the Tunnards building St Michael's Church in 1863'.

How about that for style, then? 'The parish church isn't very handy, Jeeves. I think I'll build another one' – or words to that effect. Thus Frampton acquired its two churches, which was jolly nice for the Tunnards, but has left quite a burden on the present generation of villagers, who have to maintain two fabrics instead of one. As the vicar recently pointed out in the parish magazine – appropriately named *Two Spires* – it costs £300 a

ST MARY'S CHURCH, WITH SHEEP OUTSIDE IN THE PARK AND A RABBIT INSIDE ON THE CHANDELIER.

week just to maintain the church in Frampton – and on top of that, St Michael's, built by the Tunnards for their own convenience, now needs reroofing at a cost of £7,000. Maybe they should have put up with that bumpy road after all.

St Mary's dealt with its reroofing problem back in 1930; it now merely faces a £3,000 bill for 'minor repairs'. It still has its original twelfth-century tower and broach spire, but the rest of it was pulled down in about 1350 and replaced with the present building. Apart from Coney Tunnard's chandelier, with its rabbit and its twenty-five candles, which are still used on special occasions, it has a seventeenth-century oak pulpit which started life in Bourne Abbey. It was bought for St Mary's a hundred years ago after a fire at the abbey.

Across the road from St Mary's is the Moores Arms, named after a Colonel Moore who married into the Tunnard family and lived at the Hall – though the pub is actually older than the Hall. Nearby is another three hundred-year-old building, an impressive place called Cotton Hall, not because it was Frampton's answer to Halifax's Cloth Hall, but because it was built by the Cotton family, well remembered in the Boston area for its involvement in founding that other Boston in Massachusetts.

These days the Lincolnshire Boston is a little too close to Frampton for comfort, and I suspect that several of my fellow bar-lunchers in the Moores Arms had driven out from their offices in town, but happily this central area of the village is still very much a village – and best of all, it's got all those trees . . .

ELEGANT FRAMPTON HALL, BUILT BY CONEY TUNNARD WHOSE SYMBOL WAS A RABBIT.

BENEVOLENT WITCHES AND THE WICKED LADY

CASTLE RISING
NORFOLK
5 miles north-east of King's Lynn

It is a traditional English village scene: a tree-lined lane, on one side of it a fine old Norman church set among lichen-covered tombstones, and on the other a magnificent Jacobean building in mellow red brick, its gateway flanked by twin towers.

Then through the gateway comes a most striking procession. It is headed by a lady in a scarlet cloak with a three-tiered cape, and a rather dashing tricorn hat trimmed with a black ostrich feather. Behind her walk a dozen elderly ladies, two by two, also in scarlet cloaks emblazoned with an heraldic crest, but their hats are tall and black and conical. They might have stepped out of an old Welsh print, except that Welsh hats are flattened at the top and theirs are pointed. They look for all the world like a coven of benevolent witches, led by a mature version of Margaret Lockwood's 'Wicked Lady'.

Norfolk is not renowned for its quaint village customs. It is far too down-to-earth a county, more concerned with sugar beet and barley than say, well-dressing or horn dances. There is still the occasional barn dance and hog-roast, and village school-children are sometimes persuaded to frolic, rather self-consciously, around a maypole, but most reminders of the past in rural Norfolk are less romantic – a workhouse converted into a rural life museum, perhaps, or an earth closet which can't be converted into anything yet, because it is still in use.

So it is all the more astonishing to come upon such a colourful cortège in the depths of Norfolk. But in this village it is nothing out of the ordinary, just a visit to church by the Matron and Sisters of the

WELCOME TO CASTLE RISING! A STERN GUARDIAN IN STONE AT THE PARISH CHURCH.

Hospital of the Most Holy and Undivided Trinity, Castle Rising.

The title is a little confusing. The Sisters are not sisters, the hospital is not a hospital in the modern sense, and Rising Castle, far from rising, has mostly fallen; only its keep remains. The sea no longer rises at Rising either; it was a busy port on the estuary of the Babingley river in medieval times, but the river became a rivulet, the estuary silted up, and the sea receded beyond the salt marshes, so merchants sent their ships to King's Lynn instead. As a popular couplet puts it:

Rising was a seaport when Lynn was but a marsh,
Now Lynn it is a seaport town and Rising fares the wuss.

But it was not entirely bad news. Thanks to the loss of its sea trade, Castle Rising has escaped the supermarkets and industrial estates which now disfigure its larger neighbour, and it remains largely unspoilt. The coast road now bypasses the village, so its visitors mostly go there just to explore the castle ruins. Long may the castle distract them from the village centre itself, which lies off the old main road behind the church, well away from the English Heritage direction signs.

I can understand the attraction of the old keep, which is reckoned to be second only to Norwich as Norman keeps go, and it does have a fascinating history. It was built in 1150 by Lord d'Albini, who sounds like a character out of a panto, and his story reads rather like a fairy-tale. He was born the son of William the Conqueror's butler, and eventually married the widow of William's son,

Henry I. Actually that is not as spectacular as it looks; royal butlers ranked rather higher in those days, and instead of acquiring the odd bottle of port, d'Albini senior acquired the Manor of Castle Rising. When young William succeeded him he built the castle, married the King's widow, and founded a dynasty which is still linked with the village. There is a direct link with the Howard family, who have been the squires of Castle Rising for the last four or five hundred years.

It was Henry Howard, Earl of Northampton, who built the Hospital of the Most Holy and Undivided Trinity, which to my mind is even more interesting than the castle. It dates from 1614, a time when philanthropic landowners were building 'hospitals' to care for the old and needy. It was a social service provided by the monasteries until Henry VIII decided he could manage without them. Henry Howard built four altogether; the one at Castle Rising was dedicated to his grandfather,

'THE WICKED LADY' AND THE BENEVOLENT WITCHES – THE MATRON AND SISTERS OF THE CASTLE RISING HOSPITAL EN ROUTE FOR CHURCH, IN FULL REGALIA.

the Duke of Norfolk, and another at Greenwich was to his father, the Duke's son. Both of them were imprisoned by the king and sentenced to be executed within two days of each other, but the King himself died on the day between. The good news for the Duke was that his execution was due the day after; the bad news for his son was that his took place the day before . . .

Trinity Hospital at Castle Rising is built around a central courtyard. Opposite the turreted gateway is the chapel, with the Common Hall on one side and the Matron's quarters on the other. The Sisters' dwellings are along the other two sides, still in the original Jacobean style, but now equipped with central heating and double glazing.

The qualifications for entry were pretty stiff. The Sisters had to be 'of honest life and conversation, religious, grave and discreet, able to read if such a one be had, a single woman, her place to be void on marriage, to be fifty-six years of age at least, no common beggar, harlot, scold, drunkard, haunter of taverns, inns and alms-houses'. I have met the present residents and I am sure they qualify on every count – though one sweet old lady did suggest, after we had taken up much of her time with our camera, that we owed her a gin-and-tonic . . .

The scene as the Sisters cross that quiet lane between the Hospital and the church can't have changed much since the days of Henry Howard, and it's a good reason for Castle Rising to be thankful that the sea deserted it; these ladies in their long cloaks and tall hats would not enjoy weaving through the traffic in King's Lynn. Indeed the other villagers must be happier too in the peace and quiet of their secluded green, on the other side of the church. The writer of that couplet may have thought that Rising 'fared the wuss', but I suspect the present inhabitants would subscribe to my own view:

Now much of Lynn is modernised, a place for the go-getter,
And I'd say, in the long run, Castle Rising's fared the better.

WHERE THE MATRON AND SISTERS WERE HEADING, JUST ACROSS THE ROAD: THE SPLENDID PORCH OF CASTLE RISING CHURCH.

GONE FISHING ... FIRST THE MONKS, NOW A BOY FROM BOLTON

GREAT MASSINGHAM
NORFOLK
9 miles north of Swaffham

In some ways Great Massingham is an untypical Norfolk village. Its village green, for instance, is vaster than almost any other in the county; it not only occupies the entire central area of the village, but extends into a series of auxiliary greens alongside the Weasenham road. Even more impressive, it has five ponds – two big ones in the central area and three smaller ones in the 'extensions'. The duck population sometimes seems to outnumber the villagers themselves; certainly on an average day in Great Massingham you will see more ducks than people.

The other untypical feature is that, unlike many other pairs of 'great' and 'little' villages, Great Massingham is actually far bigger than Little Massingham, just down the road – eight hundred people compared with under a hundred. But in many other ways it is an archetypal Norfolk village, particularly in its history, which features a priory, a railway, and an RAF station, all now defunct. The county used to be bespattered with all three of these, but not many villages can boast the complete set.

It was the priory which Massingham has to thank for those ponds. The Augustinians founded it in about 1260, and they probably dug the ponds to make sure of a supply of fish – a different variety in each pond, if the prior was a connoisseur.

It was a comparatively modest priory by Norfolk standards, and it was winding down long before Henry VIII finished off the job. Seventy years before the Dissolution the building was getting so dilapidated that it was amalgamated with nearby Westacre Priory and reduced to the status of a cell, with just a skeleton staff of two canons and two 'poor brethren' – a term which must have meant the brethren were even more skeletal than the canons. When the Dissolution did come along there wasn't much left to dissolve. There was, however, a great deal of land, and this came into the possession of the Gresham family in 1555. That happened to be the same year that Sir John Gresham founded his famous public school in Holt, so perhaps Great Massingham can claim a little of the credit – the extra income from his new Massingham estate may have made up Sir John's mind. Today the only evidence left of the priory are some medieval walls incorporated into the rear of Abbey House, the handsome Georgian mansion overlooking the green – and, of course, all those ponds.

THE COMBINATION OF PONDS AND FLINT HOUSES MAKE GREAT MASSINGHAM ONE OF THE MOST ATTRACTIVE VILLAGES IN NORFOLK.

The railway arrived in 1879. The station was actually a mile out of the village, in Little Massingham, but it was just called Massingham and it served them both. It was a rather obscure little line at the best of times, linking King's Lynn and Fakenham but with only a few small villages in between. There was a flurry of activity during the second World War, when the RAF had an aerodrome on Massingham Heath; all its petrol was delivered by rail, and one reference book notes that 571 petrol trains arrived at Massingham Station during the war years, so there must have been a train-spotter with a notebook around, even at that remote station. But when the war ended the RAF departed, the railway had to rely on people again instead of petrol, and inevitably Dr Beeching closed it down.

So Great Massingham lost the last of its 'invaders' – the monks, the trains and the planes – but it has retained two other traditional features of Norfolk villages, a massive medieval church with a porch the size of a small chancel, and some splendid rows of old flint cottages, particularly around the smaller green. Massingham lies in the heart of Norfolk's flint-bearing chalk belt, which stretches from the North Norfolk coast down to the flint mines called Grimes Graves on the Suffolk border, where men used deer horns as pickaxes to dig out flints for their tools and weapons, four thousand years ago. In medieval times the flint-knappers toured around Norfolk, no doubt with their knapper's-sacks on their backs, and some of them must have found their way to Massingham. In some cottage walls the flints are split and set with the shiny flat surface facing outwards, to create a mottled wall of grey and black and milky white. One imaginative writer reckoned that in strong sunlight they give a colourwashed effect, but to me they just look like flints, and who could ask for a better looking wall than that.

All these traditional ingredients add up to one of the most attractive villages in Norfolk, with the extra advantage that it is well away from the holiday routes, or indeed from any other, and is thus comparatively undiscovered by the tourist guides. Alas, only comparatively. The last time I was there I chatted to a lad who was fishing in one of the big ponds on the green. I assumed he would be a local, but it turned out that he and his family had come from Bolton. Great Massingham, I learned, now features in a 'good fishing' guide and a new 'invasion' has begun. So the monks who stocked the ponds seven hundred years ago must have done a good job, but personally I rather wish they hadn't . . .

ONE OF MASSINGHAM'S FIVE PONDS.

IN WAX, IN MARBLE, AND IN THE PINK – THE HARES ARE THERE

STOW BARDOLPH
NORFOLK
8 miles south of King's Lynn

The tranquil atmosphere and unspoilt appearance of Stow Bardolph today is due to four hundred years of protective care by the Hare family, and one imaginative decision by some anonymous highway engineer. The Hares have always stood firm against the demands of the developers, but they couldn't do much about the traffic which poured through the village on the trunk road from London to King's Lynn. Then came the bypass, and more important, the decision to block off access to the old road. All too often a bypass can lose its effectiveness as the traffic increases, the new road becomes clogged, and drivers find it quicker to follow the old route through the centre. At Stow Bardolph there is only one road off the bypass, and no way to rejoin it further along.

So you can enjoy a peaceful pint in the garden of the Hare Arms, free of fumes and noise. You can stroll past the quaint little Post Office, and admire the splendid mansion of the Hare family. And you can park outside the church on what used to be the trunk road, safely protected by that 'No Through Road' sign at the end.

It is worth parking there, just to see the wax effigy of Lady Sarah Hare in the church, the only one of its kind outside Westminster Abbey. Lady Sarah is said to have done some sewing on a Sunday, which was considered rather naughty in the eighteenth century, and pricked her finger with the needle. Presumably that would have been pretty harmless on a weekday, but in her case it proved fatal. In her will she asked for this life-size effigy to be made, and it stands upright, elegantly dressed, in a sort of wardrobe in the Hare Chapel. By the 1970s Sarah's waxen features had become somewhat worn, and one visitor complained about the blotches on her hands and face. 'Instead of wax, the effigy has the look of flesh and blood, just dead but starting to corrupt . . .' Happily, she looks a lot healthier these days, after being restored by Sir Thomas and Lady Hare.

This is not the only evidence of the Hare family's continuing care for the village and everything in it. In the parish magazine their names feature prominently. Sir Thomas is of course a churchwarden, like any dutiful squire, but his interest does not stop there. In the issue I glanced at there was a letter of thanks from a visiting Scout troop for his help in providing a campsite, and for the friendly reception they had in the village. 'It shows that our small villages still have a lot to offer,' wrote 'Tom Hare', as he signs himself. On other pages 'Rose Hare' is sorting out the church flower rota and announcing the activities of the Sunday School. She also reports on how much was raised for Romanian orphans at the Stow Garden Open Day. At the time of my visit the ladies of Stow Bardolph had been invited to a game of croquet on the lawn. And so it goes on.

So the Hares are still just as involved in the welfare of the village as they were when an earlier Sir Thomas, father of waxen Sarah, had a rather different effigy erected in his memory, made of more orthodox marble but dressed like a Roman emperor. I admire the succinctness of the inscription to him and his wife: 'The Christian virtues that adorned them were too many to be enumerated here – and are recorded in a better place'. How much more convincing than those effusive epitaphs which go on so long that only the stonemason has ever bothered to read them right to the end . . .

However, the Hares don't just commemorate themselves. It was the Hare family who erected a brass plaque in the chancel in memory of Stow Bardolph's most remarkable rector, the Revd James William Adams VC. Adams served as a chaplain with the Army in India, Afghanistan and Burma, and he won his VC by rescuing several soldiers who had fallen with their horses into a deep, water-filled ditch. He dragged both the men and the horses to safety, totally regardless of his own welfare.

The VC had never been awarded to a chaplain before, and there was some dispute as to whether he was eligible, but Lord Roberts bent the rules and acquired a special warrant to grant it. One report says that during the Afghanistan campaign Adams earned five clasps to go with it, which seems to be pushing it a bit, but he was without doubt a very brave and powerful man. When he came to Stow Bardolph he kept up the pace, preaching up and down the Fens, running a school, taking at least five services on a Sunday, and in the more remote areas using the portable communion table which had accompanied him on active service. It is still kept in Stow Bridge Church, which was also in his charge.

When he died in 1903 King Edward VII was represented at his funeral, and his old commander, Lord Roberts, attended in person. He was as much loved and respected by his parishioners as he had been by the troops; I think that he and the Hare family must have made a great team . . .

SIR THOMAS HARE, WHO WAS GIVEN A SUCCINCT INSCRIPTION –
'TOO MANY VIRTUES TO BE ENUMERATED HERE'.

THE CANADIAN CONNECTION THAT PROVIDED A TOWER OF STRENGTH

WIGHTON
NORFOLK
6 miles north of Fakenham

I could have picked any one of a dozen little villages tucked away in the hinterland behind the North Norfolk coastal road, an area largely ignored by visitors. The popular attractions for most of them are the caravan sites around Mundesley, the traditional seaside entertainments at Cromer and Sheringham, or for the more discerning, the bird sanctuaries and nature reserves that lie along the salt marshes from Cley to Holme-next-the-Sea. Few motorists turn inland, and if they do, they head for the art galleries and antiques shops of Holt or Burnham Market, and the much-publicised shrines at Walsingham. What they miss, in the secluded valleys of the Glaven and Stiffkey rivers, and on the rolling hills between – yes, Norfolk does have hills! – are tiny communities like Langham and Field Dalling, Saxlingham and Binham, Cockthorpe and Glandford, and the five 'W's – Wiveton, Westgate, the two Warhams and Wighton.

I chose Wighton because, in many ways, it is typical of them all, but it is also the envy of them all, thanks to another small 'w' – a windfall of quite magnificent proportions. The village is linked with two famous Norfolk families, the Bedingfelds and the Bacons, but the windfall came through a family whom nobody had heard of outside the village, until a Mr Leeds Richardson arrived from Ontario, Canada, and in effect, dropped a bag of gold in their laps.

Very little is known of Wighton's early history. A couple of miles outside the village are some earthworks called Crabb's Castle, but who Crabb was and why he built a castle is a matter for debate. Roman coins and other relics were found there, and when Wighton Vicarage was being built in the last century they found human bones and ancient pikes thought to be relics of a battle between Danes and Saxons. However, the church records don't start until the thirteenth century, and the present church was built about the middle of the fifteenth. We can be much more precise about the age of its tower. It may look actually older than the church, but it was only started in 1975 and finished in 1976.

The tower it replaced was indeed much older, added to the original Norman church to celebrate, it's thought, the English victory at the Battle of Crecy in 1346. Two years later came the Black Death, when so many Norfolk villages were virtually wiped out, or moved to uncontaminated land well away from their parish church, but Wighton survived and continued to cluster under the shadow of the tower.

Two centuries later the Manor of Wighton passed into the possession of the Bedingfelds of Oxburgh Hall, thirty-odd miles to the south, a Catholic family who kept their property, and their heads, throughout the religious eccentricities of the Tudors and their successors, and still live in the same hall today. They held the manor for two hundred years, through five generations, and the church still has a brass in memory of one of them, Francis Bedingfeld. Much more imposing, though, is a black marble tomb with chequered sides in memory of a seventeenth-century member of the Bacon family, Lady Elizabeth, who died, as the Latin inscription says, 'with her new-born twins, whom she took away with her, one on either arm ...' Her husband, Sir Robert, was the fifth Baronet, and the fifteenth, Sir Nicholas Bacon, Premier Baronet of England, still lives in Norfolk today, at Raveningham Hall near Norwich.

So the Bedingfelds and the Bacons are two of the oldest-established 'county' families, and both are connected with this obscure little village. They have survived for several centuries, faring rather better, in fact, than Wighton's church tower. On November 27th 1965, it decided to fall down. Any thought of rebuilding it was far beyond the villagers' resources and, as a result, it lay in ruins for some years.

Enter Mr Leeds Richardson, apparently just another Canadian looking for his Norfolk roots, but as it turned out, he was a knight in shining armour. He came, he saw, he coughed up – to the tune of a hundred thousand Canadian dollars. It was enough to build a new tower, based on the original design, but strengthened inside by a frame of steel and concrete. It had only one bell, but Mr Richardson decided it deserved more than that, so he bought another four from a redundant church in Kent and had the old one recast.

In Wighton they call it the Trillium Tower, not because of the trilling of the bells, but after the emblem of Mr Richardson's home state of Ontario. What they call Mr Richardson himself one can easily imagine. As for all the other Norfolk churches with massive repair problems – only in 1991, for instance, the round Saxon tower at Cockley Cley collapsed in much the same way – they must have started searching their parish records for a Canadian connection.

Alas, that is not quite the happy ending that it sounds. Less then twenty years later, the story has come full circle. As I write I have a cutting before me from the local paper: 'At Wighton Parochial Church Council meeting it was reported that repairs to the church would cost £91,940. English Heritage has offered a grant, but a large sum is still needed and all ways of raising further funds are being considered . . .'

Who has been the first, I wonder, to suggest a phone call to Ontario?

WIGHTON CHURCH'S TRILLIUM TOWER, REBUILT BY A CANADIAN BENEFACTOR.

'BRANDY FOR THE PARSON' – AND TROUBLE FOR THE NANNY

LEVINGTON
SUFFOLK
5 miles south-east of Ipswich

If you drive along the dual carriageway which now slices through the centre of the Felixstowe peninsula, dicing with the juggernauts which shuttle between the container terminal and the Midlands, it is difficult to believe there is any quiet corner left, but at least this new trunk road has brought some peace to the one it replaced, and to the lanes off it which are no longer accessible to through traffic. If you do manage to find a way off the A45 and head a couple of miles to the south, with any luck you will end up in Levington, a secluded little coastal village which still has the flavour of the old smuggling days, 'when strange lights twinkled at night, and many a queer craft crept to the landing stage, there to disgorge her precious cargo whose toll the king would never receive' – as someone more poetic than I once wrote.

Levington has a modern Yacht Club now, but mercifully it is well away from the village itself, and certainly the yachts would have a few problems in the muddy creek which is the nearest access to the sea. In the eighteenth century, however, the creek was made-to-measure for the smuggling fraternity, and Levington was one of the main centres for it along the Suffolk coast.

For once the most fascinating feature of the village is not the church, pleasant though it is. Historians, romantics, and not a few photographers are more likely to head for the Ship Inn, the thatched hostelry at the head of the little lane which winds down to the creek. This was the route for the contraband, and on a misty winter's evening it is still not difficult to picture the line of men coming up the lane from their boats, laden with kegs of brandy and bales of silk – and perhaps the Excise men lurking behind the hedge . . .

The inn is said to have been built from the inverted hull of an old sailing vessel, and indeed there are plenty of ships' timbers in the walls – though if every 'ship's timber' quoted by estate agents actually came from a ship, then bow to

stern they could have blocked the English Channel. However, the Ship Inn is genuine enough. It features in many of the old smuggling tales, including the most famous of them all, the story of Margaret Catchpole.

I once expressed surprise that a film producer never made it into one of those bodice-rippers of the 1950s, with perhaps Margaret Lockwood in the star role; it would have been a wonderful combination of *Jamaica Inn* and *The Wicked Lady*.

THE SHIP INN, ONCE THE HAUNT OF SMUGGLERS.

But at least there is a novel based on it, written by the Revd Richard Cobbold, a member of the well-known Suffolk brewing family. It may seem a strange subject for a clergyman, or even a brewer, but Mr Cobbold was in a unique position to write it, because between her nocturnal excursions to Levington and elsewhere, Margaret Catchpole worked for his family as a children's nanny. She was a very devoted one too, according to Mr Cobbold, and he even painted a portrait of her, 'the picture of a demure and proper young woman who has applied care and strong principle to the bringing up of her mistress' children ...

a servant girl whose work has always been thorough to a degree, and whose solicitude for her employer's family was never failing ...' Maybe it wasn't a part for Miss Lockwood after all; perhaps Jean Simmons?

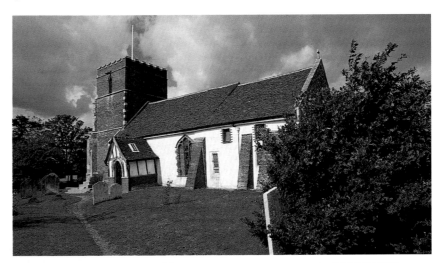

THE PICTURESQUE CHURCH AT LEVINGTON.

That was just one side of her complex character. She was a great horse-rider – a rider, in fact, of great horses, because she galloped around on Suffolk Punches, which her father looked after on a farm at Nacton. The story goes that when she was only thirteen she was delivering a message to a woman in an isolated farmhouse who fell into a fit. Margaret ran to the stable, mounted a young Punch without saddle or bridle, and rode six miles into town to fetch a doctor, 'her skirts and her hair flying in the wind'.

A year later she met the infamous Will Laud, smuggler and philanderer (Stewart Granger?), and for the next decade remained devoted to him. The Ship Inn was one of their favourite rendezvous. In due course this liaison resulted in another dramatic ride, this time with an unhappy ending. Laud led her to believe he would marry her if she met him in London, and she stole her employer's horse to go there and meet him, only to find he had deceived her. Penniless, she sold the horse, was arrested, taken back to Suffolk, tried for horse-stealing and sentenced to death. Public opinion, however, was on her side, and the sentence was commuted to seven years' imprisonment.

That might have been that, but Laud sent her a message saying he would give up smuggling if she

escaped and joined him in a new life abroad. Poor Margaret, besotted as ever, got out of prison by scaling a twenty-two foot spiked wall. This time Laud actually met her, but the coastguards caught up with them on the beach and he was shot dead at her side. She was taken back to prison, sentenced to death again, and again had the sentence commuted, to transportation for life. She was twenty-eight years old.

That would make a pretty depressing end to any film, but in fact Margaret made good in Australia and was granted a full pardon. She got married out there, had three children and lived happily ever after. Back at the Ship Inn they no doubt toasted her memory.

Now surely that's worth a film, or maybe a television series, and Levington would make a delightful location – though I doubt the residents will thank me for saying so. Perhaps it could be made in collaboration with Australian TV if money is short – even if Margaret Catchpole has to be played by Kylie Minogue . . .

THE CREEK BELOW THE SHIP INN AT LEVINGTON, HAUNT OF SMUGGLERS, EXCISE MEN AND MARGARET CATCHPOLE.

THEY CAME TO BURY ST EDMUND – AND TO PRAISE HIM

HOXNE
SUFFOLK
4 miles south-east of Diss

I was caught out so often by the pronunciation of place-names when I first moved to East Anglia – Happisburgh is 'Hazebro', Hautbois is 'Hobbis', Postwick is 'Pozzik', and so on – that I was quite certain Hoxne would be boiled down to 'Hone', but in fact it rhymes with oxen. It is a discreet little village tucked away in the Waveney Valley, just south of the Norfolk border, with very little to distinguish it, to the casual eye, from many other Suffolk villages. It does have a handsome church with some rare wall-paintings of the Tree of the Deadly Sins and the Works of Mercy, but Hoxne's claim to fame is not its church, but its bridge. The story behind Goldbrook Bridge involves at least two deadly sins, but no works of mercy at all.

Again, Hoxne's bridge looks like many another one built in the eighteenth and nineteenth centuries; the

GOLDBROOK BRIDGE, SCENE OF KING EDMUND'S CAPTURE BY THE DANES.

original, going back to Saxon times, has long since been replaced. But it was here, according to most of the experts, that the Danes captured and martyred King Edmund, patron saint of East Anglia, in a particularly unpleasant execution in AD 870.

There is in fact a much-worn plaque on the bridge, recording the event, and nearby there is a fresco on the wall of St Edmund's Hall depicting what happened. A stone cross marks the site of the tree where he died, and the tree itself was standing there until 1848. When it was felled an expert counted the rings and reckoned it was a thousand years old, and embedded in it, so they say, was one of the arrowheads that killed St Edmund. His body lay in a wooden chapel at Hoxne for thirty-three years, until the Danes had finally been disposed of and his friends took it

away to Bury St Edmunds – to bury St Edmund.

After a thousand years there are naturally arguments about where he was killed, how it happened, and indeed the origins of Edmund himself. One theory was that he was actually German, the younger son of a king of Saxony, who made such an impression on the ailing King Offa of East Anglia, a friend of his father, that Offa named him his heir when he died. I am relieved to say this has been rubbished by other experts who say there never was a King of East Anglia called Offa, and Edmund was probably born in Kent – not an East Anglian, alas, but British through and through!

Some also argue that he was killed at Sutton, near Woodbridge, but the popular version is that it happened near Heglisdune, the Hill of Eagles, which was later called Hoxne. Certainly the good folk of Hoxne are in no doubt about it, and the best account of what happened was told by an aged local inhabitant some fifty years ago to the young Suffolk writer, Julian Tennyson, who recorded it in *Suffolk Scene*.

He wrote it entirely in the local dialect, and a solid slab of it might prove a little daunting to a non-Suffolk reader, so let me translate. In 870 the Danes were rampaging around East Anglia, crushing all opposition – 'they din't give a cat's ear for nobuddy'. Edmund's modest army was defeated, and he was on the run when he found himself at Hoxne. Exhausted, he hid under Goldbrook Bridge and fell asleep.

A courting couple came and lingered on the bridge, 'a scroogin an a noodlin one nuther like willy-oh, silly young fules'. They spotted something shine under the bridge, and it turned

HOXNE'S PEACEFUL MAIN STREET.

out to be Edmund's spurs. And the first deadly sin rears its head (assuming they hadn't committed any already); in a very un-Suffolk-like display of treachery they went off and told the Danes where he was.

He was dragged from under the bridge, tied to a tree, and told the only way he could save his life was to renounce being a Christian. He refused to do so, and the old Suffolk story-teller gives a graphic account of the deadly sins that came next.

'They took the whip to im, like a lot o' savidges they was, han't no mercy for the pore boy. Howsoever they din't kill im that way, they shot all their arrers into im, and they cut his hid orf. And thass how they left im under the ould tree, and went orf arter a lot more davilry all ower the country.'

The end of the story is a mite far-fetched, even for Suffolk. Edmund's friends came for the corpse when the Danes had gone, but the head was missing. While they were searching for it they heard a cry of 'Here! Here! Here!'; it was the head calling out to them from between the front paws of a wolf, which was guarding it until they came. 'They took that hid, an so sune as they set that

down, that went an jined up wi the buddy, roight afore their bloomin eyes, time they stood a gawpin like a lot of ould fish. "Well, thass rum doin, that is," they say, "there's ony one meanin to that. This ere Edmund, he's a blessed saint, boy!"'

So that is how East Anglia got its patron saint, and how Bury St Edmunds got its crest as well as its name – a shield surmounted by a wolf holding the crowned head of St Edmund between its paws. It is also how Goldbrook Bridge got a bad name: there is said to be a curse on young couples who pass over it on their way to be married.

St Edmund's story spread far beyond East Anglia. There are over fifty churches dedicated to him, he has chapels in three cathedrals, his effigy is on at least a score of rood screens, and he even has a stained-glass window in Amiens Cathedral. But the best tribute, I think, came from that old story-teller in Hoxne, where it all began.

'Young Edmund was a good sort o' boy, thass whully a sad life he had an he dint desarve it neither. I allus think we could dew with some more of is sort these days; dessay a few like im could larn some of em to be proper good kings, and thass the trewth.'

ALL RHODES CONVERGED ON DALHAM; PERHAPS OUSDEN ONLY CONFUSED 'EM

DALHAM AND OUSDEN
SUFFOLK
6 miles east of Newmarket

I can't resist this passage from an early *History of Suffolk Parishes* – and nor could Cecil Rhodes. 'A veritable arcadia of dense woods and thickets of sylvan parkland and pleasant glades, a district whose cool green freshness seems to typify the great verdant heart of England ... the greenness and freshness which to one of English blood must ever stir the emotions.'

The writer's *nom de plume* was 'Yeoman' – what else? – and the verdant heart of England in this case was a corner of Suffolk which is not that far from the featureless flatlands of Cambridgeshire. You might not form quite the same rosy picture as you belt along the dual carriageway to Bury St Edmunds, a few miles to the north, but that hadn't been built when 'Yeoman' was around,

and although the secondary road through Dalham is now busier as a result, there are still woods and parklands and even the odd glade, and Dalham still has its little wooden bridges across the River Kennet where it runs alongside the street, and thatched cottages on the far side. It still has its smock mill too, fifty feet high with a 'pepper-pot' cap, giving the finishing touch to what a more modern gazetteer calls 'a show village', while 'Yeoman' reckoned that 'in this village we find all the delectable features so appealing to lovers of the countryside'.

Actually, I wouldn't agree with either of them. I am always wary of a 'show village', which makes it sound as artificial as a film set, and I can think of a few 'delectable features' which Dalham lacks, not

least the absence of through traffic. However, Cecil Rhodes must have been taken with it, because in 1900 he bought Dalham Hall and three thousand acres – or maybe it was just a shrewd investment, because he never lived there. He bought it from the Affleck family, whose name is perhaps more familiar in its original spelling of Auchinlech. The pub was named after the Afflecks, while Rhodes' name is linked with the village hall. It was erected in his memory by his brother, Colonel Frank Rhodes, who inherited the estate. He was succeeded by another brother, and after his death Mrs Rhodes lived on at Dalham Hall until 1937.

So for nearly forty years all Rhodes converged on Dalham, but I would commend the quiet little lane that runs off through the hills to Ousden. It has 'Yeoman's' woods and parkland too, and in the park is a dovecote, which is not very unusual, and a fifty-foot clock tower, which is. They were part of the original mansion which stood there until about forty years ago, when the main building was demolished and the coach-house and outbuildings were converted into more manageable accommodation.

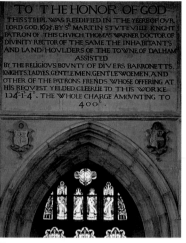

DALHAM'S CHURCH STEEPLE WAS 'RE-EDIFIED' – BUT NOT FOR LONG.

Nearby is Ousden church, and although its guidebook, with rare modesty for such a publication, calls it 'humble and unprepossessing', I found it just as interesting as the one at Dalham, where the only unusual event in its history was the loss of its spire. It blew down in a gale on the day that Oliver Cromwell died, one of the few acts of destruction against England's churches in that period which can't be blamed on Cromwell himself. It must have been particularly irritating for Sir Martin Stuteville, because thirty years earlier he had had a whip round among the local gentry, and 'by the religious bounty of divers Barronetts, knights, ladies, gentlemen, gentlewomen and other of the patron's friends', he had the steeple 're-edified', as an inscription above a stained glass window records.

The Stutevilles were Lords of the Manor through nine generations, over a period of nearly three hundred years, and Sir Martin wasn't the first to lend a hand with the church. When Thomas Stuteville died in 1468 he left enough money for a new window in the chancel, and twenty shillings towards the repair of the tower. The window is still there, but the tower, of course, looks rather different.

The gateway to the churchyard at Dalham is ingeniously constructed of oak beams from the old chancel roof, but presumably they couldn't find any use for the dislodged spire. Ousden, on the other hand, seems to have found a use for everything over the centuries. It is a marvellous hotchpotch of different styles and periods; they obviously preferred to tack things on, rather than throw things away. Where else, I wonder, could you find a twelfth-century flint tower above an eighteenth-century grey-rendered chancel, a nave which is thirteenth-century at one end and nineteenth-century at the other, with a red brick chapel sticking out of the side and a twentieth-century mock-Tudor porch over the door?

The final touch is the doorway, which I suspect was designed by a medieval mason with a sense of humour, to baffle the experts. Here's the problem he set. One side of the doorway has a Norman capital, the other has a circular Early English pillar; the decorative moulding on the arch is Norman, but the arch itself is pointed, which should make it Early English. So which period was it actually built in? In a few hundred years' time I like to think that the experts will be just as confused by that mock-Tudor porch . . .

I started by quoting 'Yeoman', and he must have the last word. It's not actually 'And so we say farewell . . .' but it's not far short. 'All around there is the fragrance and the freshness of the bounteous English countryside, there is the attraction of quivering leaves and shaded bower, of cool parkland and friendly copse, of all those glorious features which make Suffolk and the Suffolk countryside so full of solace and infinite content.'

Well done, 'Yeoman'. Rest in peace.

PRETTY AS A WHOLE SET OF PICTURES – AND YET, AND YET . . .

ICKWELL GREEN
BEDFORDSHIRE
3 miles west of Biggleswade

'This is the kind of village,' says one gazetteer euphorically, 'that used to appear in magazine Christmas supplements under the title "This England . . ." to remind expatriates of what they were missing.' It goes on to rhapsodise over Ickwell Green so enthusiastically that I almost hoped to find just another reasonably attractive village. But I have to confess that as I drove on to the green it was almost like driving on to a film set. In fact, three or four film sets, because the green is cut into quarters by the roads that intersect on it, and each quarter looks like a different location for an episode of *The Darling Buds of May.*

On the right is the cricket pitch, complete with picturesque little pavilion and ancient oak tree. On the left is a maypole with red and white stripes, like an enormous barber's pole sticking out of the grass, with a smart gold crown on top. The quarter beyond it has the War Memorial as its centrepiece, and although the fourth quarter doesn't seem to have any focal point, I imagine this is what the local historian calls 'an area of longer grass to encourage flora and fauna, and to discourage indiscriminate parking'.

For good measure, one of the roads across the green leads to an imposing gateway, beyond which there stretches Ickwell Bury Park, where horses graze around the former home of the Lord of the Manor. The Lord has long since departed, and the Manor House became a school, but when it was destroyed by fire in the 1930s they promptly built another one which looked just like it. These days it is owned by a Trust and used as a yoga centre, but for filmic purposes it still looks the part. So does the old smithy on the green, now used as a football changing room, and the wheelwright's shop, now the village hall.

All around the green are assorted houses and cottages, mostly thatched, often painted in the traditional 'Ickwell Peach', always highly photogenic. To complete the picture a couple of horse-riders appeared ahead of me, as if on cue, from the stables round the corner . . .

I drove gently past them, then gently back again. It was all so perfect, yet something seemed to be missing. Then it dawned on me. It was not one missing item, but two; there was no pub, and no church.

I pulled up beside a man walking his dog (at least the green had that essential ingredient, a man walking his dog) and asked him where I could find the village inn and the parish church. He shook his head. 'You won't find them here, you'll have to go on up the road into Northill. But you'll hardly notice the difference.'

In a way, I suppose, he was right. Northill and Ickwell Green adjoin each other so closely it is difficult to spot the join, and they are actually the same ecclesiastical parish. But in another way he was quite wrong. It was like driving out of the idyllic eighteenth century into the workaday twentieth. Here was all the modern housing which Ickwell Green seems

DANCING ROUND THE MAYPOLE AT ICKWELL GREEN.

to have avoided, or at least hidden very discreetly; the best and the worst of what the developers have given the English countryside over the past sixty-odd years.

In the midst of it was a reminder of what Northill must once have been like, a small green with the church, the pub and the village hall. But the Crown Inn has been much enlarged in recent years, the hall is a modern replacement for the original, less than twenty years old, and elsewhere along the road through the village I only spotted one thatched roof, which looked very lonely among all the red brick and tiles. I must not be too unkind to Northill, and in many ways it looks much more like the real world than the picture-postcard scenery of its neighbour – but even its most enthusiastic local chronicler, seeking to name some 'interesting buildings', had to make up his list with the disused Methodist Chapel . . .

The list in Ickwell Green, of course, goes on and on. There is Tompion's Cottage, birthplace of the famous clockmaker, with a plaque recording that he was born there in 1639 and finished up in Westminster Abbey in 1713. There is the Old House, dating back to medieval times, and still partially surrounded by a moat. Although the original manor house has gone, the seventeenth-century stable block still survives, adorned by a clock said to be the work of a local boy. The dovecote in the park is just as old, with nesting accommodation for nearly a thousand birds, and there is even an old bee house of rare design, with holes in the gable ends for the residents to buzz in and out.

Yes, it's all there at Ickwell Green, enough of Olde England to warm the heart of the most hardened tourist – and on May Day he would be positively ecstatic. The maypole and its predecessors have been danced around for at least four hundred years, and they dance there still. Some May Day customs have lapsed, like taking may bushes to people's front doors – I gather some of the newer residents objected, and even threatened to call the police. But the festivities on the green still attract crowds from the neighbouring villages, just as they did in the days when hobby-horses and dragons took part, and even 'the fashionable populace of Bedford' came to see them. It is a very picturesque occasion in an extremely picturesque setting, and is ideal material for the magazine supplements, just as the gazetteer says.

And yet, and yet . . . It is not just the absence of a church or a pub, though you could argue that no village is a real village without at least one of them. It is just that faint sense of unreality that nags at me. I can't help feeling that, next time I go to Ickwell Green, someone from the studios will have folded it up and packed it away for the next series . . .

THE MAY QUEEN'S ELEGANT PROCESSION.

BOG RHUBARB IN THE SLOUGH OF DESPOND
STEVINGTON
BEDFORDSHIRE
3 miles west of Bedford

John Bunyan and I don't have too much in common, I suspect, but we both share an affection for Stevington. Vernon Edwards, for many years doctor to the England football team and a lifelong friend from our school-days together, lived at the Old Vicarage, and it was always a great relief to escape from the baffling traffic system in Bedford, turn off the busy trunk road to Northampton, head across the hills into the Ouse Valley, and drive through Stevington into the cul-de-sac leading down to the river, the church and the vicarage, where I would soon be sampling the contents of Vernon's excellent cellar.

Bunyan undoubtedly appreciated Stevington too, even without the cellar. It was not merely the Bedford traffic he had to contend with, it was

twelve years in Bedford jail, but he must have retained happy memories of the village, where he probably preached, because it almost certainly features in *Pilgrim's Progress*. Remember the part where Christian comes to 'a place somewhat ascenting, and upon that place stood a cross, and a little below, in the bottom, a sepulchre'? The cross still stands at the crossroads in Stevington, though it is likely these days to be draped with bingo posters. The iron upright was removed at one time to act as the shaft for a weather-vane on the church tower, but this act of vandalism was suitably punished when the heavy iron pole swayed so much in the wind that it made the roof leak. They put it back in its proper position in 1905, I trust looking suitably shamefaced.

'A little below, in the bottom' – at the bottom, in fact, of the lane running down to the church – is Bunyan's 'sepulchre', the holy well under the churchyard wall. It was a notable place of pilgrimage in the Middle Ages, and it is said the spring never freezes or dries up. The Slough of Despond could well be the boggy area around it, which is full of butterbur or bog rhubarb – 'an extraordinary and interesting proliferation,' as the church guide puts it, and indeed so extraordinary it is protected by the Naturalists' Trust. I don't think bog rhubarb is mentioned in *Pilgrim's Progress*, but apart from that, everything fits.

The church is still much as Bunyan would have known it, even down to its two ruined chapels, which have been roofless since Tudor times. 'For no particular reason,' one gazetteer says, but there is a theory that it was done deliberately during the Reformation to discourage pilgrims coming to the well, and nobody has got around to repairing them since. Everything else about the church has been well preserved, particularly the jolly bench-ends on the front pews, which were taken off their original fifteenth-century benches and attached to the replacements. There are two little men drinking from a bowl, who are thought to be connected with a church ale which was provided from the proceeds of some church land. This may be confirmed by an adjoining bench-end, showing two men (the same

ones?) lying prostrate on the ground . . .

The lane peters out at the church, and a path continues into the meadows beside the Great Ouse. Those who only know the Ouse after it has reached the Fens, where it becomes a broad expanse of rather menacing grey water between high, straight banks, the water level often higher than the land around it, wouldn't recognise this peaceful stream meandering through the water-meadows. A mile or so downstream it flows under the narrow and tortuous Oakley Bridge, and on the lane back into the village is Stevington's other historic landmark, the two-hundred-year-old post-mill, restored in 1951 for the Festival of Britain and the only complete windmill left in Bedfordshire.

It was probably the last one in the country to use cloth-covered sails, which had to be reefed by hand like the sails on a ship, to suit the prevailing wind. The sails worked the mill wheel and the hoist for the grain, but no amount of reefing or unfurling could produce enough power to operate both at the same time. This was bad news for the mill-hand, who sometimes had to hump fifteen-stone sacks to the top of the mill on his back if the wheel was in use. I am surprised Bunyan didn't think of an allegory to fit that . . .

The key of the mill is kept at the Royal George, which is the really old pub in the village, not the one with the bogus 'Brewers' Tudor'. Elsewhere in Stevington there are more recent additions – 'some uneasy modern buildings', as one writer says – but the old almshouses remain, albeit rebuilt in 1839, and there are some genuine old stone cottages; best of all, there is that quiet lane down to the holy well which Bunyan must have pictured so clearly, as he picked up his pen and sent Christian on his way . . .

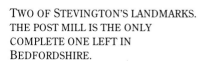

TWO OF STEVINGTON'S LANDMARKS. THE POST MILL IS THE ONLY COMPLETE ONE LEFT IN BEDFORDSHIRE.

NO DANIEL IN THIS DEN –
JUST A BOY BISHOP

BERDEN
ESSEX
7 miles north-west of Bishop's Stortford

The first problem Berden has got is its spelling. How many combinations of different vowels have cropped up in its mail, Burdon, Burden, Burdun, Birden, Birdon, Birdun, Berdin, Birdin, Berdon, Berdun . . . No doubt people have doubled the 'd' as well, or added an 'e' or even a 'g' – the permutations are endless. But Berden itself has no doubt about its name or how it originated. It comes from the Saxon words 'bear' and 'den', which are not as wildlife-orientated as they sound. 'Bear' meant barley and 'den' meant valley, and that just about sums it up. Berden is in a valley, and the fields that surround it still grow a lot of barley.

The second problem is that Berden is at the unfashionable end of the county, tucked away in the top left-hand corner, close to the borders of Hertfordshire and Cambridgeshire. If it was further east, close to the Suffolk border instead, it would come into Constable country, where the planners might have taken more care over the new developments they allowed. As it is, Berden's picturesque old thatched cottages, its magnificent Elizabethan manor house, and its half-timbered priory are now interspersed with modern dwellings, ranging from bogus Georgian to what I think of as Unashamed Angular. They have also allowed a large National Grid station a couple of miles away, with its attendant army of pylons marching across the landscape, though mercifully you can't see it once you are in the village.

This little-known corner of Essex, however, has its compensations. The Constable coach tours give it a wide berth, the sight of that National Grid complex frightens off the casual tourist, and although some of the newer residents no doubt commute to Bishop's Stortford or Saffron Walden, both towns are far enough away not to have turned it into a dormitory suburb. Berden retains its original identity and functions as a remote agricultural village, its population still under four hundred, its finest buildings still standing.

The most historic one is the priory, on the outskirts of the village down a 'No Through Road' which offers a good example of Berden's assorted architecture. There is a row of featureless semi-detached houses, a sprinkling of modern villas, one or two stockbroker-type four-bedroomers, then unexpectedly a splendid thatched and timbered house, The Old King's Head, formerly I suppose the village pub, now privately occupied. Beyond that are open fields, a farm, and finally the priory, also privately owned but once a House of Augustinian Friars. After the Dissolution it was given to Christ's Hospital, along with its lands, much of the village, and the Elizabethan Berden Hall. It was all sold off in bits and pieces in 1919.

The Hall stands next to the church, near the centre of the village, but again you have to negotiate some un-distinguished modern deve-lopments to reach them. The Hall is a lot more imposing than the church, but it is the church which holds the key to Berden's special signi-ficance. Inside it, clamped to the wall, are a bishop's crook and cross, the metalwork very simple and the staffs shorter than usual, but a lot more interesting than most, because these were the symbols of office carried by the Boy Bishops of Berden.

The appointment of boy bishops was quite

widespread in English cathedrals during the Middle Ages, but virtually unknown today, certainly in a village church, yet Berden has had them within living memory. The custom was to choose a boy on 6th December, the Feast of St Nicholas, patron saint of children. He remained in office until the Feast of the Holy Innocents on 28th December, and in the old days in cathedrals like Salisbury and Winchester the boy and his attendants performed all the ceremonies and rites except for the most sacred offices. If, by some misfortune, a boy bishop died during his three weeks in office he was buried with full episcopal honours, and their tombs still exist to prove it, with effigies of the unfortunate youths dressed in all their vestments. The story of the boy bishop who is buried in Salisbury Cathedral is particularly bizarre; he is reputed to have been tickled so strenuously to make him giggle during a ceremony that he literally died laughing.

Boy bishops were not entirely popular with the church authorities, particularly when this sort of thing happened, and the practice was prohibited in Europe in 1431. England, not for the only time, didn't take much notice of what the rules were in Europe, but eventually Queen Elizabeth clamped down on it, and the custom died out. It would be nice to record that Berden's boy bishops evaded the ban and survived through the centuries, but I have to admit that they only date back to 1899. They were introduced by an enterprising vicar, the Revd H.K. Hudson, who not only adopted the idea of boy bishops, but actually made the crook and cross for them himself. It was all treated with proper solemnity, but one of the principal duties of the young prelate was to help raise money for the maintenance of the church. He led an annual procession through Berden and the neighbouring villages, collecting contributions. His final duty was to preach a sermon from the pulpit.

Throughout Mr Hudson's incumbency, from 1899 to 1936, a boy bishop was appointed every year, but when he left enthusiasm waned, and the war caused a further gap. The custom was revived for a couple of years in the 1950s, and again between 1961 and 1966, but that was about it.

So perhaps it is time to reintroduce it, or even to revive another custom to go with it. In a Norfolk village near my home, for instance, the Palm Sunday procession is always headed by a real live donkey. If that idea were adopted, what a splendid combination to offer my successors writing future books on English villages: the boy bishop – and the Beast of Berden . . .

BERDEN PRIORY, ONCE A HOUSE OF AUGUSTINIAN FRIARS, NOW PRIVATELY OWNED.

THE M11 BUSY?
YOU SHOULD HAVE SEEN THE ICKNIELD WAY

ICKLETON
CAMBRIDGESHIRE
5 miles north-west of Saffron Walden

You could hardly imagine a less promising site for a peaceful English village. To the west is the M11. To the south is the dual carriageway that links it to the A11 trunk road. To the east is the main railway line between London and Cambridge, and to the north is the B-road from Cambridge to Chesterton. Inside this square of busy road and rail traffic lies Ickleton; the motorways are just outside the village, the railway line is on its outskirts, the B-road actually cuts through one end of it. All in all, it sounds like a recipe for Bedlam.

Miraculously, it is nothing of the sort. Ickleton's centuries-old houses, the winding village street, the splendid church and the little triangular green surrounded by mellowed cottages provide a picture of timeless calm which not even the traffic hum from the M11 can mar.

Actually, the traffic situation affecting Ickleton has come full circle, though it has taken nearly two thousand years to do it. Right through the middle of the village ran the earliest equivalent of the M11, the Icknield Way, which was the main route into East Anglia from the south before the Romans came, and the Romans used it too. Just outside the village it crossed the River Granta (in Cambridge they prefer to call it the Cam), which was an obvious place for ambushing people and thumping them, so the Romans established an extensive military headquarters at Great Chesterford, on the other side of the river, and at Ickleton they built an elaborate seventeen-roomed villa, complete with the Roman version of underfloor heating. Nearby they put a basilica, a kind of Latin office block.

Maybe the villa was the home of the Roman commander and the basilica was used by his general staff – who

AN ILL WIND . . . THE WALL-PAINTINGS UNCOVERED AFTER THE CHURCH FIRE.

knows? But obviously there was plenty of activity in the area, and the Icknield Way must have carried heavy military traffic, as well as the local ladies thronging down to Chesterford for a night out with the soldiery. Incidentally, I assumed that Ickleton derived its name from the Icknield Way, like so many East Anglian villages, but the local guidebook says it comes from Icel's Farm. I suspect Mr Icel took *his* name from Icknield and passed it on to the village, but I doubt we shall ever know.

There are very few traces left of those busy days – there was a long gap before the village prospered again in the Middle Ages. The site of the villa has long since been covered up, and the Roman tiles and stonework in the church are thought to have come from elsewhere. Much more remarkable in the church are the wall-paintings; they proved to be the silver lining to a dark cloud which affected it in 1979. It was in fact a smoke-cloud. An arsonist started a fire which destroyed

much of the building, and it took nearly two years to restore it. However, the restoration work involved cleaning the walls, and that was how the paintings were rediscovered – a series of twelfth-century pictures on the north wall of the nave, and a fourteenth-century 'Doom' over the chancel arch.

The antiquarians were intrigued as well as delighted. It was not only the rarity of the earlier paintings, it was the controversy that arose over the 'Doom'. Like those in other churches it illustrates the Day of Judgement, with Christ as the central figure on the Judgement Seat and the kneeling figures of St John and the Virgin Mary at his side. But hang on – take another look at Mary – she appears to have bare breasts.

Impossible, they argued. It must be Mary Magdalen; after all, the church is dedicated to her. But that only happened after the period of the painting; in the fourteenth century it was dedicated to the Virgin. Very well then, they said, perhaps she is baring her breasts in supplication, on behalf of all sinners. But in that case, why don't any other wall-paintings depict her in that way? Well, they said, maybe the Puritans thought they weren't decent and destroyed them all when they were generally smashing up the churches. Yes, but how did they miss this one, because they were in Ickleton church in 1644, breaking the stained-glass windows and pulling down the crosses? Ah, well . . . And so it goes on.

There is rather more certainty about the rest of the village's history. Indeed, much of it is still illustrated by its impressive collection of historic houses – Ickleton had several manors, and each one had a manor house. In the twelfth century it also had a priory of Benedictine nuns. Abbey Farm, on the site of the priory, is a mere three-hundred years old, but in the garden there is still the fish-pond which provided the Benedictine nuns with their suppers.

Hovells is probably the oldest house in Ickleton, dating back to 1450, but there was a Ralph Hovel around as early as 1284. Limburys is

ICKLETON HAS ITS FAIR SHARE OF WELL PRESERVED HOUSES.

early seventeenth century and The Valence is late eighteenth, but the Limbury family and Sir Aylmer de Valence were the respective owners of these manors in the days of Edward I.

Fullen House takes its name from an old fulling mill, where cloth was thickened in the Middle Ages with 'fuller's earth'. The seventeenth-century Priory Farm still has its original brew house, and one of the fifteenth-century cottages called the Nook and the Crannie (recent names, I imagine – rather too coy for the fifteenth century) was licensed to sell beer just once a year, on the day of the fair. The oddest house name must be Frogge Hall, the four-hundred-year-old house at the entrance to the village, which apparently became infested with frogs because of the surrounding damp. Happily modern drainage has cured the problem and Frogge Hall is now froggeless, but the name remains unchanged.

Just one final example of how Ickleton's history lives on. A devoted local researcher discovered in the parish registers that nearly a dozen village families have lived there for at least three hundred years – three of them for four hundred. 'In the light of this continuity,' he comments, 'those who have lived here less than thirty years should not be astonished when they are still considered as "newcomers from away".'

It is only after those thirty years have passed, I expect, that the locals will ask newcomers to Ickleton: 'And do you think you're going to like it here?'

THE ROMANS MAY HAVE DEPARTED, BUT THE CAESARS RETURNED

BENINGTON
HERTFORDSHIRE
4 miles east of Stevenage

I approached Benington from the Icknield Way, the chalk track down which Boadicea led her Iceni tribe out of East Anglia in her sortie against the Romans, and up which she hastily returned when the Romans had got over the shock. Where she drove her chariot down, and where the Romans marched their legions up, is now the dual carriageway between Baldock and Royston, and its ancient origin is only indicated by the Olde English lettering which some road maps use for it. I have travelled that dual carriageway scores of times on my own sorties out of Norfolk, but I have been too busy concentrating on the switchback road ahead to notice the little lanes turning off to the south, into the empty Hertfordshire countryside.

I soon realised what I had been missing. The contrast with the traffic on the Icknield Way –

better known as the A505 – was most refreshing. I met only a couple of cars in a dozen miles, as the lane wandered between the hills and led me through the confusingly named villages of Redhill and Cromer. There were tractors and muddy farmyards and even a post-mill on a hill, to confirm that this was real countryside, not the sanitised sort you get around the London suburbs.

Walkern was a bit depressing – too big, too many Victorian terraces, too much traffic. But I did pass a couple of horses in the main street, and I could see more open country ahead. It might get better again. 'Walkern, Walkern,' I found myself humming, 'with hope in your heart . . .'

The hope did not seem misplaced. A sign to Benington took me up a narrow road and into a brief encounter of the horse-box kind, which left me slightly twitching but much encouraged. If a

horse-box used this winding lane, it could hardly expect to meet heavy traffic; I was off the beaten track again.

Then I saw the concrete water tower, as ugly as all such objects are. I came into a street of modern bungalows and suburban pavements, and my heart sank. This was what I had feared; what else could I expect, less than four miles from Stevenage New Town?

But I was wrong. I drove into the village centre, and suddenly it was a different world, and a different era; a closely-cropped green with a duck pond, timbered cottages, an old pub, the imposing gateway to a stately home, and a church with a venerable yew tree in the churchyard, which looked even older than the church. Now I could understand why Benington is considered one of the most attractive villages in Hertfordshire, in spite of being so close to the New Town and the Great North Road.

The lane ahead of me passed the church and disappeared down the hill, straight into open country, and I realised where I had gone wrong. That was the lane to Stevenage, the route most visitors arrive by, and it brings them straight into this halcyon scene, without negotiating any water towers or bungalows. So I drove down it a little way, turned round, and drove back into Benington, to start all over again.

From this direction, across the churchyard, I could see Benington Lordship, the Georgian mansion built as a dower house for a descendant of Julius Caesar. Yes, I blinked when I read that too. Was this a little Roman enclave which stayed behind when everyone else had gone, and survived through the centuries? Alas, nothing so romantic. This Julius Caesar was the son of Queen Elizabeth's doctor, whose actual name was Dr Cesaro Adelmare, and when Julius bought Benington from the Earl of Essex in 1614, maybe he felt that the Lord of such a very English manor should have a rather more Anglicised name. He managed to combine the jobs of Chancellor of the Exchequer and Master of the Rolls, in the way that shrewd operators did in those days, and he was knighted about the same time that he bought Benington and its manor house, Benington Place.

The last of the Caesars, Sir Charles, rebuilt it about the same time he built the Lordship, but it proved ill-fated; the Place burnt down almost immediately. He rebuilt it a second time, and again it burnt down. When the estate was sold to the Chesshyre family they didn't bother again – they moved into the Lordship instead.

By doing so, they brought history full circle. Just beside the Lordship there still stands the ruined keep of a Norman castle built by a much earlier Lord of the Manor, Roger de Valoigne. The castle was just as ill-fated as Benington Place, when, in 1177, Henry II took a dislike to it and had it demolished. The next Lord to live on that site was John Chesshyre, in 1743.

The Chesshyres gave way to the Proctors, and it was George Proctor who built the neo-Norman gatehouse. He was not expecting another attack from Henry II, it was just that neo-Norman gatehouses were all the rage in 1832.

These days the big attraction to visitors is not the gatehouse or the ruined keep, or the tombstone of a Greek slave in the summer-house, brought back from Troy by a friend of the Proctors, Benington's answer to the Elgin Marbles. It is the garden, created out of a nine-hole golf course by the Bott family when they bought the estate in 1905 (it would probably be the reverse today), and maintained and improved by them ever since.

The garden is open to the public, and as a result the entrance to the Lordship is placarded with times of opening and direction signs to car parks and refreshments, and inevitably the delightful village green gets somewhat over-run. But I went in February, when the green was empty of people but the garden was full of snowdrops, particularly the ancient moat, which was quite overgrown until they introduced an ancient but efficient and highly economical moat-clearing device – a goat.

The view is still spectacular in spite of the proximity of Stevenage, and I could imagine why the de Valoignes, and Kings of Mercia before them, chose this hilltop site as a headquarters. King Beortwulf held a Great Council here in AD 850 to plan the defence of his kingdom against the invading Danes. Where his palace probably stood is now the main car park – a reminder that, eleven centuries later, Benington is still subject to invasion . . .

THEY RACED ON IT, THEN THEY RAMBLED ON IT – BUT WHOOSE HOO?

LILLEY
HERTFORDSHIRE
3 miles north of Luton

If you are familiar with Luton, or with that virtual New Town called Luton Airport, you may find it difficult to believe that any village has managed to survive within a radius of many miles. Certainly if you drive into the outskirts of Luton from the east, on the main road from Hitchin, you could hardly imagine that less than a mile from this busy dual carriageway there still exists a traditional English village with eighteenth-century cottages, a whitewashed pub, a triangular village green. This is Lilley, now separated from the valley of Lilley Bottom by the dual carriageway, but otherwise still preserving its original village identity, and still having a greater affinity with the ancient Icknield Way, just to the north of it, than with the A505 just to the south.

However, it has lost one of its key features over the years. In the old days one would not have thought of Lilley without Lilley Hoo, the area of heathland which was once the home of the Lilley Hoo Races, supported by the nobility and one of the important entries in the racing calendar. The first record of them was in 1693, when a plate worth thirty pounds was competed for on Michaelmas Day. The idea caught on, and the village pub was renamed 'The Running Horse' to fit into the newly-created racing scene. By 1710 it was in the rules of the meeting that 'every horse must be shown at the new stables in Lilley', which suggests, as one local historian observes, that the place was becoming a miniature Newmarket.

It never, in fact, reached Newmarket proportions, but thanks to the racing, and no doubt the influential people involved in it, Lilley Hoo escaped the Enclosure Acts and was officially described as a sheepdown. The annual race meeting now lasted for three days, and there was even a Gold Cup presented by the redoubtable Lady Salisbury, Master of the Hatfield Hunt, who was still riding to hounds in her distinctive blue and silver riding coat when she was eighty and almost blind. The story goes that she was strapped to her horse, which was on a leading rein held by her groom, and when they came to an obstacle the groom cried: 'Damn you, my lady, jump' – and she did. There is no record of her ever taking part in the Lilley Hoo Races, but I wouldn't have put it past her.

In spite of the backing from the likes of Lady Salisbury, the meetings started to decline, although nobody is quite sure why. Finally, in 1798, it is recorded that 'Wm Stevenson forbade Lilley Hoo Races, and Lord Melbourn transferred them to his park at Brocket Hall'. Who this Wm Stevenson was, why he objected to the races, and how he had the power to stop them remains a total mystery. Perhaps he was acting for Lord Melbourn in an eighteenth-century take-over bid, or perhaps it was Lady Salisbury being more eccentric than usual, but not even the book on Lilley's history, which runs to nearly two hundred pages, can offer a solution.

Lilley Hoo was left to become heathland, much enjoyed by the villagers, but there always seems to have been uncertainty over its origins and its ownership. There is a delightful theory that it

'HOO GOES THERE . . .' LILLEY HOO'S UNSPOILT OPEN SPACES.

belonged to medieval Lords of the Manor called Hoo, a name which must have led to enormous confusion in introductions . . .

'This is Thomas Hoo.'
'Who did you say?'
'Yes I did.'
'What do you mean, you did?'
'It's Hoo.'
'Who? How do I know?' And so on.

Anyway, there was certainly a Thomas Hoo involved at one stage, who sold some land at Lilley which may have been the Hoo. In the sixteenth century sheep could be grazed on it, but no one could cut down trees or gather firewood. It was referred to as a common, and there was that reference to a 'sheepdown' when the Enclosure Acts were avoided, but in 1863 Colonel Thomas Sowerby, member of an old Lilley family, successfully brought an action against a number of people for trespassing 'on a Common called Lilley Hoo' – which seems to confuse things still further. Many people seemed to assume it was common land, and for a long time it was possible 'to lose oneself among shrubs and trees, woods and spinneys, along sheep tracks and broad walks', as the local history puts it, but it goes on to record, with obvious regret, that it has now been ploughed and cultivated.

Lilley's other claim to fame in earlier days was its straw plaiting, part of the famous Luton straw hat industry. In the last century Lilley produced a special type called 'plain-and-twist wholestraw', and the local history paints a lyrical picture: 'In summer, women and girls walked around the village or sat on stiles and gates or on the grass, plaiting . . . In winter they sat round the fire in their cottage homes, plaiting and reading, or plaiting and singing'.

It sounds idyllic, but it was hard work, poorly paid, and I suspect they felt they'd drawn the short plain-and-twist wholestraw . . .

'LAND OF LIBERTY, PEACE AND PLENTY' – BUT IT DIDN'T WORK OUT THAT WAY

HERONSGATE
HERTFORDSHIRE
2 miles south of Rickmansworth

'It's not a village,' said my friend who lives there, quite firmly. 'Only the newcomers call it a village. Some of them ...' and she wrinkled her nose, '... some of them even call it an estate.'

'But it's a self-contained community in fairly rural surroundings,' I protested. 'It has its own church, its own hall, its own pub, it even had two schools. That's as much as a good many villages have these days. If you don't call it a village, what do you call it?'

She just looked at me. 'We call it Heronsgate,' she said.

She's quite right, of course. Heronsgate is not your traditional English village. But when Feargus O'Connor dreamed up the idea in 1845 of buying up tracts of agricultural land, selling shares, dividing the land into two or four acre small-holdings, and running a lottery among the share-holders to see who would live on them, he must have had a village community in mind, a self-sufficient group who would earn enough off their smallholdings to make a living, provide enough worshippers to keep a chapel going, and produce enough children for a village school (the second one was a private prep school and came much later). It was an idea which proved a monumental and disastrous failure, but many years later there were more practical methods of creating new communities in the Hertfordshire countryside, which led first of all to garden cities like Letchworth and Welwyn, and after that to new towns like Stevenage and Hemel Hempstead.

Heronsgate was not O'Connor's only settlement. He set up four others at Lowbands and Snigs End in Gloucestershire, Great Dodford in Worcestershire and Minster Lovell in Oxfordshire, but Heronsgate was the first, and he called it O'Connorville, though it never really caught on. He was an Irish MP who took up the cause of the People's Charter for the reformation of Parliament – vote by secret ballot, fairer constituencies, no

property qualification for MPs, proper payment for them, universal male suffrage, and annual Parliaments. All of these finally came about except for the annual Parliament (and thank goodness for that – imagine a General Election every year!) but the Chartists sank into obscurity long before it happened. O'Connor turned his attention to co-operative land investment, which seems to have rather tenuous links with parliamentary reform, but he formed the Chartist Land Company to buy, first of all, what was then the Herringsgate estate.

I was always fascinated by Heronsgate, long before I knew its full history. It can only be reached by a nine-foot-wide lane called, bizarrely, Stockport Road, and this leads into a network of other nine-foot lanes with similar names – Bradford, Halifax, Nottingham. There is no way that two cars can pass in these lanes; as my friend told me, the first thing you learn in Heronsgate is how to back up. The little church is in Stockport Road, and it is fortunate that the entire congrega-

ONE OF HERONSGATE'S NARROW LANES, JUST WIDE ENOUGH FOR A WAGON.

tion is within walking distance, because parking doesn't exist. It is in the midst of the thirty-five original smallholdings, now handsome houses and gardens, well fenced and hedged with the odd tennis court and swimming-pool, and mostly occupied by the well-to-do. There is no other way out of Heronsgate by car; you have to turn in somebody's gateway – not always a popular move – and go back along Stockport Road to the comparative spaciousness of Long Lane, between Rickmansworth and Chorleywood.

Through traffic in Long Lane would probably not know that Heronsgate existed, except for the pub further up the road with its distinctive name, the Land of Liberty, Peace and Plenty. I always assumed O'Connor built it there, well away from the settlement, because he was against drink, but I have learned since that a beer shop was there before Heronsgate existed, and it was only when the Chartists arrived that it shrewdly adopted an appropriate-sounding name. The signboard has changed frequently over the years, but when I last saw it there were a couple of top-hatted gentlemen on one side, standing on a platform and waving pamphlets, and on the other was a medieval king signing some document, watched by a disapproving bishop. I assume this was King John and the Magna Carta, which must quite baffle the casual customer and might even surprise Feargus O'Connor.

'COME TO THE LAND OF LIBERTY, PEACE AND PLENTY . . .'

His Chartist Land Company was based in the north of England, and most of his clientele came from there, hence the road names. For the thirty-five lucky ballot winners, Heronsgate must have seemed like the Promised Land, but they were soon disillusioned. They still had to pay O'Connor a rent, most of them were artisans with no knowledge of farming or country life, and anyway the plots were too small to be practical.

It took only five years for the project to fold up; Heronsgate and the other settlements were sold off to private buyers, O'Connor's land company went bust, and O'Connor himself, always volatile, cracked under the pressure and finished up in a clinic for the insane. It was a sad end to a basically quite good idea. The founder of Heronsgate would be astounded to see it now, and even more astounded by what has happened along its boundary. Long Lane is now an access road for the M25, and the motorway itself passes close by the edge of O'Connor's smallholdings.

If you drive to the end of Nottingham Road, where it peters out into a footpath, and you get out of the car, the noise is quite deafening. The end houses are all double-glazed, but sitting in the garden must be like relaxing beside a runway at Heathrow. The noise fades a little as you retreat, and the commuters who live in Heronsgate no doubt consider that having a motorway so handy outweighs any noise problem. There is still open country on the other side, and a riding stables to add to the rural flavour. So if I try very hard indeed, I can visualise those settlers arriving from the industrial cities of the north, full of enthusiasm and hope, to start independent new lives in the green fields of Hertfordshire. It was not their fault it didn't work out.

Heronsgate may not be a village in the conventional sense, but it was a unique social experiment in rural community life. If it had worked, it would be as famous among 'villages' as, say Milton Keynes is among 'cities'. I suspect my friend who lives there is rather glad that it didn't.

INDEX

ACKNOWLEDGMENTS

Photographs on *pages 24* – Clive Davies, Western Gazette,
49 – Geoff Staff, *80 and 81* – Derbyshire Countryside Limited, Derby
and as detailed on the dust-jacket.

The following is a select listing of people and organisations consulted.
Dr J. Holborow, Mr D. Stanbridge, Mr N. Payne, Mr R. Pinnock, Dr J. Bharier,
the family of the late Mr Douglas Gillard, County Libraries Association,
The Federation of Womens Institutes,
The English Tourist Board, The Rural Community Council,
The National Trust and The Society of Friends.

The publishers also wish to express their gratitude to the many other individuals
and organisations whose material and specialised knowledge was
invaluable in the preparation of this book.